Displaced Person

By

Helen Kish Hastman

Library and Archives Canada Cataloguing in Publication

Kish Hastman, Helen, 1945-, author
Displaced person / Helen Kish Hastman.

ISBN 978-1-927678-17-6 (paperback)

1. Kish Hastman, Helen, 1945-. 2. World War, 1939-1945--Refugees--Austria--Biography. 3. World War, 1939-1945--Refugees--Canada--Biography. 4. World War, 1939-1945--Personal narratives, Austrian. 5. World War, 1939-1945--Personal narratives, Canadian. I. Title.

D809.C2H38 2015 940.53'145 C2015-904715-3

Canadian Cataloguing in Publication Data

Displaced Person / Helen Kish Hastman 1945—

Contact the author at:
www.kishhastman.com

Book design and layout by BK Publishing
www.bkpublishing.ca

Cover and interior photographs from the personal collections of the author.

Illustrations in chapter headings come from the author's Austrian school primer, "Frohes Lernen."

Front Cover: Helen and her mother in front of Austrian farm house, Helen in Austria 1950 and a page from her mother's passport showing all the countries they traveled through
Back Cover: 1954, the emigration ship *Groote Beer*.

Cupar photos reproduced with permission from the Cupar Archives.

Memoir is written from memory and we all know that human memory is deeply flawed. The events are portrayed to the best of Helen Kish Hastman's recall. If the author could not remember the exact words said by certain people, and exact descriptions of certain things, she has reconstructed such moments to the best of her ability. To her sadness she could not recall the names of her Austrian foster sister nor the Sisters of Service.

Acknowledgements

A serendipitous meeting with a stranger named Pat Narynski really began this journey. After a brief chat whereby she learned of my desire to write a memoir for my grandchildren, she steered me to the Selkirk Library Writers Group. It became the catalyst and guidance I needed. The leadership and fellowship of this group, along with their gentle critiques, allowed me to gain confidence and improve my craft. Thanks to Pat and to you wonderful people in the group.

In relating my story, I reveal my family's and friends' histories. I am grateful to them for their eager encouragements. Thank you to Ethel Sulea, Helen Kovach, Mary Ann Mitchell, Lenny Kallichuk, Susie Fox, Jenarae Spence and Gary Kayter for providing me with some of your confirmations and photos .

A special thank you to Ishbel Moore, editor extraordinaire, whose courage and persistence ensured that my manuscript went forward. God bless you Ishbel for your patience and insights.

Then there is Tyra Masters-Heinrichs, talented publisher, who transformed the manuscript into a “real” book. Thank you Tyra for all the thousands of extra things you do.

A lovely lady by the name of Maria Antal assisted me with my written Hungarian. I thank you ever so much for your generosity Maria.

My gratitude also goes to the archives of the city of Linz, Austria and the town of Cupar, Saskatchewan for providing me with the historical data necessary.

Last but not least, I would like to thank my beloved husband, Lawrence for his interest, patience, and support in helping make my dream come true.

This Book is dedicated to my granddaughters
Charley, Lara and Emma

Displaced Person

Austria had been bullied and threatened to annex with Germany before the war. Some Austrians protested this move. Others wished to again be a part of a larger picture as they had been under the Austro-Hungarian Empire. They believed that joining with Germany was not just advantageous for financial and political reasons, but also because they shared the same language, culture and religion.

alpine village

The Abduction

Fall 1950—Farm in Austria

"Don't let her take me!" I cried and ran back to my family. I hid behind my mother and clung to her skirt. "I'll be good!"

My mother, *Mutter,* turned, knelt down and hugged me. I could feel her wet cheeks on my face. "We love you, Helene, but you must go now."

"I don't want to go with her!" I pleaded.

"I'm sorry, Helene, but we have no choice."

My older sister, Greta, who stood nearby, had also begun to cry. The three of us huddled in a circle just outside the door of our farmhouse. Dark clouds had been gathering all day, and now even *they* let a few tears fall.

My father, *Vater*, who had been watching all this, now stepped between us, gently took my hand in his and guided me back to the woman. As he relinquished his hold, he patted me on the head. "There, there, you'll be fine." I noticed a slight tremor in his usually steady voice.

The woman now took my hand and began to walk away with me. We had only gone a few paces when I heard *Mutter* call out, "Be good,

Helene, and be brave."

Be brave? How can I be brave? I'm only five years old!

I knew I shouldn't have looked back, but I couldn't resist. My family was waving and crying. I decided I wasn't going anywhere. As I struggled to free myself from the woman's grasp, she tightened her grip, so I planted my feet firmly and sat down. Surely, she wouldn't drag me on the ground. Before I knew it, she had swung me into her arms and was carrying me away. Why was she taking me from my family?

As I was being transported away, I tried to search my mind for any clues in the past that would explain this event. There must have been, but I may have missed them or not realized their importance at the time.

What *did* I know about this woman? I only knew her as the olive-skinned, dark-eyed woman who frequently came to the farm. I had been told to call her *Tante* Lisi although I was told she wasn't my real auntie. I sensed she was not a family member but rather an acquaintance of *Mutter's.* She would arrive in the early morning and be gone by supper time. In return for sweets, she demanded I remain by her side. The woman would speak very little and wouldn't take her eyes off me. She showed no such interest in Greta who was much smarter and prettier. But as long as she continued to bring me sweets, I didn't mind, although her dark appearance and cool manner made me a little afraid of her.

On this dark cloudy day, "*Tante* Lisi" had arrived again. I had sensed that this was no ordinary visit. My *Mutter's* usual cheerfulness was gone. Even my father's stern face had looked somewhat softened. And Greta wouldn't even look me in the eye!

What's wrong?

The visit had gone on as usual except that everyone hovered around us. I accepted the bribe and her constant scrutiny but was eager to be away from her. I felt better once we had said our usual goodbyes to her and headed out the door. *Mutter* had passed a small suitcase to her, and "*Tante* Lisi" had thanked her with a great deal of enthusiasm.

My mother had bent down and whispered in my ear, "Helene, Tante Lisi would like you to visit with her in the wonderful city of Linz.

There are so many things to see and do there; I know you will like it." She had hugged my shoulders, kissed me on the cheek then had steered me over to the woman.

This can't be real. I must be dreaming.

***

Still in a fog, I allowed myself to be carried away. I suspected this woman of being a witch—the same one who had taken Hansel and Gretel captive. I had not gone into the forest, yet I had taken sweets from her. Did that make me hers? It appeared so because my parents had done nothing to stop her. And only witches stole children from their parents!

Money had passed between them. Was I being sold? I didn't know what was happening, and it frightened me.

Only after we were out of sight and earshot, did she finally put me down. We walked for quite some time and landed up at a busy, noisy place with lots of well-dressed people. Near a large building some sort of iron tracks ran on the ground. I continued to cry and snivel, hoping someone would hear my distress and come to my rescue. No one did!

Out of the corner of my eye, I spied a huge one-eyed black dragon. It chortled and snorted, huffed and puffed, hissed and whistled as it came to a screeching halt in front of us. I had never seen such a monster! It must have been very angry because hot steam came from the top and the sides. People were actually entering this creature. With her hand fastened firmly around my wrist, the witch-woman also began to step into this dragon.

"We are going to be eaten by this monster!" I screamed as I held back.

"Don't be silly. This is a train and it will take us home." She tightened her grip and pulled on my wrist again.

Everyone entered without a fuss, so I yielded, but I wasn't entirely convinced. Once inside, she found a space for us on one of the hard benches. The seats soon filled with people and, before long, the dragon screeched and lurched again. It carried me away from my father and mother! I started to cry, louder than ever. People stared at us and shook their heads. *Maybe now someone will rescue me!*

But no, it was not me that they were looking at but rather at this witch-woman. I could see a red blush creep over her face. She took my chin in her hand, and with her cool brown eyes and an even cooler voice, she said, “Shush! I won’t have you embarrassing me. People will think I can’t control a child. Be quiet and behave!”

Had she forgotten to say “or else”? Would she eat me right here in front of these people?

I didn’t think she could get away with that.

Once I lost my fear of becoming her supper, I began to calm down a little. No one else seemed concerned about being in this dragon. Everyone laughed and chatted, even the children. Most importantly, no one recognized this woman beside me as a witch. On the farm, she had not posed a danger. Now, without the protection of my parents, I was truly afraid. But my parents loved me and would never do anything to hurt me. That was the thought I clung to. However, witches can cast spells.

How far away is Linz? What will she do with me once we get there?

These thoughts raced through my mind as the dragon hurled into the dark night, until the voices, the rhythmic clickety-clack of the wheels and the gentle rocking lulled me to sleep.

country kitchen in Austria

Before the Abduction

1945 to 1950—Farm in Austria

I was happy. I had just awakened from a wonderful dream and tried to relive it. The details were blurry, but the happy mood lingered. My eyes were drawn to a crisscross pattern on the wall created by the sun as it shone through the open grated window in our bedroom. The wooden shutters had not been closed since the rain last week. I heard the wind murmuring through the pines near the house and felt its crispness remove any remaining cobwebs of sleep.

I pushed the light feather quilt aside and stretched. My movement disturbed my sister beside me and she groaned. Our wooden bed was so narrow that the slightest motion from either of us during the night could land the other on the floor. In the winter however, I was grateful for its narrow space that allowed us to snuggle and share a heated log that warmed our feet. But in the summer, our close proximity caused us to fight whenever we merely brushed against the other.

I listened for any sounds from the other side of the curtain where *Mutter* and *Vater* slept in this single large bedroom on the second floor of our stone house. There was none. That meant that both were already up and about. Sure enough, I heard someone moving in the kitchen downstairs. Turning to my sleeping companion, I nudged her shoulder.

"Get up, Greta. It's time to eat. And I'm hungry."

"Go away, Helene," she mumbled.

My sister Greta was much, much older than I—a whole three years. She was taller, slimmer and smarter. When we stood side by side in front of our mirror, I looked like a Bratwurst with my chubby cheeks, stubbly arms and legs, and small facial features. I also had a forehead that entered a room well ahead of me.

Being careful not to bump myself as I had a hundred times before, I straddled the high ledge on the side of the bed. This ledge rose well above the top of the mattress and prevented the quilt from sliding to the floor, but I was convinced that its main purpose was to reveal my clumsiness. Today, my agility proved to be perfect—no extra bruises. I used the chamber pot, replaced the lid and gently shoved it back under the bed.

Slipping out of my nightgown, I grabbed my favourite dress—the sky blue one with tiny flowers. It had once belonged to Greta and to someone else before that. Now it was too short for her, but on me, its hem hung around my calves—just perfect. Over this, I pulled on a full bib apron and fastened it at the back of my waist. I had two aprons, one I wore at home, and another better one was worn when we went visiting. Women always wore aprons everywhere. Being summer meant I did not have to wear an undershirt, garters or stockings. Best of all, I wore no shoes. I loved running around in my bare feet.

I gave Greta another nudge then scurried downstairs. *Mutter* was putting out a cold breakfast at the kitchen table. I cherished her familiar shape—short, plump with a round face, laughing eyes and rosy cheeks. Her thick long hair, worn in a bun, was now covered with a kerchief tied at her nape. A crisp white apron covered her grey, calf-length dress.

She had her back to me, so I tried to sneak up in order to frighten her, but I was unsuccessful again. She had eyes and ears at the back of her head!

Mutter turned, smiled and greeted me, "*Guten Morgen, meine Liebchen.*" Always calling me her sweetheart, she now bent down and beckoned with her arms. I ran into her waiting embrace. She was always eager for a hug, and I demanded it often. With my face pressed against her neck, I inhaled the clean fresh scent of the laundry soap that she used. That scent made me feel loved and worthy.

As we hugged, we would often play a game. She would begin with "What ever would I do without you!"

And I would reply, "Don't worry *Mutter*, I will never leave you." I would giggle, and she would feign a sad smile. Sometimes though, her sad smile seemed much too convincing, and I had to remind myself it was just a game.

I knew what came after this ritual. "Have Greta comb and braid your hair then wash for breakfast."

I ran back up the stairs calling Greta's name. When I reached the top, I saw her roll out of bed complaining, "*Ja, Ja*, I'm coming. You're such a pest!"

Me? A pest? The sooner I get ready, the sooner I can eat.

"While you get dressed, I'll make the bed." I offered. I could never do as good a job as Greta because the flat sheet had to be all tucked under the mattress again. Also, the large feather quilt was too cumbersome for me, but I would do anything to speed things along. We were ready at the same time.

Reluctantly, I sat down on a chair by the bed to await my morning torture—the untangling of my long hair. We had a brush, but its bristles were too soft to effectively loosen anything. Using only a comb, Greta worked hard to pull out the knots in the thick mop that reached to the small of my back. It was not an easy task, considering that I yelped and squirmed with each stroke. Once the comb moved smoothly through to the ends, she parted my hair down the middle. She then worked tight braids along both sides of my temples, ending with two long braids tied in ribbons. Though this style accentuated my big forehead, I loved it. *Mutter* sometimes did my hair, but she had no time to fuss, so she would simply gather it back and make one braid. I didn't like that style but would never complain. Greta took the extra time to make me pretty, and I thanked her.

We both ran downstairs to the washbasin by the wood stove. Greta poured some water into the bowl and waited for me to wash first. I dipped my finger tips in the cold water, dabbed my eyes and groped for the towel. Most of the time Greta caught me doing this and would give me a glare, then make me wash properly. Today I got away with it.

I sat on the bench by the table near the kitchen window and waited for the rest of the family to join me. Bored quickly, I turned, knelt and looked out the window. *Mutter's* flower pots sat on the very wide window sill and obstructed my view. I pushed past them to grasp the iron grill attached to the outside edge of the sill. As I breathed in the cool morning air, my eyes were drawn to the flower-carpeted meadows on the distant hills. *It is going to be a gorgeous day*!

Mutter admonished me."Helene, turn around and sit down before you knock over one of my plants."

I did not obey right away, but when the door to the lean-to stable opened and our father came through, I immediately did as I was told. He carried a pail of fresh milk which I knew came from our goats. I wondered if he had treated our two cats with some of that rich milk.

"*Guten Morgen, Vater*," Greta and I chorused together. It was the polite thing to do.

He turned towards us and acknowledged our greeting with a nod. His head almost bumped the thick beams that crossed the low ceiling. He handed the pail to *Mutter* and waited as Greta poured clean water over his fingers at the washstand. After a quick scrub of his hands and a good rub of his face, he held out his hand for the towel from Greta. I watched as the towel slowly revealed first his scraggly eyebrows, then his thin scruffy beard. With a feigned deep growl, he pounced on Greta, laughing. She jumped back and shrieked in delight.

I liked him when he was like that, but Greta and I both knew when he meant business. A stern look from him got our full attention when required. If that didn't do that, his booming voice soon commanded respect and obedience. We had heard him say to *Mutter* once, "Children should be seen and not heard." Greta and I had discussed this and couldn't figure out how, if he could see us, why would he not want to hear us? *Mutter,* on the other hand, insisted that she see *and* hear us all the time.

Vater finally sat down at the table. Greta and *Mutter* followed. Our mother cut the bread and cheese into thick slices while Greta passed them around. I was so hungry, I wanted to grab the bread and stuff it in my mouth but knew better than that. Prayers first! *Vater* clasped his hands and we all bowed our heads.

He prayed, "Thanks be to God that Hitler is dead and the war is over. We are grateful that You put us into the hands of the Americans and not the Russians. We ask that You bring peace and prosperity once again to our beloved Austria. We thank You, Lord, for this bountiful food and the safety and health of our family."

We all chimed in our "Amens". I did not understand any part of that prayer except the part about the food.

Why are we thanking the "Lord" when it had been Mutter who had baked the bread and made the cheese? Why are we not thanking her?

The rest of the prayer had nothing to do with my tummy, so it flew over my head. As *Mutter* poured the fresh warm milk into our cups, I couldn't help but blurt out, "I'm so hungry!"

"Your are *always* hungry!" said Greta.

"I am glad that you have a good appetite, Helene. It means that you are healthy," *Mutter* replied. As usual, she headed off our argument before it got out of hand.

Vater also had to have his say. "Be very grateful for everything you have, children. For quite some time now, there has been a terrible war. Then the famine came. Our countrymen were hungry, homeless and afraid. The only job available was survival." He took a deep breath and shook his head. "Our folks in the city had to scrounge, barter or pay exorbitant prices on the black market for the very food you are eating now. Because we were able to grow some food here on our farm, we *were* and *are* the fortunate ones. The only thing it costs us is time and labour."

Vater is so serious most of the time!

Mutter bowed her head and said her own silent prayer.

I slathered big globs of homemade butter on my bread. When the bread was not as fresh as today, I would soak it in milk and spoon it out of my cup. Either way, I loved that heavy chewy bread. *Where's more cheese?*

When breakfast was over, Greta helped *Mutter* clear up the table and wash the dishes. We only had enough plates and cutlery to serve six, so it became necessary to wash them after each meal. When company came, *Mutter* would relinquish her place at the table, and Greta and I would have to wait until the adults were done. That was particularly hard for me.

With *Mutter* and Greta busy doing their chores, I swept the floor under the table. Being short, I was the only who could reach all the corners and crevices where bread crumbs liked to hide—or so I was told. I swept them out past the threshold of the door and wondered why I had to clean up other people's crumbs. I knew which ones were mine—or did I? But then I realized that my mother always cleaned up *our* mess, and she never complained. I wanted to be just like *Mutter*.

Mutter and Greta remained busy, so I decided to play in the lean-to stable where I would usually catch the cats napping. Entering the dark interior, I waited for my eyes to adjust. I looked for the familiar places that the cats used for their beds—the hayloft and under the manger. Even though the ceiling hung low, I had to jump high to peer over the deep shelf that served as the hayloft. The hay was gone and so were the cats. The livestock had also left for the meadows making the interior appear larger than it really was. In the winter, it became cramped with the two oxen, three goats, cats, chickens and uninvited pigeons, but their crowded bodies made the stable snug and warm.

I finally spied one cat under the manger, coaxed her out, picked her up and rubbed my face in her belly. She purred as I gently blew on it. I heard a distinct cluck, turned my head toward the sound and there, atop the straw in the manger, sat two fat white chickens. I let go of the cat and stuck my hand under the hens to check for eggs. The grouchy one pecked my hand. I yanked my hand away and screeched.

"*Das ist nicht schön!* That is not nice," I scolded her as I cautiously clung to the two eggs I had managed to steal. I left the stable through the door that lead directly into the kitchen.

Our chores done, Greta and I were now both free and heading outdoors.

Still sitting at the table, our father called after us, "Stay near in case we need you. And remember the forest is *verboten*—forbidden."

"*Ja, Vater*, we promise not to go into the forest," Greta called back. We had discussed this before and decided it was wise to obey our father's command. Not just because we were afraid of what his punishment might be, but because we had heard the horrifying stories about what happened to children who had ventured into the woods. We knew that Hansel and Gretel had been lured with sweets by a witch who wanted to roast them in the oven. Little Red Riding Hood had almost been eaten by a wolf. We weren't about to let that happen to us.

Content to play in the surrounding hills and orchard, we were good children who always obeyed our parents—most of the time! Sometimes, we raided our orchard and gulped down vast quantities of whichever fruit was in season like plums, pears, apples or cherries. Today, it was cherries, our favourite. In order to get to them, we had to climb the tree. I tried first, but every time I bent my knee or lifted my leg, my long dress got in the way.

Greta interrupted my attempts. "I think I have a solution to our problem. Watch me."

She bent over, grabbed the back hem of her skirt, pulled it forward between her legs and tucked it into her waist band to create a makeshift set of trousers. She was then able to scamper, unhampered, up the tree. I always knew she was smart. Following her lead, I quickly joined her on a strong limb that supported both of us. There, perched side by side, our legs dangling beneath to give us balance, we grabbed handfuls of cherries and crammed them into our mouths until the juices squirted everywhere. Then began the contest.

"I can spit the farthest!" I squealed.

"No you can't!"

"Yes I can!"

The cherry pits flew from our mouths like stones from a sling shot.

After filling our tummies, we shimmied down the tree and skulked away smirking with delight that no one had seen us steal that forbidden fruit. But as soon as we neared our mother, she looked at us, grinned and asked, "Have you been in those cherries again?"

How does she know?

"Not us!" we replied with some indignation, slipping our stained hands into our apron pockets.

"Really? Then what is this?" With a knowing smile, she touched Greta's chin and cheek

Oh, no! Stupidly, we had forgotten about the blue-red stains on our faces.

"Don't eat too many," she warned. "You will get a bad tummy ache!"

But the warning came too late. We had very few treats available to us, so those sweet, juicy temptations were too much to resist. We soon felt the effects of our gorging—it was not so sweet! No other punishment was required!

The European war ended in May of 1945. Austria was then occupied by the four liberating Allied countries—England, France, Russia and United States. The Soviets considered the Austrians to be Germans and thus treated them accordingly. They occupied the northeastern part of Austria and continued to plunder, expropriate businesses and did nothing to help its people. I was fortunate to be born that August, in the part of Austria that was occupied by the Americans. It was because of their help that we recovered more quickly and less painfully than any other area of Austria.

flailing the crop

No Idle Hands Here

1945 to 1950—Farm in Austria

Though Greta and I had plenty of time to play, it seemed to me that our parents never did. So if we wanted to spend time with them, we'd simply follow them around, and thus were often tricked into helping them.

We decided one day to tag behind *Vater* as he did his work around the farm. Because we knew he had no patience for chattering children, we never spoke a word, just made sure to be underfoot. Today, he didn't shoo us away like flies, so we trailed him everywhere. His long stride made it difficult for me to keep up. As he loped, I scurried—my short legs and arms pumping—but I never could catch up to him. Thankfully, he stopped often enough for me to catch my breath. Greta didn't have my problem. When in *Vater's* company, we learned a great deal about him. He spoke only when he had something important to say such as "There is too much work to be done to waste precious time and energy on frivolous things!"

When he caught us doing "frivolous things", he would shake his head and mumble in his beard, "Idle hands are the devil's workshop."

I would then turn to my older and wiser sister and ask, "What does that mean?"

Greta, with her three-year age advantage, took her role as my mentor seriously. With a flick of her head and an air of authority, she replied, "It means that when our hands are not working, the devil will set up a workshop and do the work for us."

Sounds good to me!

***

Each season on this farm had its own chores and its own fun. The best time for Greta and me involved gathering the hay. *Vater* would cut it with a long-handled scythe and let it dry in the sun. Once dry, it had to be removed before any rain came. If that didn't happen, it would rot and not be good for the livestock. Everyone had to work. As the oxen pulled the hay wagon, our parents forked it from the ground and heaved it onto the rack where Greta and I tried to disperse it evenly. She had a pitchfork, but I used only my hands.

"*Achtung*! Look out!" was the warning for us to get out of the way as the forkfuls came in. Our responsibility was to arrange it so that it wouldn't slide off. The hay stayed on, but it took everything I had to keep *myself* from sliding off. Every time the wagon lurched to a start or a stop, I would scream and go flying into the soft hay.

Greta would say, "Helene, are you alright? Did I poke you with my pitchfork? So sorry!" She hadn't of course, but this continued until she caught on. She stopped apologizing and glared at me after each scream.

I did not always land on my bottom, sometimes it was face first. The sweet scent of hay became embedded in my brain—up through my nose!

Harvest time brought another very busy time for our family. I watched as *Vater* and *Mutter* cut the crop with a sickle or scythe, tied it into sheaves, and left the stalks to dry by leaning them upright against each other in stooks.

Once ripened and dry, they needed to remove the grain from the seed pods. My parents placed the loosened sheaves on a large cloth on the ground, then beat the heads of the grain with a flail—a handle with a freely swinging stick at the other end. Fascinated, I watched as *Mutter* placed the freed grain into a large, shallow basket, gently tossed the contents into the air and allowed the wind to blow the light chaff and dirt away. The heavier seed fell back into the basket. She repeated this until only clean seed remained.

"I can help. Let me help!" I squealed as I chased the chaff in the breeze. They only allowed me to beat the *straw* with a stick and throw it in the air. Mostly, the short, stiff stems were driven straight back to me with a vengeance, piercing my hair and clothing until I looked like a hedgehog. Everyone laughed except me.

Vater gathered the leftover straw to be used as bedding for the animals. The cleaned grain had to be taken to a mill in the nearest village to be ground into flour, then returned for *Mutter* to make tasty, chewy bread in her big clay oven just outside the house.

As a result of the severe winter of 1946 plus the drought in summer of 1947, food shortage became the worst problem for Austria. Sixty-five percent of Austrian agricultural output was concentrated in, and kept in, the Soviet zone and hoarded.

the village

Protected

Fall 1950—Farm in Austria

A little after the harvest, *Vater* invited me to join him for a ride into the nearby village. I didn't know what I'd done to deserve this honour and pleasure. We headed out with the oxen yoked to the wagon.

"There will be many new things for you to see and do today," my father said as we entered the village. Sure enough, one of the first things that caught my attention were the horses—strong, graceful and much faster than our snail-paced oxen.

"Why don't we have horses, *Vater?* They are so pretty."

"Oxen are so much better," he replied. "They cost less to buy, feed and upkeep. They're more rugged and don't get injured or ill as easily as horses. Oxen are stronger, gentler and easier to train and control. I would never trade my magnificent beasts for any horse!"

I had no idea how much he knew and loved these "magnificent" plodding beasts. My attitude towards them also changed.

I had never seen so many people and buildings crowding around in one place. My head swivelled this way and that until I was sure it would unscrew itself from my neck. Our cart finally stopped. *Vater* tied the oxen to a post and helped me down. He led me to the front door of a building and opened the door. I pinched my nose at the strange and acrid stench. "What is that stink?"

"That's just medicine," answered *Vater.*

The room was filled with people, all seated in chairs. *Vater* found two that were empty, sat down and motioned for me to sit beside him.

I looked around and asked, "What is this place?"

Vater explained it was a doctor's office. He was about to continue when we heard a most horrendous screech from behind one of the doors. Soon after, the door opened and a young boy, about my age, came out with his mother. He had tears in his eyes but grinned at a lollipop in his hand. One by one, adults and children passed through that door. More screams, more lollipops.

"Helene Kiraly, please," called out the doctor.

Vater took my hand and we walked toward *that* door. We entered. Everything appeared blindingly white in there—the walls, the furniture, the sheets and even the doctor. He looked like a ghost—white coat and white hair. Even his skin looked pale. His mustache would also have been white, had it not been for a yellow-brown stain on it. My father lifted me unto what looked like a high bed. The white man approached.

"*Guten Tag,* Good day, Helene, I'm Doctor Schultz."

His voice seemed kind enough. He studied me and prodded my neck. Placing a cold metal device on my bare chest, he asked me to breathe deeply. I laughed when my knees jerked on their own after he hit them with a rubber hammer. Then he pulled down a shiny round disc strapped on his forehead and looked through the hole in the middle. As he did, he asked me to open my mouth wide and say, "Ahh".

I overheard him instruct *Vater* to hold my left arm very firmly. *Why does he want him to do that?*

Both men closed in around me. The doctor had some sort of tube with a needle at the end. Alarmed, I kicked, squirmed and screamed with all my might as the needle came closer. The doctor and *Vater* were unable to hold me still long enough to give that needle.

First, Dr. Schultz tried to coax me. "This will only take a second and won't hurt at all. Most importantly, it will give you protection from bad germs later."

Then he tried to flatter me."Come now, you're a big girl, and big girls aren't afraid."

Oh yes, they are!

When that didn't work, he sighed and attempted to entice me through a more lowly form of persuasion—bribery. "If you stop your squirming and squealing, I will give you a candy, *Ja?*"

I gave in. The pain was great, but the reward was not. I recovered quickly from that needle wound, but it left a round dip in my arm that looked like one of the valleys in the mountains.

Upon my return home from the village, I complained to my mother for not warning me about the downside of that village trip. She simply replied, "Sometimes it's best not to know everything."

I disagreed—I always wanted to know what was ahead of me. How could I prevent a fall, if I didn't see the cliff's edge? I also wondered if that needle could really protect me from bad things to come.

In the post-world war II period, Europe remained ravaged and susceptible to exploitation by an internal and external Communist threat. In 1947, George C. Marshall issued a call for a comprehensive program to rebuild Europe. Fanned by the fear of Communist expansion and the rapid deterioration of European economies, Congress passed the Economic Cooperation Act in 1948, later known as the Marshall Plan. It provided food aid and money of over $12 billion to rebuild not only Austria but most Western European countries devastated by the war.

plowing the land

After the Abduction

Fall 1950—Linz, Austria

A strong scent of cinnamon awoke me. Nothing looked familiar—it was not the farm, and it was not the noisy train. Where was I?

I sat up and found myself on a huge couch in an undersized room filled with oversized furniture. A tapestry of a beautiful white horse harnessed to a plough hung above the couch. He was pulling with all his might. I thought about what *Vater* had said about how oxen were stronger than horses. That thought immediately brought a lump to my throat. *Mutter* had told me to be brave, so I shook my head and continued to look around.

Opposite this wall—so close that if I stretched real hard, I could touch it—stood a large, ornately carved grandfather clock. I had never seen such elegant furniture. At the foot of my couch/bed was an immense wooden desk littered with papers, pencils and other items I did not recognize. There seemed to be more furniture in this one room than in the whole of *Vater's* farm house.

The only floor space not occupied was a narrow strip leading to a door. Through this door now came that same witch-woman. She no longer looked like the elegant lady that had visited me on the farm but was dressed rather plain, more like *Mutter*. Instead of a hat and high-heeled shoes, she now wore a small kerchief tied at her nape, and loafers on her feet. The tailored dress had been replaced by a simple smock covered by an apron. Only her attitude remained the same—aloof.

So, this is not just a bad dream. This nightmare is real!

I began to cry. I asked for my parents, but she did not reply. Instead, she neared my couch, pulled the blanket off and explained it was time to get up and get dressed.

Can't you see I'm scared? Don't you have any feelings?

She gave no sympathy, no greeting, no explanation—just the order to get dressed. I thought it incredibly rude, and it made me angry. I sat up and faced her. "I want to go back to my family. I know who you are! You're the witch from the woods, and you want to fatten and eat me! Don't you?" I hoped that if she knew her game was up, maybe she'd let me go.

Her eyes widened, her mouth dropped open, then she laughed. Or was that a cackle? She sat down on the couch beside me, put one hand on my shoulder and said, "Don't be silly child! I am not a witch, and nobody is going to eat you!"

That is good news, but can I believe you?

Her face became serious. She removed her hand from my shoulder and placed it on her lap beside the other one. Her whole body and voice took on a controlled tone as she said, "I see it's time you learned the truth. The people you have been living with are not your family! *I* am your real mother, and you will be living with *me* from now on!"

My chest hurt. I couldn't breathe. My ears were buzzing! I couldn't grasp her meaning. All I could do was blurt out, "I have a mother!"

"No, no, she was your foster mother."

"What's a foster mother?" I didn't know there were different kinds of mothers.

"That's someone who takes care of you for only a little while."

A little while? I'm five years old, and she's been the only mother I have ever known. I started to whimper again. "My *Mutter* loves me, and she would have told me if this was true."

The witch-woman squirmed little but carried on with a conviction in her voice, "She didn't tell you because I had given her strict orders not to do that. I thought if you knew who your real mother was, you wouldn't want to stay there. Besides, it would only have confused you and made you unhappy." She looked away and wouldn't meet my eyes.

Well, I certainly was confused and unhappy now. I had just lost the only people I have ever known and loved. I wanted nothing to do with this woman or this city. I began to sob uncontrollably!

"Shush, shush. If I promise that you can see them again next summer, will you stop your crying?" She certainly had perfected the art of bribery.

I had no choice, but that promise helped calm me down a bit.

She gave a sigh of relief and continued. "We are now living here in Linz and are guests of the Stöbers. I will call you Heli and I want you to call me *Mutti.*" It was not a question, but another order. Both were terms of endearment.

Ha! I will not agree.

The witch-woman, however, carried on as if I had. "Now, let's get you cleaned up."

She led me to a room filled with wondrous things. She pointed to what looked like a potty, but it looked heavy and attached to the floor. *Was ist das?* What is this? How was she ever going to be able to empty it? I sat on its comfortable seat and did my business. I hoped she didn't expect me to help her carry it out. Instead, she pulled a chain and *whoosh*, my "business" was gone! *Wunderbar*!

Then she took me to a big basin that was attached to the wall. With a flick of her wrist, she turned one of the knobs on the top, and I saw steaming water gush from it. She turned the other and mixed it with the water already in the bowl, as if she was testing the temperature.

"Here's a facecloth and soap. Wash your hands and face, but use only a little of the soap. We must not be wasteful."

I rubbed a little of the soap on the cloth and brought it to my face. It smelled like the small violet flowers on the hill by our farm. I rinsed off the soap with that lovely warm water. As I dried myself, the witch-woman pulled a plug to release the dirty water. I gasped and jumped back, expecting the water to splash all over my feet. I looked underneath, but to my surprise, there was no spilt water. *Magic!*

Back in the room where we had started, she helped me dress, then combed and braided my hair. She eyed me up and down, tucked in a stray hair and straightened up a crease in my blouse. Then she pinched both my cheeks, hard!

"Ouch! What did you do that for?" I asked, rubbing my sore face.

"That makes your cheeks pink and gives you a healthy glow," she explained.

If you're not going to eat me, why do I need to look healthy?

One more quick inspection, then she led me out. "It is time for you to meet some people. You will address the lady as *Frau* Stöber and her son's name is Willi. She is my employer, so be polite, and don't speak unless you are spoken to, and be sure to curtsy."

She quickly showed me the proper way of bowing the head, bending one's knee slightly while holding the hem of the dress. *Am I meeting a king and queen?*

As we entered the kitchen, I could only see a pretty woman with her light brown hair drawn back in a bun. My new "mother" made the introductions.

"Guten Morgen, Frau Stöber," I said as I wished her good morning and performed my clumsy curtsy.

Frau Stöber smiled. "*Guten Morgen, Heli. Wie geht es dir?*"

When she asked me how I was, I should have met her eyes and answered, but I became distracted by a movement from behind her. Out came a young boy, slightly shorter and younger than I. Of slight build with a small triangular face, his straight black hair was swept to the side of his forehead. He looked cute in his knee high socks and short *Lederhosen*. He smiled shyly.

This must be Willi! I hope he will be a friend.

After the introductions, Willi and I sat down for breakfast. Thank goodness! I had been hungry ever since I had been awakened by the scent of that cinnamon. A sweet roll sat on a plate beside a cup half filled with hot black liquid that Willi explained was called “coffee”. I had never had anything like it before and was about to sip it when Willi stopped me.

“Wait! You don't drink it like that!” He grabbed the bowl of sweet whipped cream on the table and kept spooning it into my cup until it mounded over the lip. “Now taste it.”

I lapped up that velvety cream like a cat. Eventually the mound dissolved into the coffee. If this was any indication of things to come, I could live with that.

gathering the hay

New Home

Fall 1950—Linz, Austria

The place where I now stayed turned out to be a bakery, so every morning the sweet roll would be different, but that luscious coffee remained the same. However, there seemed to be something still nagging at the back of my mind—this could still be a trick, and all these goodies were meant to fatten me before I would be eaten!

After breakfast, Willi was ordered to familiarize me to my new surroundings. Willi was willing. For the next several days, I explored my new home with the help of my private guide.

Our tour started with the street just outside the main door. As we stepped out over the threshold, I immediately felt closed in. A solid row of housing, looming five stories high, flanked either side of the long narrow street. Each private property was defined only by a street number or business sign on its door. Ours was Wurmstrasse 20, Stöber Bäckerei. Whiffs of that mouth-watering baking wafted into the street and swirled into our nostrils as we surveyed our surroundings.

Those towering buildings blocked the sunshine—a blessing in

disguise. The resulting dark shadows partially hid and softened the jagged edges of a rubble directly across the street. An entire portion of the row of housing had been reduced to pancake slabs of concrete. The exposed, charred wall of the remaining unit rose starkly from the gaping hole that was at its centre. No fence or guard rail surrounded it. This was an invitation for me to explore the rubble, but Willi stopped me with a sharp yell.

"*Halt, das ist verbotten!*"

I grudgingly stepped back onto the sidewalk. "Why is it forbidden, and why is that building *kaput*?"

"Bombs from aeroplanes during the war!" he explained, proud that he knew something I didn't.

I knew nothing of bombs, aeroplanes or war, but I didn't like the damage they caused. I was glad it hadn't been done to Willi's home. I would have to ask my new mother about things like this.

Back inside, Willi ushered me around the first floor. I began to get my bearings. We crossed the kitchen where we had eaten breakfast and entered the room where I had slept. My bedroom was actually their business office with the bakery shop right next door. Willi explained that we were not allowed in the shop. I could understand. No one wanted sniffling, drooling children around bakery to be sold. The kitchen, dining room and living room were open to everyone. A set of stairs led up to the private quarters of his family. I was never to go up there!

Fine! What else is there to see?

"Let's go outside and play in the courtyard," Willi said as he pushed open a big wooden door.

Courtyard? I imagined a formal garden with well-groomed trees and grass, like the courtyards of the kings and queens in fairytales. My mind saw lush green gardens, but my eyes saw only grey stone walls! Walls on my left, walls on my right and walls straight ahead. Stone slabs even covered the ground. It was a prison! There was one solitary scraggly vine, and *it* was desperately trying to escape over the wall. A tiny patch of blue affirmed itself overhead. This was certainly a far cry from my parents' farm. Compared to this, it had been pure Eden where I could run barefoot and free on its lush meadows with the sun on my face, the wind in my hair, and the scent of flowers in my nostrils.

Will I ever experience these again!

That night, as my new mother tucked me into the sofa-bed, I asked her about bombs, aeroplanes, war and why the building across the street was damaged. Her initial response to my question was surprise. Then she became quiet and a sadness crept into her eyes. "Before you were born, the world was a bad place. There was much fighting and hurting going on. Many people suffered, many died. We were living here, with you still in my tummy, when the American planes came and bombed Linz." She stopped, sighed, took a deep breath and crossed herself. "The rubble across the street is a reminder of how thankful we are that God had spared the Stöbers and us."

I didn't understand all of that, but I did get the impression that Willi and I had both been fortunate. After she left, I tried to make sense of the war. *Vater* had frequently talked about it. I knew only that it had been a terrible time. Everyone said so. Aside from all that, I was more befuddled by the idea of me being in her tummy.

Had she eaten me then? Will she do it again?

So many questions, so few answers. I tried to sort things out, but nothing made sense. I was not impressed or convinced that everything would be all right. Despite the good friend, great food and a grander home, I became very sad. Every night I would return to this same small room, and listen to the echoing tick-tock of the grandfather clock. There in the dark, I would lie alone, my whole world turned upside down. My *Vater* and *Mutter* were *not* my father and mother. My *Schwester* was *not* my sister. *Mein Haus* was *not* my home.

So then, who am I, where am I, and what is to become of me? Mein Gott im Himmel, my God in heaven, I do so miss my Mutter and family!

Linz's history goes back as far as the Romans, but it

became infamous when Adolf Hitler decided to make it his "home town". He had been born in Braunau, Austria but moved to Linz and lived there briefly in his youth, as did Adolf Eichmann, one of the major organizers of the Holocaust. Adolf Hitler planned to make this small town into an industrial city, a cultural centre where all the looted arts would be housed, and his place of retirement. He used slave labour from the Mauthausen-Gusen concentration camps just twenty miles north of the city for construction and factory workers to build an armament industry and marshalling yards. These, along with the ordnance depot and oil plant gave the Allies a good reason to send twenty-two air raids into Linz from Italy.

Questions

Fall 1950—Linz, Austria

Every night I would dream of my time and my family on the farm, and every morning I would awake to the crushing reality that I no longer lived there. I had to remind myself that my name was now Heli, and that I now lived in Linz, *a.d. Donau, OberÖstereich,* (Linz, on the Danube in upper Austria). A new name, new home, new life and supposedly a new mother. What was I to make of this?

My supposedly new mother, *Mutti,* had black hair, brown eyes and darker skin. With light brown hair, hazel eyes and light skin, I didn't resemble her at all, so how could I be her daughter? Bewildered by these doubts, I had lots of questions that I wanted to ask her. However, I needed to wait until we could be alone without interruptions or, more importantly, until we knew each other a little better. Many opportunities came and went, but I just didn't have the courage at those times. I sensed that personal questions were never asked directly by any adult, and most certainly not by a child.

Then one day while sitting at the kitchen table slurping my *Rind Suppe*, soup made from beef ribs, I found myself alone with my new mother. She had her back to me and was stirring something in a pot on the stove. Whatever it was, it smelled delicious! She seemed in good humour, so I decided this was the time and place. But as my heart began to beat quicker, I had second thoughts. What if she gets angry and throws me into the pot? I needed answers badly, so I swallowed what food I had in my mouth, gulped, then peppered her with my questions.

"Why did you send me to a foster home? Where is the rest of my family? If you are my mother, then who is my father and where is he?" Might as well get them all out at once. I was surprised at my recklessness.

The arm stopped stirring. She didn't move. I held my breath. After what seemed an eternity, she turned, wiped her hands on her apron and wagged her finger at me, "You shouldn't be asking questions like that. It is impolite! You are too young to understand my reasons for sending you away. When you get older, I will tell you all you need to know." She returned to stirring. I waited. Nothing more came.

"Do I have any other brothers or sisters. What about aunties, uncles or grandparents?" I felt like I was digging for gold, but very few nuggets were forthcoming.

She continued stirring but turned to face me to say, "We do have relatives in Hungary and Romania, but with the war, I'm not sure where they might be now."

"What about my father? Where is he and when will I meet him."

She stiffened and had again turned her back to me. I waited even more eagerly for this answer. "Your father died in the war!" Her voice had become low, slow and even, without emotion. She sounded as if she had written and rehearsed it. Why wouldn't she look me in the eye? Was she lying or holding something back? I waited again, but I could see that there would be no further discussion. I thought sarcastically, *God forbid children should get too much information; they are liable to get too smart. That's not good for them! Perhaps I shall try again later.*

I finished the rest of lunch in silence. I had hoped to at least meet my father, but then I realized that I hadn't seen Willi's father around either.

My mother, Elisabeth Méhész, née Kiraly, was born and

raised in Kolosvar, Hungary along with two brothers, Pál (Paul) and György (George), and a sister named Rosie. Because Hungary became an Axis member in 1940, both brothers fought against the Russians on the German side. After the war, Kolosvar was taken over by Romania and became known as the town of Cluj-Napoca. Pál and Rosie survived the war. Both married and had children. György went missing in action.

Proper Young Lady

Fall 1950—Linz, Austria

Eventually I was introduced to the rest of Willi's family. I knew now that he had no father, but he did have grandparents that lived with us and two brothers that I had not yet seen.

His grandparents were both portly and pleasant. His grandfather, *Opa,* had only a few wisps of white hair on his head, but compensated for it with thick white bristles on his chin. *Oma,* his grandmother, on the other hand, had a thick mop of white hair and only a few whiskers on her chin. I performed the required curtsy and was greeted with a smile. Was the smile for the curtsy or for me?

I learned quickly that good social graces and etiquette were very important in this household. There had been no real rules on the farm—just work hard, be kind and stay out of trouble. Here, bad manners would not be tolerated and swift punishment followed from any adult, be it family or stranger. I had actually witnessed a total stranger discipline a child that was not his own. One day during an outing, my new mother and I were about to step on a bus, when a young lad cut in front of us. Suddenly, a hand shot from behind, grabbed the boy's collar and plucked him back.

"Women first!" bellowed a deep voice.

I turned to follow the voice and saw an older gentleman yanking on the ear of the young man and scolding him soundly. No one challenged the man's action, only nodded in approval. It seemed that there was no place for a misbehaving child to hide from the consequences of any bad manners or deeds.

When I came to Linz, I had no idea of what was acceptable and what was not. No one gave me a book of rules, so I learned mostly by trial and error. With my eyes and ears open, I had seen Willi receiving many a cuff to the back of the head or a pull on his ear. So thanks to him, I didn't have to learn them all by myself, the hard way. However, nothing prepared me for the endless new ones that kept emerging. I began to suspect that the adults created new ones daily just to torture us children. A stern look or raised voice in my direction reminded me that I had to always be wary. I learned never to question the established rules nor dare to consider going against them. By hook or by crook, this new place was going to teach me all the social graces, feminine etiquette, and respectable behaviour necessary for a proper young lady.

Brothers Three

Fall 1950—Linz, Austria

Willi and I spent a great deal of time together and became good friends. He never complained, picked a fight or called me names. I couldn't say the same for myself. What belonged to him, belonged to me. What was mine, he didn't want. How could such a small frame hold such a big heart?

Despite the fact that I was maybe a year or two older and a girl, we played well together. The small courtyard that I had moaned about at the beginning leant itself well to playing *Fusball,* soccer. No great distances had to be covered either in moving the ball towards the net, or retrieving it. With only one goalie and one striker taking turns, points were scored every few minutes.

"Go-oal! Your turn!"

Wc switched positions.

"Go-oal! Your turn!"

Somehow, Willi scored more quickly and more often than I did. We did not play roughly because that hard stone surface was not something we wished to come in contact with—accidentally or voluntarily with a feigned injury.

On rainy days, we played the indoor games like cards and board games such as Snakes and Ladders. I had never played cards nor board games, so he won most of those too. I was familiar with only one game —Hide and Seek. Even there, he had the advantage because he was familiar with all the best places to hide, and how to sneak home without being detected. He also owned a wooden train set that we played with for hours. He took the engine, and I held the caboose, and together we followed invisible train tracks under the dining table and chairs.

I began to realize that we always played the games that he chose, never what I wanted.

"Why won't you play house with me?" I asked. "You could be the Papa." I didn't even own a doll, but I used a small towel knotted at three corners to represent the head and two arms. The look of horror on his face translated as a definite "No!"

***

We attended the same kindergarten, where mostly we were taught to socialize but not much about numbers and letters. One day at kindergarten, I was asked to replace one of the girls who played a dwarf in a stage production of Snow White. She had become ill, and they deemed it a perfect role for someone short and rotund like me. With makeup and costume on, all I had to do was follow closely behind the other dwarves. I had no lines, but merely served as a required seventh body. Of course, I gave a stellar performance and was sure the applause was meant exclusively for me.

During our time together, Willi had more than once talked about his brothers, Hermann and Ziegfried, whom I had not yet seen around. I assumed that they were fostered out somewhere, as I had been. Then one day Willi came to get me.

"They're home! They're home!" He grabbed my hand. "Come, you must meet them!"

When we entered the dining room, I expected to see two young boys, but there were only two grown men. Willi let go of my hand, ran and jumped into the arms of one of them.

"This is my brother Hermann, Heli," he squealed with pleasure. Then he pointed to the other man and introduced him as "Ziggy". I curtsied and shook their hands as required. Were they really brothers—they resembled each other so little? They reminded me of the sisters, Snow White and Rose Red, in my fairytales. Although both of Willi's brothers were tall and handsome, Hermann resembled Snow White—fair in appearance with thin blond hair, blue eyes and light skin, while Ziegfried or "Ziggy" had the same features as Rose Red—black hair, dark eyes and complexion. I could see that Willi was overjoyed to have them home.

In the evening, everyone, including the grandparents, gathered around the dining table and celebrated their return. I tried hard to remember my newly-learned table manners: remain standing until given permission to sit, place my napkin on my lap right away and do not begin eating until after the head of the household does. With the knife in my right hand, I must cut only enough of a portion for one bite. Then, using the fork still in my left hand, with tines down, guide the food to my mouth. I should not talk with food in my mouth nor wash it down with the drink. No food was to be left on the plate. When done, my fork and knife should be placed parallel to each other with the handles facing right. I must ask permission to leave the table and thank Frau Stöber.

I found all these rules silly and difficult to remember since I was always too hungry to wait or eat slowly. To them I must have seemed as though I had been brought up by wild animals, for everyone at the table could and would correct me at any time. Thank goodness I was not invited to every meal.

Between concentrating on my manners and properly wielding my utensils, I could not listen in on the conversations. Thus, I never learned where the brothers had been, what they had done or why they returned home now. It didn't really matter; their return lightened everyone's spirit and filled the house with laughter and happiness.

There was nothing that Frau Stöber wouldn't do for her sons. She fussed over them like a mother hen with her chicks. *I wish my new mother had welcomed me like that!*

I did pick up on the fact that Hermann was her favourite. He was more quiet and serious than his brother, and his mother couldn't help but smile with pride and cluck over him with fondness. Ziggy, on the other hand, always appeared to be in trouble with his mother. Each time he greased back his thick black hair, put on his leather jacket and headed out on his motorcycle, I could hear Frau Stöber plead, "Do you have to go out again? There is much work to be done here." After he had gone, she would let out a sigh of resignation, shake her head and mutter, "*Schurke,* (scoundrel)," under her breath.

To me, he was the only adult in this household who was relaxed and laughed easily and often. The scent of his cologne and diesel fumes from his jacket lingered long after he left each time.

Lisi

Fall 1950—Linz, Austria

As time went by, I learned my new mother's Christian name and her position in the Stöber household. Elizabeth or Lisi, as she was affectionately called by all, worked as a live-in servant, doing all the things necessary to allow the Stöber family to carry on the business of the bakery. Before I came to live there, she had also been a nanny to Willi. Now, she cooked, cleaned house, did the laundry and probably considerably more than I knew about, including sanitizing the large bakery room at the back. Very few people were allowed to enter that area.

On a day when there was no one to keep an eye on me, *Mutti* had no choice but to allow me into the bakery while she scrubbed the immense steel drums necessary for mixing the dough. As I entered, I felt an immediate drop in temperature. I became blinded by the white tiles that covered the ceiling, walls and floor—the only two objects not white in this room were my mother and me. The space was so huge that when we spoke, our voices reverberated. That was all I needed to entertain myself. I began to yodel and sing so I could hear the echoes. This did not go over well with my new mother.

"You are driving me crazy. Get out of here and go play in the courtyard."

Even though the ovens were not on at the time, when I left, the aroma of freshly baked bread, flour and the musky yeast remained in my nostrils.

Roaming around the courtyard, I noticed a man on the flat roof of a small shed. A staircase led to the top and before I knew it, I was on the roof and watching him brush some black sticky goop on its surface. I must have startled him for he jumped when he saw me.

"What are you doing up here? Get off immediately! This is hot tar and it's dangerous!"

As he applied the black goop, it spattered everywhere—including on the top of my naked foot.

It hurts! It hurts! I shrieked. I screamed. I hopped.

The man dropped his broom, picked me up and carried me down the steps to the courtyard. I guess my mother heard my screams and came running out. Together in the workman's car, they took me to the Emergency at the nearest hospital. As the doctor tried to remove that sticky stuff, I screamed even more.

My new mother kept looking at the doctor and the workman. "I'm so sorry for all your trouble my daughter has caused you. I told her to play in the courtyard. She never listens."

On the way home, she began scolding me."I can't take my eyes off you without you getting into trouble. Why can't you stay put? I hope you've learned your lesson."

The only lesson I learned was that throughout this incident, my new "*Mutti*" hadn't offered me any sympathy, hugs or encouragement. I also learned that the louder I screamed, the better the bribe. I had walked out of the Emergency department with a bandage and a chocolate bar.

It seemed as though everyone accepted and loved Lisi, especially Willi. But not me! As my real mother, she should at least have shown me the same depth of love as my foster mother had. This new mother did not measure up to my expectations. There were no physical or verbal indications of any affection. I believed what I had been told—that I was such a "lovely child". Why didn't *she* think so? Very little had changed since I first came here. As a result, I still did not trust her, just accepted her as someone who instructed and provided for me.

She did however, dote on Willi a great deal.

I wonder if she would love me better if I was a boy?

St. Nicholas and Krampus

Weihnachtzeit

December 1950—Linz, Austria

Celebrations for Christmas in Austria began on December 6, St. Nicholas Day. The evening before, Willi and I were summoned into the dining room and ordered to stand by the table and wait. When the glass double doors opened, two figures entered.

One in particular frightened me terribly. He looked like a devil or demon with his long protruding tongue, blood-red horns and twitching tail. He wore a black fur cape and carried a willow switch in one hand. I recognized him as *Krampus*—the horned creature who punished bad children by carrying them off in his sack to his lair in the forest. This was the first time I had come face to face with him, and I cowered in fear.

The other figure was dressed like a bishop with fancy robes, a conical hat and a sack over his shoulder. That was kindly St. Nicholas who wouldn't hurt anyone. They both approached us. I wanted to back away, but I felt myself pressed up against the dining room table.

"Remain where you are!" bellowed *Krampus.* He raised his switch as he neared Willi on my left. He was questioned first. "Have you been bad this year?"

Willi mumbled words that no one understood, so *Krampus* lightly tapped his bottom with his switch. He let out a tiny shriek and jumped back. Now St. Nicholas stepped in front of him. "I'm sure you must have done some good deeds, haven't you Willi?"

How does he know his name?

Of course, he couldn't remember anything after the switching! St. Nicholas patted Willi on the head, blessed him and handed him some treats from his sack.

Now my turn came! My knees felt weak and my lower lip trembled. Both figures drew near, studied me then covered their mouths with their gloved hands. No questions were asked. The bishop hastily gave me my treat, then both bolted for the door, their shoulders shaking with barely concealed laughter. At that moment there was something about them that I recognized.

Ziggy and Hermann? Couldn't be! Could it?

No one asked us what we wanted for Christmas, nor did we tell St. Nicholas what we would have liked. That would have been rude and selfish. The Christ Child would choose the presents and He would know what we needed.

After St. Nicholas' visit, serious Christmas preparations began all around us. More than ever, the scent of spices and baking filled the whole first floor. Willi told me what delightful and delectable cakes and cookies would follow soon. "We'll get *Lebkuchen, Springerle* and *Stollen.* My favourite is *Pfeffernüsse.*"

Little by little, I had the chance to taste them all, and I, too, loved the dark moist pepper nuts. I could not believe that I, who loved food so much, became so lucky as to live not just near a bakery, but *in* a bakery. I grew even more chubby, but I still hadn't been eaten by my new mother whom I had thought to be a witch.

A few days before Christmas, the dining and living rooms were off limits to us children. Big secret things were happening! On Christmas Eve, after a light supper, we all sat in the dining room awaiting the arrival of the Christ Child. It was He who would decorate the pine tree and leave the presents under it. He would let us know when everything was ready by ringing a small bell.

We sat as patiently as possible. Finally we heard it! Willi and I jumped up and stood by the living room door in great anticipation. When it burst open, a most wondrous sight filled my eyes. The lights in the room had been turned off. The only illumination came from small burning candles clipped onto the branches of the decorated Christmas tree. Their flickering flames reflected off the shiny ornaments and bounced off the walls and ceiling as if they were coming from heaven itself! The Christ Child had done great work!

Everyone then hugged and wished each other "*Frohe Weihnachten!* Merry Christmas!" Now we were allowed to open our presents that were tucked beside the Nativity Scene. Again, order and etiquette had to be followed. Only one person at a time could open his or her present so that everyone could take part in their delight. Thank goodness, they allowed us children to go first this time!

"Don't tear the wrapping, children," said Frau Stöber. "Give it to Lisi. It needs to be saved for another time."

The adults watched carefully as Willi and I took turns opening our presents. Each of us received one toy and some clothing items. I noticed that the clothing gifts were handed to us first, then lastly our toy gift. Appropriate gratitude needed to be shown either on our face or in our actions, regardless which item showed itself.

I had celebrated Christmas on the farm but never like this. There had been no fancy bought decorations, only what we made by hand. There had been no candles. I had received a few nice clothes and only home made toys.

I opened my presents that first Christmas in Linz and was thrilled. I received a very elegantly embroidered dress, some pretty socks, fine underclothing and a warm cardigan. But the Christ Child knew what I really needed—a doll! She had a delicately sculptured head and a soft cloth body. Dressed in traditional Hungarian clothes, she even had red boots stitched on her feet. Being my first real doll, I named her Greta, after my beloved "sister".

I was happy, but Willi's gift also looked interesting. He received a train set *with tracks*. This engine pulled the cars along without any help from us. It even had "smoke" coming from its chimney. All Willi had to do was drop a pellet down the smokestack and watch the magic! I was fascinated and wanted to play with his new toy.

"Can I please play with your new train. I'll let you play with my new doll."

His eyes opened wide and he shook his head vigorously from side to side. I couldn't understand why he didn't want to play with my doll.

Now, with the flickering candles still moving light and shadows, we stood in a half-circle around the tree. Willi and I were in front of *Opa* and *Oma*, then Frau Stöber and *"Mutti"*, with Hermann and Ziggy at the back. With our faces aglow from the lit tree, we sang our favourite carols starting with *Stille Nacht,* (Silent Night), and *O Tannenbaum,* (Oh Christmas Tree). There was a voice amongst us that seemed to come from heaven. It was so rich, full and vibrant that it made me shiver. I craned my neck around to find its source. To my utter amazement, it was coming out of the mouth of my new mother! I did not know what to make of this. All I knew right then was that a witch simply could not have the voice of an angel! I could not take my eyes off her for the rest of the night.

As the evening went on, we all sat down to a proper meal because soon we would be going to midnight mass. Tonight, everyone was more lenient with my bad table manners. Cookies, candies and chocolates hung amidst the decorations on the tree and were eaten as dessert.

I had a lot to think about, especially about my new mother. Maybe now I could call her *"Mutti,"* but I was not quite ready to allow her into my heart. *I suppose I could rent out a little room in there for her, but my foster mother still occupies most of it for free.*

Faschingssamstag

February 1951—Linz, Austria

Willi and I had good times, but nothing excited me more than the time when we had the chance to dress up in costumes. This took place during Carnival week in February and was called *Faschingssamstag.*

We had gone to the parade in the afternoon and now everyone was preparing themselves for the evening parties. My mother helped Frau Stöber step into her costume for her fancy evening ball. She looked stunning in her long ornate dress and mask.

Willi and I still wore our costumes and had just come back from our own party at kindergarten. I had worn a traditional Hungarian outfit—white embroidered blouse with puffy sleeves, a fancy black skirt and boots. My long hair lay loose, held back by a magnificent headdress made of flowers and wheat heads.

Willi portrayed a Romanian gentleman and wore long white trousers with fringes at the bottom of each leg. His matching white fringed shirt was covered with a black embroidered vest. On his head he wore a round, flat hat called a fez. A charcoal-painted moustache completed his outfit. He looked downright handsome.

Ziggy, too, would soon be getting dressed to go out, but he was now in the office taking photos of us.

"Did you know that in America they get dressed up like this for a celebration called Hallowe'en that takes place in October?" he asked as he moved us around into different poses. "They believe that the souls of the departed wander the earth that night, looking for vengeance. In order to prevent any harm coming from these souls, the people would wear costumes to disguise themselves. But they don't wear costumes like ours. They are costumes of witches, ghosts and ghouls. Some wear horrible looking masks."

"Stop frightening the children, Ziggy," his mother interrupted. "We are not pagans. We are Roman Catholic and don't believe in ghouls."

"Yes, well in America, they allow the costumed children to go door to door to beg for treats. They don't just beg, they threaten them with a mischief if the home owner doesn't give them any," he said, then chuckled. I suspected that he knew this was going to upset his mother.

"Such behaviour from children is outrageous! It is rude and selfish," she said, her voice rising. "Shame on the parents for letting their children beg in the streets like gypsies, especially when everyone knows there is more than plenty of food in America."

Ziggy grinned, his eyes crinkling in glee. He snapped a few more photos before he left the office.

trains in Austria

The Lager

Summer and Fall 1951—Displaced Persons Camp

Mutti's word was good! As promised, the following summer, I rode the train all by myself out to the farm. *Vater* picked me up at the railway station with the same oxen and wagon he had used for my disastrous doctor's appointment. I ran so fast towards him that he had to open his arms to prevent me from flying past. Intentional or not, it resulted in a hug. I knew he was happy because I caught him smiling.

Once we reached the farmhouse, *Mutter* and Greta ran to greet me. My heart skipped a beat upon seeing them again. We squealed with delight as we hugged each other tightly. I couldn't let go of either of them. Finally, *Mutter* asked Greta to do an errand which left me alone with her. I wanted to apologize before anything else.

"I'm so sorry," I said. "I broke my promise never to leave you, *Mutter,* but I had no choice!"

Mutter shook her head, took my hand and led me inside. We sat on the familiar bench by the window where she pulled me towards her. She held me for quite some time, kissing my cheeks and my forehead.

I snuggled closer to breathe in the familiar clean, soapy smell of *Mutter.* I was happy again! When we finally pulled apart, I looked into her face and saw tears in her eyes.

"Don't you apologize to me, *meine Liebchen.* I am the one who should apologize. My baby had just died when you came into my life, and you made it bearable. I nursed you and loved you like my own. Your mother paid me to take care of you and made me promise never to tell you who she was. I didn't agree with her decision, but I had to abide by it. Now I realize that despite her orders, I should have prepared you, at least a little, for that eventual day."

"Why *did* my mother send me to you?" I asked. "Didn't she love me? Was I too much bother?"

She wiped her eyes with her apron. "Helene, you may not understand what I am about to tell you, but the most important thing is that you know that your mother did what she did *because* she loved you and wanted to protect you." She pulled me to her again, and held my hands in hers. "The war had just ended, but Linz was still in ruins. No transportation, no businesses, and most of all, no food. At that time, everyone was doubtful that the war was really over, and if truly so, who or what kind of people would hold our future in their hands. Would it be the Allies or the Russians? Your mother didn't know either, but she knew you would be well fed and safe on this farm. Do you understand now?"

Not really, at least not about the war part, but it was good to hear that my new mother loved me. Too bad she couldn't tell me or show me herself.

I said, "Yes, but you will always be my real mother."

"Why did you say that? Are you not happy?

"I am happy now."

"No, no, she is your real mother, and you must give yourselves the chance to know each other."

Well, I hope we get to know each other soon.

Mutter then gave me one more quick hug and said, "I baked you your favourite. Cherry pie. Would you like some?"

Everything and everyone was forgiven. I was finally away from the high stone walls and narrow streets. Free also from the thousands of rules that I continuously forgot to follow. Once again I felt the warm sun on my face, the cool grass on my bare feet, and smelled the flowers in the meadows. All my problems with *Mutti* disappeared from my mind. It was a glorious time! Eventually though and much too quickly, I had to face reality. Back to the bleak surroundings and constant rules; it took me a little while to get used to them again.

Not long after my return to Linz, my mother ordered me to gather all my things and help her pack our suitcases.

"Who are we visiting?" I asked with growing excitement. "How long are we staying? Are we going to see our relatives? Why are we taking all our stuff?"

"We are not going to visit anyone. We are moving to a different place."

What? I have just become used to this one and to Willi!

"Are Willi and Frau Stöber coming with us?"

"No, no, they will remain here. I am still going to work here, we just won't be living here. You'll get a chance to visit them often. Now get going."

How many times is "often"?

The taxi ride did not take long, and soon we arrived at a place that looked like a compound with many rows of long, low wood buildings. This stark place had no surrounding lawns, trees or sidewalks. We briefly stopped in at an office where an official led us to one of these units. With our luggage in tow, we entered its long dark hallway which had closely spaced doors on each side. The official unlocked one of them and handed the keys to *Mutti.*

"This one is yours. Welcome, and be sure to come to the office once you are settled."

The door opened into a tiny room that held furniture pressed against all four walls—stove, single bed, narrow wardrobe, kitchen cupboard, table and one chair. The center of the room only had enough space for one person to pass at a time. A sliver of daylight shone through a small, grimy window opposite this door. My mother threw the suitcases on the bed and began to unpack.

"Where is my bedroom?" I asked, eager to explore my new home as I had done in Linz.

"There are no other rooms. We are allowed just one. Only larger families get two."

This is it? The kitchen, dining, and bedroom all in one room? This is our new home?

I now felt bad that I had complained about Linz where we had plenty of room, tons of yummy food and lots of good friends. Puzzled, I asked, "Why did we move here?"

"That is not your concern. We will be fine here. Soon you will start school, and you will meet new friends

So who did it concern then? Why did my mother never prepare me for changes? I wonder if she thought like *Mutter* who believed that sometimes it's best not to know everything. Were they both protecting me?

By the way, what is this place?

I kept my eyes and ears open for clues. Through bits of conversations here and there, I learned that this place was a temporary shelter, a displaced persons' camp called a "*Lager*". This particular camp was *Lager* #67 in Wegscheid, near Linz.

"What is a displaced person, *Mutti?*" I finally had to ask.

"A displaced person is someone that had been forced from their home," she replied. "We are not like them, so don't worry your little head about it."

I certainly *felt* like a displaced person—forced away from my foster mother's love and my original home on the farm!

Once I had a chance to look around, I learned that the buildings were called barracks. They were made of unpainted wood and all looked alike. Most, like ours, housed people. Others were used for a bathhouse, or laundry. My mother always brought back our laundered clothes and hung them on a line just outside our window where we could keep an eye on it. "There are many thieves and gypsies here. We have to guard our belongings!"

We had lights, but no running water in our room. It became my job to fetch water from a pump not far from our barrack. We used that water for drinking, cooking, and washing a few items of small clothing. My mother used the bathhouse occasionally, but most of the time we would both bathe in our room with a washcloth and a basin of warm water.

Other buildings in the compound included a store, two churches, and brand new pit toilets. *Mutti* would send me to the store in the *Lager* for the occasional item, but she preferred to bring food from the Stöber's or buy it at a store in Linz. We did not attend the Roman Catholic Church in the compound. I asked my mother if we could go to the *Orthodoxe Kirche* for a change; I wanted to see what it looked like inside. She reacted as if I had asked her to go to the place where the devil dwelt.

"That is not the church our Lord wants us to go to. Don't you go near that place or talk about this anymore," she said, her eyes wide with fear. She crossed herself and muttered, "God forgive her!"

Again, I did not understand. It had the title "Church". I thought God lived everywhere?

The front of the compound seemed to be the place with the most activity. If anyone needed anything or had a question or a problem, they would go these offices. That's where I noticed new folks coming in and old friends leaving, never to be seen again. Where did they come from, and where did they go?

***

We no longer had sumptuous meals or luxuries like pastries and whipped cream coffee. We had to switch to tea, but *Mutti* did not like the bland taste of it.

"It tastes like dishwater!" she moaned, then promptly added a tablespoon or two of rum. I loved it but was allowed to have it only in the evening or bedtime. I didn't know why. On special occasions, my mother made her famous chocolate wafer cake that required no baking and consisted of thin round layers of wafers filled and covered with chocolate icing that also contained rum. Needless to say, she wouldn't let me have too much of it.

My mother had the oddest taste buds. One day she came home with some dried salami. She cut it very thinly, placed it on a plate and added oil and vinegar to it. I knew it would taste awful, but after watching *Mutti* gobble it down, I had to try it. It was heavenly! Was there anything I wouldn't eat?

The victorious Allies had to solve the problem of the vast number of refugees from all over Europe. Some were inmates of the Nazi concentration camps, others had their homes destroyed or confiscated and still others had fled in fear of the Soviet onslaught. They all required shelter, nutrition and healthcare along with psychiatric care. Some were even beyond help. The Allies built these camps where the displaced people could stay until either they returned to their homes, found new ones on their own, or were sponsored by another country.

school children

Precious

Fall 1951—Lager

Even though my mother still worked at the bakery, there were times when I would accompany her as she cleaned offices and homes.

My job was to go to school. We children were bussed to a school north of the camp on Niedernharterstrasse. I was eager to start school, but once there, I wasn't so sure any more. All children beginning grade one were guided into a room; there seemed to be quite a few of us. Knowing no one, I searched for a friendly face and found none. Some glared at me,while others wouldn't even meet my eyes. Still others looked around in terror. Several of the boys acted up, while a few of the girls cried.

Appearance and language differed vastly—from fair skinned to dark skinned, from reasonably dressed to rags, all speaking their own homeland language. I also noticed that not everyone was the same age. Some were older but were still placed in grade one. At first, I thought it was because they had failed some grades, but soon learned they were behind in their schooling because of the 'war'. That word again—war. Many things seemed to be blamed on it, but I still didn't understand what it was.

Herr Tomaschewsky, our schoolmaster, introduced himself and told us to find a desk and sit down. A few of us immediately found a place, but several didn't seem to understand German, and so only copied the rest of us. He watched and shook his head as if in despair. Later I overheard him moaning to one of his colleagues, "I don't know how I am going to gather these precious, unravelled threads of children and mould them into loving and useful human beings."

My mother had bought me an attractive wooden pencil case with a hand painted gnome, snail and toadstool on it. Inside was a pencil I had used many times before. My mother had shown me how this pencil served two purposes. It could be used as an ordinary pencil that was erasable. Or, by wetting the nib with my saliva and using it before it dried, the markings came out purple and permanent. In order to maintain the ink version of this pencil, I had to wet the nib every minute or so resulting in purple, bruise-like markings on my lips and tongue. *Mutti* and I had both laughed the first time that happened.

Now, my school mates had a good time with it also. "Helene's been bad again, and the teacher had to beat her."

The more I tried to explain the marks, the more they taunted me. I gave up and tried not to wet the nib anymore. So, with one scribbler, one pencil and one reader titled *Frohes Lernen* (Happy Learning), I discovered the magic of reading and writing. I also formed a friendship with two sisters, Eva and Maria, who were in the same grade and from the same camp. We became inseparable at school and at home.

At the beginning of grade one, we learned to print with pencil, but by the end we were using ink. Writing in ink made me feel like a grownup, but it came with many difficulties. The "pen" consisted of a metal tip inserted into a wooden holder. The nib had to be refilled every few minutes by dipping it into an open inkwell. I had no idea that ink was so mischievous. At one time, it actually leapt into my new pencil case, ruining its beauty forever! Then another time, it ran off my overfilled nib and deposited itself on my nice clean white paper. The nib also caused me grief. As I attempted to write, it produced lovely scratching sounds, but if I applied just a smidgen more pressure, it objected by tearing the page.

Each time I did not end up with a perfect piece of work, I crumpled the page into a tight ball and discarded it into my desk. I started again with a nice clean sheet of paper. No one was going to see that the ink and the nib had got the better of me! No one except Herr Tomaschewsky—the person who I least wanted to be aware of it. He opened the desk top and looked horrified to find several of these balls. He took them out, unrolled one, smoothed out the paper and laid it on top of my desk.

"Do not waste paper, Helene! Do you know that during the war, paper was as precious as gold. Every bit of white space was used up on every piece of paper available. From here on out, you will unroll each and every one these and write on them until they are used up. When they are gone, show me, and only then will I give you fresh ones."

There goes that word "war" again. How am I supposed to know what went on before I was born?

My mother also had reason to scold me for being wasteful. *Mutti* had allowed me to wear one of her lovely scarves to school one day. I don't know how, but it hid from me, and I couldn't find it before I had to leave for home. My mother became incredibly upset and screamed at me in anger. "I have had this scarf for over twenty years and have taken good care of it. You wear it for one day and it's gone. How could you? It was precious to me." She blinked back tears.

I felt really bad but couldn't undo what I had done. I wanted to say I was sorry, but before I could open my mouth, she interrupted in an even sadder voice. "I don't have very many beautiful things, so the ones I have, I take good care of. You need to do the same. Look how you have ruined your precious pencil case. You are a very careless child."

This was about the third time I heard the word "precious" in a very short time. I thought about what my teacher and my mother had said about their precious items. When I began to think about what was precious to me, I realized that when I'd had an abundance of my *Mutter's* love, I did not respect and appreciate it. I learned that day that it was the lack of a thing that made it so precious.

Wegscheid 67, also known as Maurice Tyler #337, was originally erected to service the German anti-aircraft personnel, regiment #38. When the Americans arrived, they converted these barracks into a settlement for the displaced people of Europe.

Saving Babies

1952—Lager

The following summer holiday, I again joined my foster family on the farm. My time there was still my happiest; it made me new again.

Once back, I headed into grade two at the same school. This year, for the first time, I had a class called Catechism where I learned about a man called Jesus. *Mutti* and I had gone to church, but I knew very little about God and Jesus. I enjoyed the bible stories but did not understand the importance of Jesus and the sacraments.

Besides Catechism, there was another class that we girls took to prepare for our First Communion. We were taught to crochet so that we could make a small handbag to go with our outfit for that day. We used a very fine thread and hook. I struggled to get even tension. My teacher would accept nothing but perfection.

My mother had me fitted for a dress by a seamstress in the camp. The lady showed me a picture of what it would look like—long, white, with ruffles at the bottom. I loved it, thanked my mother and could hardly wait.

The night before my First Holy Communion, my mother washed my long hair and instead of rinsing it with vinegar, she used sugar water and rolled it up in small white rags. The next morning, the rags were removed to reveal delicate curls that held their shape. A white floral headband held back my long loose locks. My mother helped me into my dress, white socks and shoes. White gloves and my crocheted bag completed my outfit. One look in the mirror on the clothes closet, I knew I was beautiful!

I danced in front of the mirror. *"Ich bin schön, Ja?* I am beautiful, yes?*"*

"Ja, Ja, du bist schön," my mother replied. Then in the next breath, "Don't be vain!"

When we arrived at the church for the ceremony, I was eager to show off my great outfit to Eva and Maria. I caught a glimpse of them, but they had their backs towards me.

"Can we please join them?" I asked my mother.

She agreed, and we began to move towards them. Just as we approached, the two sisters turned around. I took one look at them and gasped. To my surprise, they were outfitted in the *same dress*, *same bag* and *same hairdo* as I! I guessed the seamstress at the *Lager* only had one pattern. We looked like identical triplets. Some very uncharitable thoughts crossed my mind towards my best friends at that moment. But soon, with all the excitement around me, I forgot my irritation and sidled up between them for the photo taking. With all that sugar in our hair, I hoped no flies or bees would show up to ruin our day.

***

Aside from that small hiccup, my friendships with Eva and Maria grew. The *Lager* grounds had no play areas for us, not even a patch of grass, just loose dusty soil. We became bored hanging around the crowded barracks where people were constantly yelling at us to be quiet or to go away. We decided to explore outside our compound for greener pastures. Near the edge of its perimeter, we came upon a field of green grass on a small hill.

As we cheered and jumped around at our success, we discovered what looked like underground dwellings. These were made of thick cement in the shape of a loaf of bread with only the crust or top peeking above the grass, and the rest was hidden underground. Wide excavated paths led down into the earth to entrances on either side. We searched until we found one that had doors missing. Cautiously, we followed the path to its interior. Our eyes needed time to adjust, but with the sunlight coming from the opposite open end, we could make out a low, narrow space. The ceiling followed the same curvature as the exterior, and an electrical wire snaked its way to a single burned-out bulb hanging low in the centre. We had to be careful not to break the bulb with our foreheads. Two long benches were braced against the length of each opposing wall. Dust and rubble covered every surface. In some places, broken concrete exposed jagged supporting rods. Though it was dark, dank and scary, we thought they would make good play houses. There were six of them—more than enough for all three of us.

"This one's mine!" Eva took possession by brushing off the dust accumulated in the benches and clearing the rubble from the floor.

Maria and I each searched for our own. Both entrances at each end had to be open in order to have enough light. We followed Eva's example and cleaned each one up as much as we could. Rushing back to the barracks, we brought our dolls to our new "homes". I did not want to be secretive like my mother, so I explained everything to my doll, Greta. After we cleaned our houses a bit more, we visited each other for tea. From then on, we spent all our playtime here. We talked about how lucky we were that no one else had discovered this "village".

One Saturday morning, as I was heading out to meet my friends in this village, my mother called me back. "Stop for a moment. Where are you going, Heli? You haven't been at your friends' house because I asked their mother, and she thought that you were all playing here. If you're not here nor there, then where are you girls spending your time?"

I didn't want to share our special secret, so I just pointed in the general direction of our village and said, "Over there!"

"You're not getting into any trouble, are you?"

"Nope, we are playing house." I wasn't lying!

"All right then, but don't stay too long."

Later, I bragged to my friends how cleverly I had fooled my mother without lying. We giggled and carried on with our household duties.

It couldn't have been more than ten minutes when Maria was knocking at my pretend door. "Heli, your mother is coming up the hill towards us. I thought you said you didn't tell her!"

"I didn't!" *How did she find out where we were? She must have followed me! Darn those mothers—they are always so nosy!*

I stood inside my "house" holding my doll and waited until my mother drew near. "Come see my house. Isn't it wonderful." I invited her in. She would be proud how clean and tidy it was.

She hadn't even stepped over the threshold when I could see the blood drain from her face as a look of total horror crept across it. She leapt upon me like a cat, grabbed my arm and yanked me out with such a force I thought my arm would come off. As soon as we were both out, she ordered me to stay put. She ran to the other units screaming at the top of her lungs, "Get out! Get out! Get away from here!" As Eva and Maria popped out, *Mutti* hauled them to where I was standing. With me in one hand, Eva in the other and Maria in tow, she dragged us down the hill to the barracks. I looked up at my mother's face trying to get a reading as to what was going on. Her face was white, her lips were drawn tight, and she was breathing heavily. Something had frightened her, but for the life of me I couldn't guess what.

She took all three of us to Eva and Maria's mother. They were speaking so fast that we couldn't understand a word. All we could hear was the shrill, terrified voice of *Mutti* and the slow, composed voice of my friends' mother attempting to calm her. We stood there dumbfounded until Eva's mother led us over to the table and sat us down.

Her voice was low and grave. "You must never go and play there again. It is extremely dangerous. Your playhouses are actually bomb shelters."

I knew that bombs were bad because I had discussed that with my mother when I was in Linz, but I still did not have a full understanding of “bomb shelters”.

“What are bomb shelters?” we asked in unison.

“They’re places where people stayed to be safe when the bombs fell. Now, they are in ruin and can collapse and crush you. There might be live electrical wires or live ammunition left behind. All those things can hurt you very badly! You must promise us that you will never, ever go there again. It is v*erboten*!”

I knew nothing of live ammunition or live wires, and I could see that Eva and Maria didn’t either. I did understand *“verboten”*, and that was good enough for me.

Later, Eva, Maria and I talked about this amongst ourselves. We were sad that we were forced to leave our “homes”, but considered ourselves brave and happy that we had saved our “babies”’.

Initially the US military managed Wegscheid 67's operation, but from 1946 and on, it was run by various international committees like UNRRA (United Nations Relief and Rehabilitation Administration), IRO (International Refugee Organization) and UNHCR (United Nation High Commissioner for Refugees). After 1950, it was given back to Austria, but there was still money and other aids coming from the international communities.

Talking Mind

Summer 1953—Lager

Mother kept her word again, and we visited the Stöbers regularly and especially on holidays like Easter or Christmas. Willi had grown taller and more handsome, but he was not as attentive to me as before. I felt sad but realized that we had both moved on to new friends and adventures. It was still nice to see him, though.

Ever since mother and I had moved to the *Lager,* our close quarters forced us to spend more time together. I had thought this would be the time when we could get to know each other. I began to know her all right, but found her odd. She still didn't talk with me, but rather at me, and then only if there were orders or instructions that needed to be given. The only person she did talk to, was herself. Without realizing it, she would speak her thoughts. In so doing, she accidentally allowed me into her mind, and I came to know her better than if we had had an ordinary conversation. Mostly, I did not agree with, nor understand, her opinions or reactions.

On one of our many outings, my mother and I were seated on a trolley bus in Linz. I didn't care where we were going, as long as I was able to get out of that crowded room. Peering through the window, I tried to count the number of buildings still in ruin. My concentration was broken by the sudden jerk of the bus as it stopped to pick up passengers.

I also loved watching people and was fascinated by a striking blond woman who entered our bus. She was not look like the other women, and it wasn't because she had a short, stylish haircut or wore red lipstick. It was because she was wearing slacks—beige, wide-legged and pleated! Never having seen a woman wearing lipstick nor slacks, I thought her to be very attractive. I was about to bring her to my mother’s attention when I realized that she too was staring at her.

“*Americaner!* Only *that* kind of woman would wear pants like a man. Has she no shame!” was what came out of my mother’s mouth to no one in particular. Then, in almost a whisper, the word, “*kurva*” escaped.

That kind of woman? And what was a *kurva*? Were there different kinds of women? I studied the woman in the slacks but was unable to see any differences except that she was far prettier than all the rest. She appeared quiet and composed. So, who was really acting shamefully?

Another time, again in Linz, my mother and I were walking down a street when a young, but rather larger lady walked towards us. As she neared, I noticed she wasn’t large at all—just had a big round tummy. She wore no makeup and looked charming with her loose navy dress draped smartly over her tummy.

Mutti stared as she neared, then muttered under breath, “She shouldn’t be in public at this time! This is very offensive!”

Because she was talking to no one in particular, I asked, “Why can’t people with big tummies leave their house, *Mutti?*”

“She is with child, and it is improper to show this in public.”

I don’t see any child!

. the way one should slide down a hill

Could or Should

Fall 1953—Lager

During the summer between grade two and three, my mother again allowed me to visit my foster family. Once again, I was filled with affection and assured that I was a "lovely child".

"I promised that I would never leave you, so here I am again," I told them.

This time, my vacation with them seemed shorter than ever, and soon it was time for me to leave. Now that we had seen each other several times, we were confident that our *"Auf Wiedersehn"* really meant "see you again". So, *Mutter*, Greta and I were able to say our goodbyes with less heavy hearts than before.

Back at the *Lager*, I was generally having a good time, but my usual renewed confidence and cheerfulness did not survive long into the new school year. Once I entered grade three at a newly built school on Stadlerstrasse, I realized that everything and everyone had become more serious.

"Stop talking, Helene. Sit up straight and stop that fidgeting," my new teacher snapped at me during class. "My goodness you are a restless child!"

How can I <u>not</u> be restless? There was nowhere for us to go at recess. Because of the new construction, the grounds were still too muddy and no room had been readied for us to play inside. We had to remain in our seats, which meant no roughhousing or running. Chatting and giggling was fine, but no shouting or loud laughing were allowed.

Grade three also meant fractions and multiplication tables. I couldn't comprehend either of them. No matter how hard I practised my times tables at night, by the time I reached the classroom, I couldn't remember anything. Between my poor math skills, my squirming and chatting, I did not become the teacher's favourite. School or learning wasn't fun anymore, so I began to daydream in class which further irritated my teacher. The more she harassed me, the more I hated school, and the less I progressed.

Restless and unhappy, I was constantly attempting to find ways to amuse myself. One cloudy fall day, I stepped off the school bus and caught sight of some boys from my class sliding down a grassy slope on their school bags. The wet grass from the recent rain increased their speed and thrills. That looked like so much fun—something that I did not have much of recently. With my own new leather school bag on my back, I headed to the top of the hill. I watched as the boys laid the front of their bags down on the grass, sat on it, and used the back straps to steer the "sled" down the hill.

Nothing to it! I can do this.

But my skirt posed a problem. I used the same method as Greta and I had used when we climbed the fruit trees—pull the back of the skirt between the legs and tuck it into the front waist band. With my modesty now intact, I attempted my first run. I had barely started down the hill, when I fell off my bag and rolled the rest of the way down to the bottom. I picked myself up, climbed the hill again and studied the boys' methods more closely. They had not used the straps for steering but only their feet. Press the ground with your left foot, and it turned you left, and vice versa. I followed their lead and soon I went faster and farther than most of the boys. The boys did not cheer me on, they just looked at me in horror.

After several exhilarating slides down this hill, I realized that I better stop and get home. My mother did not like it when I was late. As I ran towards the barrack, I realized that everything on me was either wet or muddy, including my new school bag. There was nothing I could do to clean myself up. *Mutti will be furious!*

I stopped outside our door, panting and sweating and trying to gather myself, hoping with all my heart that she wasn't home, or she wouldn't notice my state.

How can I explain my appearance? What excuse will she believe? I could say that I had been pushed into some mud. Yes, that sounds good.

I opened the door and looked at my mother's face. It told me that I wasn't going to get away with anything. Before I could blurt out my excuse, my mother put me over her knee and spanked me with a wooden spoon. One, two, three painful whacks. Wishing I was wearing Willi's *Lederhosen,* I began to cry! After the spanking, she made me kneel in the corner to think.

I had never been punished like this before. As I knelt on that hard wood floor, I wondered what I had done to deserve this. Was it because I was late, or because I'd ruined my clothes and school bag? I had been careless again, and had not taken good care of the things my mother worked so hard for. But it had been such a great opportunity for fun.

Perhaps in the future I must try to remember that just because I could, doesn't mean I should.

There was one more decision I came to. No wooden spoons would ever be allowed in *my* house.

Hepatitis

Fall 1953—Lager

That fall, I became quite ill. I had no energy and, strangely enough, no appetite. When I saw myself in the mirror, my skin and the whites of my eyes were yellow. *Mutti* became alarmed and took me to the clinic in the *Lager*. After a brief examination, the doctor informed my mother that he suspected I had hepatitis.

"What is that, and how did she get it?" my mother demanded. "I keep everything clean. It must be those dirty gypsies that are bringing diseases into this camp."

The doctor seemed taken aback by her comment and said, "Now, Frau Méhész, let's not be unkind. Everyone who enters here is checked for communicable diseases. Not all can be easily detected. We try very hard to have good sanitation and clean water, but things like this will happen. That is why I am here." He took my mother's arm and gently continued. "The important thing now, Frau Méhész, is that you get your daughter to the hospital right away. We are not sure if she has the milder strain or the bad one, but either way, she still needs to be isolated and treated. I will phone ahead and let them know you are coming. Can you manage?"

She managed, but I did not. I was so weak that I could not walk on my own, so she had to carry me to the bus and then to the hospital. There, they took some blood and immediately took me to a ward. My mother was not allowed to follow. Once in a room, I was placed in a bed that resembled a baby's crib, except that it was large enough to accommodate me when I was lying down, and the metal side bars were so high that they reached under my arms when I stood up. I couldn't understand the purpose of that because I had no energy to escape even if I could. I peered through the bars. There were more beds like mine with other children in them, all different shades of yellow.

Mutti was not allowed to visit me in the hospital; all she could do is wave from the grounds below while I looked down from the third floor window. Each time she came, she brought me goodies that were later brought up to my ward. As I had no appetite, they were dispensed to other children that were almost well. I did not mind that, but I did object to the vast quantities of cooked vegetables, especially carrots, that they stuffed down my throat. I figured that was probably why we all glowed yellow. I developed a loathing for cooked vegetables from that day on.

It seemed to take forever for me to get my strength back and eventually get out of the hospital. I overheard my mother explain to the neighbours that I had the "milder form". It made her feel better, but they looked more relieved than she did.

> *When Wegscheid 67 originally opened in 1946, it was the largest Jewish transit camp in Austria housing about 4,000 inhabitants. At that time, Wegscheid was seriously overcrowded, resulting in inadequate food supply, bad sanitation, and serious health problems like pneumonia, tuberculosis, hepatitis and parasites. When my mother and I arrived in 1951, there were only about 100 barracks in relatively decent condition with good sanitation. New refugees, undernourished, in poor health and carrying diseases, were still arriving. The medical teams tried hard to assess them for communicable diseases, but some went*

undetected, like hepatitis. This disease could not be diagnosed in its early stages, nor was it tested when the person had no symptoms, but was a carrier. Once established though, it spread rapidly in the camp. The virulent form, Hepatitis B, was often fatal.

red-white-red Austrian flag and emblem

Uprooted

Winter 1953-54—Lager

That year, winter was early and surly. Grey clouds hung heavy and low, blocking out any trace of sun. The wind howled and battered at our tiny window. Temperatures swung between balmy and bitterly cold.

The grounds in the camp, bare of grass and trees, had been dusty and dry in the summer except for the occasional rain that turned it to soup. With no sidewalks, we slipped and slopped in the mud. Now, with continuous melting and freezing, we either plodded through boot-sucking mud, or stumbled in the frozen, ankle-breaking crevices hidden by the snow.

This meant I had to stay indoors in the cramped quarters with my mother. If it was dismal outside, it was depressing inside. Both of us were getting cranky, but of course, I couldn’t show mine, whereas she did—at every opportunity. I never realized how much she nattered at me until now, when I couldn't escape into the coldness outside. It took every effort not to scream back at her or cry in frustration.

I would have gone mad had it not been for the kindness of my friends. I could not invite Eva and Maria to our place to play, as it simply would have been too crowded. Also, I did not want them to see the state of my mother. They understood that there was no room and made sure to invite me over to their two-room apartment as often as they could. It was such a relief!

Each time before I left to play with them, *Mutti* would always stress, “Remember not to stay for a meal. They have enough mouths to feed. Besides I don’t want people thinking I can’t feed my own child.”

“*Ja, Ja!*” I would promise, even though I knew they would always encourage me to have some of their mother’s cabbage soup, which I didn't consider to be a meal.

The three of us enjoyed ourselves in their bedroom playing games or playing house with our dolls. I noticed that Eva and Maria’s parents never nattered at them. Maybe I *was* a pest, as Greta used to call me, and that was why my mother was at me all the time

Gott sei Danke! Thank God it will be soon be Christmas and I will be away from this stuffy room.

The holidays finally arrived, and we were once again at Stöber’s Bakery in a breathable space, amongst loving friends, luscious food, and soothing music. This small break did wonders for me and *Mutti*. The sudden change in her was startling but welcome.

How long will it last? Never mind, just enjoy.

Unfortunately before long, it was time to go back to cramped quarters, a cranky mother and an even crankier teacher. It felt like this winter would drag on forever. All I could think about was summer and the farm. But mostly I wanted out of school. I prayed hard to my Guardian Angel to make it happen quickly.

It came faster than I expected. Near the end of February, my mother announced, “I’m taking you out of school soon.”

“*Wunderbar!*”

No more sour looks or finger wagging from my teacher. No more hours of homework with no reward. Despite the fact that I wanted out, I knew that neither my Guardian Angel nor my mother would normally have granted me that wish. So what had prompted this decision and why?

To try to make sense of this, I looked back over the past few months for any clues. There had been some out-of-the-ordinary occurrences as far back as the beginning of grade three. A lady, whom I did not recognize, had come to write and read letters for *Mutti* in a language I did not understand. Secondly, my mother had paid a photographer to come to our room and take photos of me and my toys. That was not as unusual as the number of appointments we had with officials. There were also doctor's examinations and x-rays. I had to have needles for blood tests and injections. But I wasn't sick, except of school, so why all these tests?

Again, my mother had explained nothing so I had to ask."Why did I have to see a doctor? Am I sick again?"

"No, Heli. We are moving."

"Again? Where?"

"We are moving to Kanada," she said.

"Where is Kanada?"

"It is in America," she replied.

"Where is America?"

"Across the ocean."

"Where is the ocean?" There was no answer. I wondered if she really knew the answer. "Why are we moving again?" I asked, still wondering. I knew she wouldn't answer that one either because I shouldn't "worry my little head about it" or "it didn't concern me".

She did, however, instruct me to start packing.

At that time and even today, some Europeans refer to Canada as America. As far as they are concerned, we come from the same North American continent, therefore are considered "American".

Austria!

Goodbyes

Spring 1954—Lager

Grudgingly, I began to gather all my toys. Since being given my original cloth doll, I had also acquired a doll carriage and a small one-roomed doll house. I thought it resembled the very room we lived in with almost the identical furniture—stove, bed, wardrobe, table and chairs.

When *Mutti* saw me gathering them, she interrupted me. "Heli, you cannot take any of your toys. We are allowed only one large trunk for our important things that will be stored, and one suitcase to keep with us. Toys are not essential."

They're important to me!

"Can I at least just take my doll?"

"No, there is just no room! I promise when we get to America, I will buy you a new doll that will be more beautiful than ever."

No doll could ever be as beautiful as my Greta, but I also knew that my mother usually kept her promises.

After that, there was much hurrying and scurrying, and soon it was time to say our goodbyes to the Stöbers. Despite our having grown slightly apart, Willi did give me a big hug, but then he turned away quickly. *Oh well, maybe because he's older, he's just embarrassed about hugging a girl.*

As photographs were exchanged, everyone started to cry. Why were we exchanging photos? Why was everyone crying? Between the tears everyone promised to write. Why are we going to write? Couldn't we just visit each other as we had before? I thought we were just moving a little farther away and just wouldn't see each other as often. How far away was this Kanada anyway? All this made me very suspicious!

"*Mutti,* are we going to be able to visit the Stöbers during the holidays? What about my friends at the *Lager*? Most of all, will I will be going to the farm again this summer?"

"No, Heli," she said as she wiped her eyes. "We are moving far far away and will probably never see anyone from here again, so you better say your proper goodbyes."

Never see the Stöbers or my friends again? Never see my foster family again?

I felt hopeless—no more girlish secrets, no more loving, comforting hugs and kisses, and definitely no nods of approval. The thought of that made me terribly sad and anxious.

"How will I be able to give my proper goodbyes to my foster family if I don't see them again?"

"There will be no time to visit them, Heli. You will have to write them a letter when we get to Kanada."

I would be breaking my promise to see them again. It made my last *"Auf Wiedersehn"* a lie. Now, *I* started to cry.

We also took our leave at the *Lager.* I only had two good friends here—Eva and Maria. Their mother had told them about our situation, so they knew we were never going to play together again. I hugged my friends; we cried. I handed Eva my doll, Greta, and said, "Promise to take good care of her. She is a good girl and deserves a good mother."

I made sure to explain to my Greta that Mommy had to leave, and that Eva will love her as much as I did. She would be in good hands. I hoped she understood that I had no choice in this matter.

I wonder if my mother had a choice when she left me at the farm.

As we packed our final items, I came across the photographs that we had exchanged during our farewells. There was one of Willi, his mother and his grandparents. We also had individual ones of Hermann and Siegfried. In the photographs all were smiling. I was not.

> *Our train ride from Linz to Rotterdam, Holland involved several countries. I assume we were given a circuitous route due to the still damaged railways across Europe. Or, perhaps like in Canada, they also had special trains for emigrants. I'm not sure which countries we actually passed through, but our passport allowed us through Italy, Switzerland, France, Germany, Belgium and finally into Holland. There, we boarded one of the many emigration ships to Canada.*

Groote Beer

March 1954—On the emigration ship

Before long, we had crossed Europe on a rattling train to who knows where, taking me even farther away from my loving foster family and all my friends.

"Are we in Kanada yet?" I asked my mother with a hopeful heart as we got off the noisy train after several wearying days on its cold hard benches to get there—wherever that was.

She sighed. "No, we have arrived in Rotterdam, Holland and we still have a very far way to go.

I had no concept of time or distance, but I did know that I was bored and tired. Thankfully, I had a good rest that night in a comfortable hotel. It felt so good to sleep in a warm, soft bed and not be disturbed by the noise of other passengers or the rattling of the train. I was more refreshed and eager as we headed towards the dock to board the enormous ship that would take us across the ocean to America. I had not seen many boats, certainly not one this size. *Mein Gott! Surely it is larger than Noah's Ark. How can anything this big and heavy stay afloat?*

A strange odour lingered in the air. I wrinkled my nose and asked *Mutti,* "What is that smell?"

"I think it's the smell of the sea," she replied. "I don't like it."

For me, it wasn't familiar, but it wasn't unpleasant.

The officials lined us up by the gangway, checked our papers, our luggage and before long we were on board. As I looked down from the railing, the people on the dock looked like ants scurrying here and there. *Mutti* and I were soon directed to our cabin that had two sets of bunk beds and two sinks. I immediately claimed one of the upper bunks, kindly leaving my mother the boring bottom one. However, we couldn't claim it as "our" cabin because as my mother plunked our suitcase on one of the bunks, another mother/daughter pair was led in.

The mother looked around and then in clear German asked the assistant, "Why couldn't my husband and son have joined me in this cabin. There are enough bunks for the four of us?"

The man had just turned to leave when he heard her question. He patiently turned back and politely explained, "There are no private cabins on this voyage, ma'am. This vessel once transported soldiers during the war, and has now been modified to carry as many emigrants as possible. In order to make this an efficient crossing, we relegated the soldiers' dormitories to the men and older boys, and the officers' cabins to the women and young children. All are separated, even if they are married. This way, no bunk is left empty, and the women have their privacy. Remember, you are not allowed to visit the men's dormitory, nor will your husband or son be able to come to this cabin."

A look of great concern crossed the woman's face, and with a voice slightly higher than the last time, asked, "Are you saying that I will not be able to see my husband and son until the end of this voyage?"

"Oh, you can see each other in all the public places like the deck, the dining room or in the hallways. Just not here." He stepped outside the cabin and pointed down the passageway. "You'll find signs in the corridor indicating the locations of the bathrooms and showers. As soon as you have dropped off your belongings, go to the muster station for instructions." He left us to ourselves.

The woman introduced herself and her four-year-old daughter and explained she came from Germany. *Mutti* tried to be polite but was not overly friendly. I knew she did not like strangers, but she did wait for the woman and her daughter so that we could all head onto the deck together. Once there, translators of all sorts were informing their passengers. I heard our German translator explain that we were aboard the Dutch ship SS *Groote Beer*.

"It means the Great Bear," he said. "She will be tugged out to the North Sea, then on her own power, turn south. When we reach the Strait of Dover, we will inform you so that you may see the famous White Cliffs from the right side of the ship. Once past, we will steam through the English Channel, then west to the Atlantic Ocean until we arrive in Halifax, Kanada."

I heard the words, but I was too distracted by the great number of people around me with their strange clothes, strange languages and even stranger smells to pay much attention. Another translator gave us instructions for any emergency situations. He showed us how to put on our life vests and explained why we needed to walk in an orderly fashion to a specific area on the deck near the lifeboats. He explained that in case of a bad storm we may have to evacuate this liner and get into these boats.

Leave this big ship and get into those puny boats in a storm? Are they crazy? I would rather stay on board should that time come, *Danke Schön!* Surely, this Great Bear could swat down any mighty winds with her paws and devour the boiling waves.

Although this was not a luxury liner, our food and services were good. The staff tried hard to meet our needs and treated us with respect and kindness. *Mutti* only had to find the correct translator if she needed anything or had any questions.

I was pretty excited the first morning my mother and I went to the dining room for breakfast. The room wasn't fancy, but they had white tablecloths and flowers on each table. This morning, we had a table all to ourselves. I assumed the person who seated us realized that she spoke German and had arranged for a German speaking waiter. My mother was informed that breakfast would be sausages and eggs—

something we were familiar with. As we waited for our meal, the waiter brought us what appeared to be a large pale orange; each of us getting a half.

"This is a grapefruit," he explained. "It is important to eat as much of it as possible."

He demonstrated how to cut and and pry out the sections with a spoon. He tried to translate its meaning into German for *Mutti,* and I understood it as fruit of the grape. It didn't look like a grape and, as soon as I took one bite, I knew it didn't taste like a grape. My mother, too, made such a face that I started to giggle, and before long, even she began laughing.

When the waiter returned, she asked him, "Will all the fruit in Kanada be this bitter?"

He laughed, apologized and suggested we put sugar on it. It still didn't take away the bitterness, but least it didn't make our mouths pucker.

Our breakfast arrived with what looked like burned bread. *Mutti* mentioned this to the waiter, and again he chuckled. "We call it toast, and you should try some butter and jam on it.

Why would anybody burn a piece of bread, make it hard, then put butter on it to make it soft?

Meals were both delicious and adventurous, but we spent most of our time in the cabin. Being able to communicate in German with the other mother-daughter pair made it easier to get along with them in these tight quarters, but it did not result in a friendship. *Mutti* spoke to the mother only when necessary. Because I had not been allowed to bring any of my toys, I became bored and had no choice but to play with the little four-year-old girl. I found her cute and funny—but not for long.

With nothing to do in the cabin that was interesting, my mother and I began to explore the ship's deck. Our favourite pastime was to sit on the deckchairs and watch the people moving about. Some wore the strangest outfits while many spoke languages that I did not understand. My mother explained that most of the staff and passengers were Dutch.

It sounded very close to *"Deutch"*, but I knew it wasn't German. The name sounded so funny that I giggled.

About three days into our journey, an announcer explained that we have neared the middle of the Atlantic and that the seas would get rough. I had no idea how rough it could be. The temperatures dropped and the waves rose! We rode down the troughs of the waves and up the high crests. One moment my stomach tickled my tonsils, and in the next moment, plunged like an anchor to my feet. I did not know how long this roller coast ride could go on. More people became seasick, and fewer showed up for their meals. And those that did were running to the railings not too long into their meal or soon after. Arriving on time and finding a spot upwind from everyone else, was a job in itself! We were told there were no medications to ease our problems, and that we just had to "bear" it, stay in our bunk, carry a bag, or stand near the rails. I felt sorry for the staff who had to clean up all the misses and messes!

My mother became quite ill, so I had to take care of her as much as I could. I would be feeling fine until I either saw or heard someone retching, then *I* would start heaving. It became a vicious circle. The smell of vomit was everywhere! I tried to stay on deck when I could and as long as I could, but eventually all passengers were banned from it due to the severe weather.

It appeared to me that the sea had picked a fight with the *Groote Beer*. We were ordered to put on our life jackets, remain in our cabin and wait, should the order to evacuate come through. I wondered though, if this big liner capsized in these waves, wouldn't the tiny lifeboat be torn to smithereens, and all of us drown? My sense of security and confidence in the "Big Bear" washed overboard, and a proper respectful fear of the sea took its place.

Mutti and I became exhausted, and it seemed as if the sea had also grown weary for it became less fierce. After a few days, the waters calmed down except for a few trickster waves. We had survived the storm! We were allowed on deck again.

The Groote Beer was originally built in the US and used as a troop and cargo ship during the war. After the war, she was sold to the Netherlands Government for use as an emigrant ship. There, she was refurbished to accommodate 800 passengers with large dormitories outnumbering conventional cabins. She sailed not only to Canada and the US, but also to Australia, New Zealand and South Africa. Her final owners lived in Greece.

Man Overboard

March 1954—On the Groote Beer

It was great to breathe in the fresh sea air and soak in the sun again. I sought out the occasional stray wave that crashed onto the deck and allowed the wind to spray the icy water on my face. I squealed from the shock of it, then licked my salt-encrusted lips with delight. Drenched and cold, I returned to the cabin to warm up. My mother, not impressed, finally put an end to my fun and only permitted me out when the sea was completely calm.

She encouraged me to find and play with the other children as long as I didn't stray too far. However, most of these outings were unsuccessful and disappointing because my requirements for a playmate included that she be a girl, be my age and be able to speak German. I hoped that on this large vessel there would be at least one that matched my needs.

Daily I would sit and wait, watch and listen. On one such a day, as I sat alone, I noticed a girl about my size walking in my general direction. Accompanied by a woman, she carried a most exquisite doll in her arms. My hopes rose, and I listened. Were they speaking my language? Upon hearing the familiar German-sounding words coming from their lips, I leapt from my chair and ran in front of them, blocking their way.

"*Guten Tag!*" I said, wishing her a good day. "You have a lovely doll. What is her name?" I feared I had been impolite. I was taught that children do not introduce themselves to strangers, but I was desperate.

It appeared that she was just as eager to find a friend. "My doll's name is Heidi. What is yours?" We introduced ourselves. Her name was Anna and the lady with her was her mother.

"Can Helene come and play with me, Mother?" Anna asked.

Her mother smiled. "I'm pleased you've found a friend, and she is welcome to come to our cabin. She must first get her mother's permission and let her know where we will be."

With their location tucked clearly in my mind and excited by the prospect, I dived down to our cabin and surfaced quickly, back to Anna and her mother on deck.

"So everything is all right?" the mother asked.

"Yes, fine." I replied. *Everything is just perfect!*

Chatting, giggling and skipping, we soon arrived near Anna's cabin but remained on deck with her mother and family. Anna and I had a marvellous time. I told her my sad story about my doll, Greta, and how I had to give her up for adoption. She felt sorry for me and allowed me to play with her Heidi. The sun felt warm, the sea stayed calm, I had a companion, and I was happy. A perfect time, a perfect day!

We were occupied in our play, when a man in a white uniform approached Anna's mother and questioned her in what I assumed was Dutch. After her answer, she turned to me and asked me my last name. I answered promptly and politely. The man again turned to my friend's mother and, whatever he told her, made her catch her breath. She quickly turned back to me and with a slightly agitated voice asked, "Did you give your mother the directions as to where you will be? Did she give you permission to come here?"

I replied honestly. "No I couldn't. No one was in the cabin. She wanted very much for me to find a friend, so I didn't think she would mind."

This time the mother's voice became almost hysterical as she said, "*Och Mein Gott!* Your mother minds very much indeed and has been desperately looking for you. An all-out search has been called. They're afraid you might have fallen overboard!" Shaking her head, she came towards me and handed me over to the white-uniformed man. "You must go with this man immediately!"

I didn't understand why there was such a fuss being made. I didn't even have a chance to thank or say goodbye to Anna. The man in the white uniform grasped my hand and gruffly towed me away. We ended up at some official's office. The man I came face to face with, looked similar to the doctor in the village near the farm—like a ghost. He wore white from his cap to his shoes; the only colour on him was his red face. I was not afraid of this short and stout man until he opened his mouth and boomed like the horn on this ship. I trembled and started to cry. At first I couldn't make out what he was shouting about, then finally, I caught a few phrases about the dangers of tramping around the ship without my mother's knowledge or permission.

It's not my fault she wasn't in the cabin. I can't really run away from home on a ship, can I?

Moments later, I heard my mother's hysterical voice just outside the open door. Tearfully, she came towards me. "Where did you go? I told you to stay near. I've looked everywhere!"

She apologized to the official over and over again. I expected her to either grab and shake me, or hug me. She did neither, just took my hand and headed toward our cabin. I was relieved, but I knew that if anything was going to happen, it would happen in private. I had been careless again and would surely be punished somehow.

Where is the wooden spoon? Oh yes, it's safely packed away in the trunk which is in storage!

When we reached the cabin, it was empty. I braced myself for the worst. To my surprise, she did nothing. She was quiet—eerily quiet. Through the rest of the day, I expected her to spank me or at least scold me at any moment. It never came.

I had come to the realization that my mother was not as physically affectionate as my foster mother had been. *Mutti* never gave me a hug or kiss unless I gave her one first. She gave me the impression that it was my duty to her as her child. Whatever the reason, that night, before I climbed into the top bunk, I was shocked when she initiated the kiss and held me tighter and longer than normal. Every day after that and until we left the ship, she hovered continuously over me. I don't need *that* much attention!

Anna and I did continue to play with each other, but only after each mother was satisfied as to our whereabouts on the boat. Anna's mother also taught me some English words. I was surprised how closely some English words sounded to the corresponding German one. The first English word I learned was "water" which sounded very close to *"Wasser"*. I concluded learning English would be a snap or was that *Schnapps*?

Pier 21

March 15, 1954—Halifax, Nova Scotia

After nine, long, harrowing days at sea, we finally neared our destination —Kanada! The ship slowed and everyone crowded onto the deck. Mountains of ice floated by in the water. They were called icebergs. I understood that word immediately because it came from the German word *"Eisberg"*. The air was very chilly. I couldn't believe how that raw, cutting cold crept through my thin European winter coat. My mother had heeded her friend's warning about the cold Kanadian winter and had removed her heavy fur coat from the stored trunk. I now buried my hands and face in it to keep warm. Huddled against the railings and lashed by the bitter cold winds off the water, I was anxious to get off this ship. As we watched, the *Groote Beer* very carefully positioned herself along Pier 21 in Halifax.

We gathered our belongings from the cabin, said goodbye and good wishes to the German woman and her daughter, and followed other passengers off the ship.

"Are we in Kanada now?" I asked *Mutti.*

"Yes, Heli, but I think our journey is far from over."

Once on solid ground, my legs began to wobble, and I couldn't get them to do as I asked. We followed the crushing crowd into a large hall. Confusion broke out. *Mutti*, along with everyone else, didn't know the English language, where to go or which line to join. Thankfully, there were many volunteers who helped direct us to the clinic, immigration officers, railway ticket counters, and our previously stored trunks. Each of these areas in turn had interpreters.

As my mother and I sat on the hard wooden benches waiting for directions, we were offered cookies and tea by ladies in grey uniforms and hats. On their hat an emblem of a red cross on a white background stood out clearly. Even though we didn't understand them, they appeared kind. They were particularly helpful to women with small children or babies and helped move them to the privacy of another room. I finally had a moment to look around and noticed a sign that read "Welcome to Canada". I understood the word "welcome" because it greatly resembled "*Wilkommen*" in German, but they spelled Kanada wrong—the "c" in German is pronounced "tse," not "k".

We were eventually ushered into a doctor's office. Through a lady interpreter, he asked for the proper papers to check our health status. He had smiling eyes, and I relaxed immediately. Through the interpreter, he asked me if I knew any English words. With the help of Anna's mother on board the ship, I had learned to count to ten.

"Go ahead," the interpreter coaxed.

"Von, too, tree, far, fife, sex ... " I stopped as a roar of laughter came from both doctor and the lady. Neither my mother nor I could figure out what was so funny, but I was glad that there were no needles involved.

They took us into another large room where all the trunks that had been in the ship's hold were lined up alphabetically against the wall. People and trunks were being matched up while inspectors rummaged through each one. As my mother unlocked our trunk and opened our suitcase, we were distracted by a commotion to our left. A woman, clutching a large coil of sausage to her chest, wailed as another inspector attempted to take it away from her. Her husband, also involved, shouted and argued with him. Despite their noisy, pitiful objections, the sausage ended up on the pile in the centre of the floor with other foods like cheese, bread and fish—most of which had spoiled during the long journey.

Isn't there enough food in Canada that they have to take it from us?

My mother turned to our German inspector and asked for an explanation. He shook his head sadly. "Those poor folks did not know that most food items are not allowed into the country. They just wanted to bring some of the things that they are familiar with. I hope you don't have any such things in your trunk or suitcase? I will be forced to take it away."

Mutti replied with an emphatic "*Nein!*" and jerked her head side to side to convince him of it. He searched through all our stuff and removed nothing. I believed that if we had lost even one item from our meagre possessions, she too might have become very angry. However, the inspectors were indeed only looking for food items.

We passed our health and customs inspection. Only one more hurdle to cross—the immigration officer. Through the translator, I heard them asking my mother questions. Do you have any Canadian money for the train? Do you know your destination? Do you have a job awaiting you? To all these she answered, "*Ja*". The officer was apparently satisfied with her answer for he stamped "Immigrant—Landed" on our passports. I heard a great sigh of relief from my mother as we turned away. Earlier on, she had mumbled something about being worried that the officials might want some of her money for a bribe. Now she seemed at ease.

"One moment, Frau Méhész!" called the interpreter.

I felt my mother stiffen, but it soon became clear that there was no problem when the interpreter said in German, "Make sure you go to the canteen and buy some food for your journey. There are no real dining facilities on the train, so you will also have to purchase food in the towns along the way. Please have a seat over there and eventually someone will direct you onto the appropriate train."

"*Danke*," replied my mother, but she was really saying it to God for her eyes were turned upward.

Sure enough, in a very long "eventually", we were herded through a narrow ramp to the train tracks situated immediately alongside Pier 21.

***

The train ride across Canada was a blur. When I looked out the window, all I saw was whiteness, interrupted by occasional green trees and wood houses.

So much white space! So few houses and people!

> *Pier 21 was a port of renown. During WW2, all soldiers, other service personnel and supplies bound for Europe embarked from here. Wounded soldiers, and British wartime evacuee children came through this port. After the war, the volume really exploded! Returning troops, their war brides and children, along with refugees from the displaced persons camps were grateful to pass through this 'Gateway to Canada'. In 1956, more refugees from the Hungarian Revolution poured through this same port. Today, Pier 21 is a National Historic Site and hosts the Canadian Museum of Immigration.*

Mutti & I at Austrian farmhouse

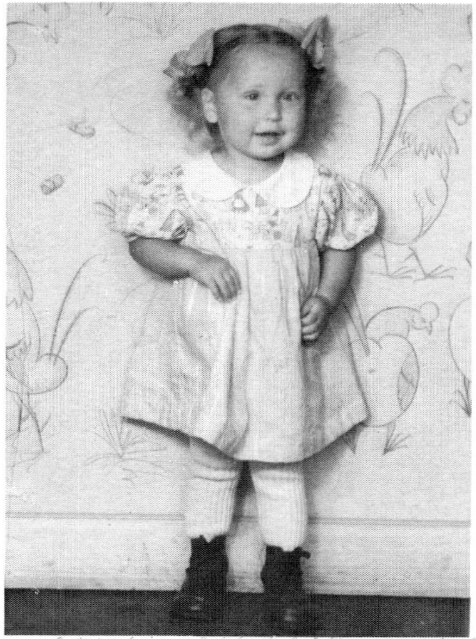

me - 1947

Mutti & I - 1949

Aunt Rosie & husband

Uncle George

Uncle Paul -1942

Mutti at age 35

Grandmother Ilka David

Photo Mutti sent to Canada - 1953

example of a narrow street in Linz

Hermann

Stober family

Ziegfried (Ziggy)

Abb. 13: Lageplan der „Wohnsiedlung“ 67 in Wegscheid (ASlL, Wohnlager 58—70, 1956, Nachzeichnung Lackner).

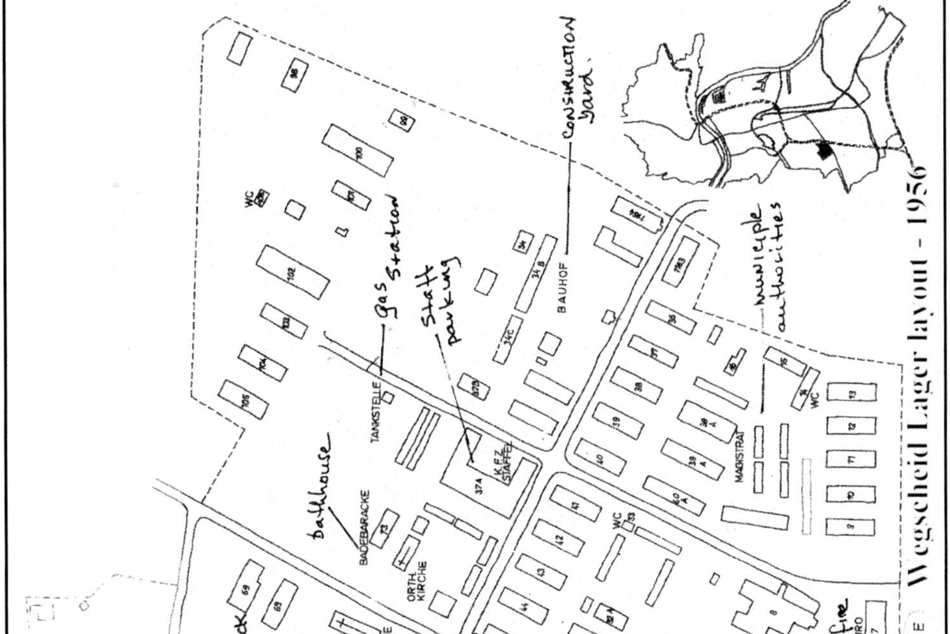

front row, fifth from the left, grade one in the Lager - 1952

Maria, myself, Eva -1952

Willi & I during Faschingssamstag

my passport photo -1953

my toys in the Lager - 1953

trains through Canada

Arrival

March 1954—Cupar, Saskatchewan

We disembarked from the train several days later. I was so glad that we were finally *there!* However, *Mutti* told me that it was only Winnipeg, Manitoba and not our final stop. They led us off the train through a very fancy hotel that had marble everywhere. It reminded me of some of the buildings in Linz. The one thing that really caught my eye was a huge semi-circular set of stairs that must have led to somewhere magical. These steps looked very similar to the steps on which Cinderella might have lost her slipper. I heard a woman say that this was thc Royal Alcxandra Hotel. Officials checked our papers again, questions were answered and everything seemed to be in order.

Several more wearying days on a lurching train, rattled us into a city called Regina where we changed trains. *Will this ever end?*

Not long after, we stood on the platform at the railway station in Cupar, Saskatchewan. At least that's what it said on our ticket. I did not need to ask if we were there yet; my bones told me so. Falling snow whirled around us as we were quickly ushered inside and seated near warm stove. I hadn't been warm since we boarded that first train in Halifax. We waited with our trunk and suitcase beside us.

It had begun to get dark when the stationmaster indicated that our receiving party had arrived and was outside. My mother stood up, took a deep breath, then with one hand on our small suitcase and the other nudging my shoulder, we headed out the door. The snow looked deeper, the wind felt stronger and the air more bitterly cold than when we had arrived. My ankle-high shoes and wool stockings soon became wet from the knee-deep snow. My flimsy kerchief and wool coat were no match for that icy wind, and I shivered uncontrollably. *Mutti,* despite her fur coat, also gave a slight shiver. Somehow I sensed that it was not due to the weather. I hid behind her for both warmth and security.

A very handsome man and a striking young woman emerged from a car. They looked like movie stars! A short older man stepped out from the back seat. All three approached us. I could see that introductions were being made, but I could not understand a word. My mother pulled me forward, and I heard my name used. The younger couple exchanged glances then questioned the older man. They seemed surprised at my presence. *Didn't they know I was coming?*

Despite my unease, they were soon smiling and hugging me.

By the time our big trunk was loaded, the world outside had turned completely dark and the snow fell even more heavily. We all crowded into the car, left the town behind and drove into a black void. The swirling snow against the headlights hypnotized me. Inside the cold vehicle, our breath soon frosted up the small windows. I buried myself even deeper into my mother's fur coat. By the time we arrived at our new "home", I was freezing, hungry and utterly exhausted.

Once inside, *Mutti* removed my wet shoes and clothes and replaced them with a heavy flannel nightgown. Not long after, a young woman appeared who fed me and put me to bed, covering me with a large feather quilt. It was familiar, comforting and warm. This was the first night since we had left Linz almost three weeks ago, that the ground did not move beneath me, but the motion of the ship and train was still in my brain. It rocked me to sleep. I felt full, safe and fell asleep almost instantly. Sometime in the night, someone crept in the bed beside me. The person did not smell like my mother but did wear a hint of perfume.

It is estimated that 95% of immigrants who passed through Pier 21, boarded a train to get to their destinations in central and western Canada. The train station, located in the Annex Building, was connected to Pier 21 by a pedway. This transport was independent of regular passenger service. Although the Canadian National Railway (CNR) was the dominant carrier, the immigrants, depending upon their destination, may have required the service of the Canadian Pacific Railway (CPR).

Solid Ground

March 1954—Canadian farm

I awoke again to unfamiliar surroundings. *So many mornings in so many different places! Where am I? Aha, I am in Canada!*

An immense feather quilt obstructed my view. As I sat up, it fell away and a chilly draft fell on my shoulders. When I exhaled, my breath was misty white. I pulled the quilt up until only my eyes were exposed, and surveyed my surroundings. Chunks of crystallized ice filled each corner near the ceiling. *Frost? Inside a house?*

The large room held three beds, each one against a corner. On my left, under a draughty window, sat a wooden chair, and perpendicular to that, stood a mirrored oak dresser. Hanging from a string from the ceiling, two large bed sheets were now tied back, but would have provided privacy around this space when pulled together. At the foot of my bed stood a large wardrobe closet. The distinct smell of moth balls wafted from it. An open doorway led to the rest of the house. I could hear voices but could not recognize any familiar words. I didn't want to get out from the warmth of the bed, but I was getting hungry and needed to use the toilet.

The clothes that I had worn yesterday were on the chair beside me, but they felt ice cold. I snatched them and placed them under the quilt to warm them. Under the covers, I clasped on my garter belt, slipped on my wool stockings, and fastened the front and back of them to the suspenders. I was proud of the garter belt I had crocheted that consisted of a wide waistband with four thinner straps leading to the rubber clasps. I pulled on my warm flannel panties with the extended legs that covered the bare thighs above my stockings—more like bloomers. I took off the nightie and, with my undershirt still on, slipped out from under the covers. Quickly I pulled on my sweater, skirt and shoes. Dressing under a quilt was a skill I had learned from my foster mother. It certainly served me well now. I reminded myself that I must learn as many skills as I can because one never knows when they could be useful.

Fully dressed, but still cold, hungry and needing to pee, I slipped into the next room. It was large and held a heavy dining room suite, a substantial buffet and an elegant china cabinet. Two couches were against one wall with rugs made of some sort of hide at their feet. Near the middle of the room sat a heater that gave off a strange odour. It kept this room warm, but it had done nothing for the bedroom. A row of windows stretched along the opposite wall, but each pane was coated with a thick latticework of frost, thus, not allowing me to see what was beyond the house.

I followed the voices coming from a room off this one. As I stepped into that room, a blast of soothing warm air surrounded me. Before I had a chance to look around, I realized that conversations had stopped and all eyes were on me. Three people sat at a table—an old man, a young woman and my mother who already headed towards me. She took me by my shoulders and directed me in front of the older man. I recognized him as one of the people who had picked us up at the station.

"Heli, I would like you to meet Herr Kish. We are going to be living with him for a while. Say good morning," my mother ordered.

"*Guten Morgan, Herr Kish.*" I curtsied.

His eyebrows rose in surprise, but he smiled broadly and said something in that strange tongue. My mother then guided me to the young woman seated directly across from him.

"This is his daughter, Etal. She can be like your sister. Say hello nicely."

Again I said my good morning in German and curtsied. Again, there were raised eyebrows and this time a hearty long "Yoi-ee", along with laughter.

What is so funny? I thought my etiquette was perfect.

I turned to my mother for an explanation. "Why are they laughing at me? And why can't I understand anyone?"

"They are not laughing at you," she said. "They are impressed with your good manners, but they say that you will not need to curtsy like that here. We will decide about that later. Right now, we are all speaking Hungarian, but soon you and I are going to have to learn to speak English."

What was Hungarian? How did *Mutti* know that language? We had always spoken only German. I thought Canadians spoke English, at least that's what they had told me on the ship. And, what was that about Etal being like my sister? This wasn't fair. I couldn't speak Hungarian nor English. How was I going to live with these people? I guessed I would have to depend on *Mutti*, but she never had patience to explain things to me before. Why would she start now? *This is going to be very interesting!*

With all this going on, I had forgotten about my need to pee. Now it came upon me with a vengeance. I was desperately trying to get my mother's attention to explain my emergency, but it was my "sister" who understood my body contortions and came to my rescue. So there *was* another way we could communicate! With a chuckle, Etal ushered me back into the bedroom where she pointed to a large metal pail, uncovered the lid and pretended to sit on it.

What? Pfui!

Gingerly and quickly, I backed my bare bottom over it and relieved myself. Etal handed me a newspaper page and again acted out its usage. *Ouch! No toilet paper?*

She led me to a porch next to the kitchen and pointed to a basin on a wash stand with cold water and soap. I knew what that was for, but where was the hot water tap—no running water?

Back in the kitchen at the table, a glob of gruel was plopped into a soup bowl for me. They called it "porridge", and it tasted as bland as it looked. I made a face of dislike. Etal laughed and quickly added some rich farm cream and brown sugar. Now it tasted like heaven. Once more, she had understood me and had come to my rescue. I felt better now about not being able to speak either language.

Everyone had returned to their previous conversation, and I no longer was the centre of attention. Now it was my turn to study them. On my right sat Herr Kish, short and slight with thinning hair and a square patch of moustache in the middle of his upper lip. I had seen that kind of moustache before, but I just couldn't remember where. In his stocking feet, overalls and a heavy flannel checkered shirt, he appeared friendly enough. He was smoking a cigarette and drinking coffee. Occasionally he would place his cigarette into the ashtray, and pour some of his hot coffee from his cup into his saucer. Bending his head forward, he carefully brought the saucer to his lips and loudly slurped it up with a resounding "Ahh!" I was horrified! Such bad manners would never have been tolerated in Austria! I looked at my mother. There was no reaction.

I turned to Etal and caught her grinning broadly at me. Already she had shown that she cared for me in those first few minutes of our meeting. She made me feel accepted and protected in this strange new world. With her short curly brown hair, large expressive eyes and a smile as warm as the sun, she was beautiful. However, in her faded jeans and tucked-in man's shirt, she represented *that* kind of woman—the kind that my mother on the bus, had considered a *kurva,* or a bad woman. I looked towards my mother, expecting her to show some form of disapproval towards her, but whatever her mind was thinking, it did not at this time express itself in words.

I spent the rest of the morning following Etal around. She would point at things and say the name of the object in English, and I would attempt to repeat it back. Each time I replied, she laughed, chuckled or giggled. I now had to chance to point to the hide rugs in front of the sofas. She said, “cow” and went “moo”. I immediately understood her as it sounded similar to the German “Kuh”, pronouced *coo*, for cow. After a while, I began to use the German word for an item, and Etal would try to pronounce it. In the end, it became a game and both of us laughed at each other.

If my English was as bad as her German, she did not let on or correct me. She did however, correct my pronunciation of her name. It was “Ethel” not ”Etal”. She showed me how to place my tongue between my teeth and attempt the sound without spitting in someone’s face. I practised the sound of “th” all that afternoon by hopping around the house repeating her name over and over in a sing-song fashion. Eth-thel, Eth-thel. She was not amused anymore. She muttered something to my mother which when I asked her what it meant, translated as something like “I have my work cut out for me!”

What does Ethel mean by that?

As the day wore on, *Mutti* and I began to unpack our belongings and try to find a place for each item. I remembered my doll and began to miss her. I still could not understand why *Mutti* could not have packed her. But my eyes caught something familiar in the trunk; there amongst everything else, were my school books—readers, Catechism and even the detestable math text, and I was thrilled. I could now at least read something until I learned English.

As we were putting things away, my “little head” began to worry again. I did not know these people, I did not know the language, and I did not know what the future held. I questioned my mother about why we had come here. Expecting her usual brush-off, I was surprised when she actually confided in me. “People in Europe said everything is better in America. There are many good paying jobs. I will be Herr Kish’s housekeeper, and you and I will be able to buy many new things that are not available in Austria.”

Sounds good to me.

Settling In

March—1954

Daylight had faded by the time everything was unpacked. I looked for the light switches but found none. Nor were there any bulbs on the ceiling. *No electricity?*

Herr Kish must have read my mind because I could hear him rattling in the living room. I ran in just in time to see him take down a contraption from a hook on the ceiling above the dining room table. It was tall with a long handle, and it had a canister at the bottom. A glass in the middle encased two gauze-like appendages. He smiled as I watched him swirl the bottom to check its fluid level. Satisfied, he pumped air into the canister like one would pump a bike tire. When he finished, he lifted the glass, released a valve and lit a match. A loud hiss and a sudden brilliant flash of light filled the room. The two gauze-like materials inside the glass casing had now turned into blinding globes. Every corner of the room was flooded with this bright, almost harsh light.

Herr Kish then went into the kitchen and grabbed another lamp already on the table. My foster parents in Austria had one similar to this one. Its glass container, shaped like a pedestal, contained the fuel. A glass chimney surrounded a flat wick that dipped into the kerosene fuel. Once it was lit, the brightness was controlled by a knob that raised or lowered the burning wick. It offered a softer, warmer glow than the hissing one in the living room. Soon after these lamps were lit, both Herr Kish and Ethel put on their coats and left the house.

Where would they be going at this time of day?

My mother remained with me, so I asked her. She answered, "They are doing chores."

"What is that?"

"We are now living on a farm that has cows, pigs, chickens, and I don't know what else, but they need to be fed and watered daily. The cows have to be milked twice a day. Tomorrow, you and I will have to help with these daily chores, but we get tonight off."

Farm? Animals? Will it be like the farm in Austria with lots of room to run and play, with lots of animals to talk to? If this is so, then my Guardian Angel had really outdone herself. Thank you, Guardian Angel, thank you.

By the time Ethel and her father had returned, my mother had supper ready. I ate heartily. We hadn't eaten a proper hot meal since we left the ship.

But what I really wanted now was a bath. We did not use the showers on the ship; we had used the small sink in the cabin to freshen up. After nine days on the ship plus another five days or so on the train without a proper bath, I no longer smelled like a rose. But, with no hot or cold running water, nor a proper bathroom or tub, how was this going to be accomplished?

Ethel had either read our minds or smelled our bodies because she had begun our bath preparations long before we had expressed our need. Right after lunch that day, she had placed a huge metal container, she called it a "canner", on the wood stove. Throughout the day, she had continuously filled it with clean snow until the container was full of steaming hot water. After supper, Herr Kish lugged in a large oval-shaped tin tub which he placed in front of the stove. My mother ladled the hot water from the canner into the tub. Alternately adding hot and cold water, she determined the temperature to be perfect for the first bather—me. She ordered me to get undressed, undo my braids, and hop into the tub.

Here, in the open kitchen with no doors! Anyone could walk in on me!

I hesitated. My face must have indicated my thought.

"Don't be silly." *Mutti* tugged at my clothes. "Everyone will stay in the living room. Now get in. Other people are waiting for a bath."

The water was not perfect; it was very hot! I squealed in pain but soon became accustomed to its temperature. I scrubbed my body with a chunk of what looked like home-made soap. This one did not smell of violets like the one in Linz. *Mutti* shampooed my long hair with Halo, then rinsed it with clean water with a little vinegar added for shine. The rough thin towel turned my body pink, but it was truly refreshing!

After I slipped into my clean nightgown that had been warming on the open oven door, I felt like a new person in this new land. With my wet hair rolled in a towel and my body wrapped in a warm flannel sheet, I was ushered by Ethel into the living room and seated on the couch nearest the heater. She indicated with her hand for me to stay. I snuggled into the couch and began to further dry my hair. A bed sheet had gone up across the doorway between the kitchen and living room.

My mother was in the same room as I, so it must have been Ethel who was now splashing in the kitchen. I asked *Mutti* about who had discarded my dirty bath water. She explained that everyone used the original contents and simply added more hot water to keep the bath warm. As my face filled with disgust, she continued. "That is the way it is done here. There is only enough hot water to fill the tub once and to keep it warm for others. The cleanest one goes first, then everyone else goes in order of increasing dirtiness with the last one usually being the man of the house." As I turned away she added, "We only get to use the tub once a week."

In Linz, we used the tub with the hot running water whenever we felt a need to. In the *Lager*, I had only received sponge baths from my mother, but the water was always clean and warm.

"So what do we do in between?" I asked her.

She said that there was always warm water in a reservoir on the right side of the stove. We can use it to wash dishes, any delicate clothing, our hair and our private nooks and crannies.

I guess it will have to do.

I sat on the sofa, pulling the comb through my tangled hair. My tummy was full, my body clean, and I had made a new friend. Living on a farm would be exciting and familiar. The only thing I asked my Guardian Angel that night was that we stay put for a while, and that Ethel and I would indeed become like sisters.

That night as I crept into the same cold bed, I wondered why they didn't warm the bed the way my foster mother used to. In the winter, *Mutter* would take a smooth round log previously warmed in the oven and tuck it in by our feet. It kept us warm until our body heat made it cosy warm. *I'm going to have to get used to many new things and ways.*

Before long, I felt someone slip in beside me again. It was Ethel, not my mother. I didn't know what she thought of me taking up her bed space and being an all-round nuisance. I hoped she would get to like me as much as I did her.

That night I dreamed of Austria—the lush dark forest, the flower-carpeted hills and Linz. Sometimes I saw Willi on the farm, laughing with my sister Greta. Then suddenly I heard *Vater's* gruff voice echoing through the bakery. Everything seemed jumbled. But then I felt my foster mother's arms and her familiar scent around me. A physical wave of love moved through my body into my heart. I had not felt such stillness and peace for a long time.

Prior to 1949, only a small percentage of Saskatchewan farms had electricity. The province could not afford its installation due its poor economic situation and the sparsity of its farms. Finally, in 1952, T.C. Douglas promised that all rural areas would have electricity. Though some farmers could not afford the cost of the installation, most realized that electrical power would cut back on manual labour and prove to be the most efficient way to raise their net farm income.

The standard lamps used on most farms were the coal oil lamps that produced a smoky, flickering yellowish light not conducive for any close work such as reading or needlework. The solution to that was the Coleman pressure lamps that used kerosene or gasoline for fuel and two mantels to produce a steady intense light. Outside the house, lanterns encased in glass and screen to prevent any combustible materials near the flame, illuminated any work in the barn or outside.

Kasper - Austrian version of Punch & Judy

Introductions

March—1954

It was Sunday when I awoke with the memory of my dream strong on my mind and heart. No one was in the bedroom and the house sounded very quiet. The bed in the opposite corner to mine must have been where *Mutti* had slept, for I recognized her nightgown lying on it. I wondered if we were going to attend church. I really wasn't in the mood for it, being still very weary.

I snatched some clean clothes that someone had readied for me and darted into the living room. The floor felt so cold on my bare feet, so I pulled one of the cow rugs near the heater. It tickled my feet, but it was much better. I dressed quickly and crept into the kitchen, expecting someone to greet me. No one was about. The fire in the wood stove crackled, so I grabbed a chair and snuggled up beside it. The kitchen was the warmest room in the house. *Perhaps tomorrow I'll dress in here.*

Before long, the outside door rattled, and Ethel and *Mutti* burst in. A blast of icy air followed them—much colder than what I was used to. Both must have been doing chores. I'm glad they had forgotten to get me up to help.

Mutti immediately began preparing a breakfast of bacon, eggs, and fried potatoes with onions. Ethel placed two thick slices of homemade bread on a bent coat hanger and placed it on top of the wood stove. Once browned and the surface hardened, she took a clove of raw garlic and rubbed it against its surface, then drenched it in butter.

I had not liked the toast that had been served on the ship, but this stuff was incredibly tasty. I couldn't get enough of it. I was hoping for some sweet baking and whipping cream coffee that had been the normal breakfast in Linz, but *Mutti* told me that they don't give coffee to children here. The fresh milk, fried eggs, smoked fatty bacon and fried potatoes tasted delicious. I became really full and really sleepy and wanted to go back to bed, but *Mutti* explained that we were expecting company. Family members of Herr Kish would be dropping in to meet us.

"Be polite, curtsy and smile!"

It would have been better if they had come before I had eaten three slices of that raw garlic toast!

They came a little after lunch. Apparently, Herr Kish had a large family. There was Ethel's sister Alice Kallichuk with her husband Walter, and their two children, Lenny and Susie. I recognized them as the couple who had picked us up at the train station. They informed me that they lived on a farm down the road from us within walking distance. Too bad that both their children were too young for me to play with.

A girl named Mary Ann, about three years old, was also among the guests. She belonged to Joe Kish, Ethel's oldest brother and his wife. Doraphine. She eagerly told my mother that I could come and play with Mary Ann whenever I wanted. They lived across the road from the Kallichuk's.

Another couple, Helen and Frank Kovach, lived much farther away but also on a farm. Frank was very tall and thin and had a nose that reminded me of a character called Kasper, a hand puppet. Kasper's character had been very frightful, but Frank came through as kind and friendly. Helen was introduced as another of Ethel's sisters. It took me a while to understand that we had the same name.

"Isn't this great!" she said. "Now we have two Helens in our family. How is anyone going to tell us apart?" She held onto my shoulder but turned to discuss this with her other sisters. Very quickly, she turned back to me, cupped my face in her hand, and said slowly, "You, Little Helen". She pointed her finger at herself and said, "Me, Big Helen." I understood and smiled widely. She burst into laughter and hugged me hard. Everyone nodded and smiled.

I also met Ethel's boyfriend, Steve Sulea. His handsome and jovial face lit up when he laughed, in fact, his whole body shook. When we were introduced, he looked at me and his eyes opened wide like he had found a gold nugget. I didn't understand a word he said, but his big bear hug certainly endeared me to him. I had never been hugged by a man before! *Mutti* had not witnessed him do that, and I wondered what her reaction would have been. She always acted strange when any man came near me.

Last, but not least, came a tall, handsome man called Bill Kish. He smiled and winked at me when we were introduced. He was Ethel's youngest brother who reminded me of Ziggy, Willi's brother in Austria—full of mischief and acting silly. He lived somewhere else and would only drop in occasionally to help his father.

There seemed to be an unusual amount of attention given to me. Most of Herr Kish's family appeared surprised when they were first introduced to me. Did my good manners shock them? I had been at my best behaviour with all my curtsying and handshaking. Or was it, as I suspected, my garlic breath. I felt their eyes upon me and sensed that they were talking about me. As before, I had the feeling that they had not expected this woman to bring a child.

I was sure that I would never remember all their names, but maybe it wouldn't be necessary. After all, we were just the hired help. I had been nervous about meeting these strangers, especially since I wouldn't be able to communicate with them. But aside from the slight hesitation, everyone had quickly smiled and hugged me. I really loved it. It was so very opposite of what I had experienced in Linz where people acted extremely formal. There, no one touched strangers except for a handshake, nor did they laugh wildly and loudly.

The following day, when my mother and I were alone, I accidentally heard her thinking out loud about the very same thing. I wanted to hear what she had to say about the gathering.

"Wasn't it nice that all these people came to welcome us here, *Mutti*? I like these people. They are very friendly and kind." I expected her to disagree with me, but not to the extent that she did.

"People here are way too forward. They have no decorum or manners. They act like imbeciles or children with no self-control. Don't they know that there has been a war, and that we must act appropriately sombre and respectful of the dead. If you are not an earnest person and act properly, no one will take you seriously."

Thank goodness she was thinking out loud in German and not in the language that others could understand. I would have been embarrassed if Ethel had overheard her say that. If that was the way she thought and felt, did that explain why she was so aloof? Was that also why few people ever smiled in their photos in Europe?

Well, I like these people—imbeciles or not. I hope that they will like me even if I am not as earnest as my mother!

the barn

The Barn

March—1954

I also wanted an introduction to the farm. There were so many buildings out there that begged to be explored, but my mother would not allow me. Ethel finally convinced her to let me go into the barn by promising not to leave my side. Properly clothed, I ran out into the middle of the immense yard, arms outstretched, turning a slow circle. I noted rolling hills but could not distinguish between the vast blue-white sky and the white-blue mountains of snow.

When my eyes finally focused on near-by objects, I saw grey—grey house, grey barn and grey buildings all around the yard. After a closer look, I realized that all the structures were composed of wood—not painted wood—weather-beaten wood. *Why are there no brick or stone structures? In Austria only poor people lived in wood houses. Are we poor? Can't be—there is lots of food here!*

As long as there was food, I didn't care if we lived in a house made of wood. I looked around again and saw plenty of space which meant freedom to run and play to my heart's content.

But where was Spring? It was the end of March and still there was no hint of her here. In Austria, Mother Earth would have already insisted that she wear her most colourful dress. *Ah, I know why Spring is so late! She is still in Austria, and just like us, it is going take her a long time to get to Canada.*

I wanted to see what was inside the barn. It had to be at least ten times larger than the one in Austria. How could such an immense building keep the animals warm? As Ethel and I entered, I picked up the odour of a pungent mixture of manure, urine, sweat and hay. It smelled similar to the Austrian barn but stronger. Its immense size surprised me —wide, long and high. Despite this, the air around me felt warm, moist and tinged with the scent of milk. I counted six stalls with more room at the back. Five of the stalls contained two cows each which were much smaller than the oxen that I remembered.

"These are the cows that we milk every morning and every night," said Ethel. "We also have to feed and water them along with every other animal on this farm. You will soon learn how much work there is here. We call the work 'chores' because they must be done on a regular basis whether we feel like it or not."

I grasped very little of what she said while I tried to take everything in at once.

"You won't be helping us until later in spring," Ethel continued, but my attention had already locked on to the last stall and a pair of enormous flanks.

Horses! I started towards them.

"No! Get back, Helen!" I heard Ethel yell. I turned. Her eyes were large, and she was shaking her head in a "no" gesture. The fear in her voice and her eyes made me stop and wait for her to reach me. "Both of these girls are normally gentle, but never get to close. They could accidentally kick you because they don't know you yet." She pointed out their huge hooves, then to the horse on the right. "This one is Jolan." She pointed to the other. "That one is Gitzka." She repeated the names, each time pointing to the particular horse. I nodded and repeated their names.

"Yes, yes, you've got it. You can pat their noses from the stall beside them if you like. Here, I'll show you."

Ethel entered the stall next to the horses, pushed the cows aside, hiked me onto the manger and showed me how to reach across the boards toward the nearest horse. I did so cautiously, and to my joy and surprise, Jolan brought her nose up to meet my hand, sniffing for an offering. I had nothing to give her now but would make sure I did so in the future. Her hot breath smelled of hay as I stroked her velvety nose. *This is the moment I knew I loved horses!*

I wanted to stay, but Ethel had more to show me. We were sidetracked by a commotion coming from behind an enclosure at the back of the barn. I hurried there to find several calves running to the front the barrier to meet me. I leaned over the top to pet their heads, but they kept trying to bite my fingers. Ethel pointed to the left of the calf enclosure where a huge mama pig lay on her side in the straw suckling about ten pink, squealing, squirming piglets. *More babies!*

Ethel motioned for me to follow her into one of the cow stalls. I hesitated, afraid that those two broad cows would either squash me between them, or trample me under their huge hooves. Ethel pushed them aside and coaxed me to join her at the manger. She knelt down, reached under and produced a mewing kitten with its eyes only half open. Smitten by the kitten, I danced with delight and, in the process, frightened the cows.

I was in heaven! Once more, my Guardian Angel had given me what I needed without me even asking for it. That night my dreams of Austria were replaced by dreams of baby animals and horses.

Belonging

April—1954

On the evening of April 20, one month after the initial gathering, a big party took place at our house. All of Herr Kish's family plus many new strangers arrived. I had never been at an adult party, nor seen that that much fiddling, singing, dancing, eating or drinking. *Mutti* was also drinking something she interpreted tranlated to me as "moonshine", but I saw no moon in the sky that night. My mother enchanted everyone with her voice of course. She seemed happy. Everyone seemed happy. *Das ist gut, Ja! That is good, yes!*

Herr Kish's family again smothered me with lots of hugs and kisses. This time I also met Ethel's oldest sister, Margaret, who was married to John Karpa. *Mutti* had agreed that I need not curtsy any more, but trying to undo this drilled-in habit proved more difficult than learning it. Every once in a while, one would slip out, but everyone found it charming.

I wanted to ask my mother what we were celebrating, but she seemed pre-occupied.

As the night wore on, people became livelier and sillier. I had never seen adults behaving in this manner, and I laughed and danced along with them. It wasn't long before my mother noticed my good times and decided to put me to bed. Despite my objections, she escorted me into the bedroom.

I complained, "Why do I have to go to bed now? I want to stay up for the party. Why are we even having a party?"

She shushed me, steered me towards her bed, and helped me into my nightie. *She smells funny?*

"Why are you putting me in your bed? I want to sleep with Ethel."

Again she shushed me, hurried me into the bed, pulled the huge feather quilt over me and left.

The party carried on becoming louder and louder. The doorway between this bedroom and the party room next door had no barrier of any kind in order to allow the heat through. But, along with the heat came the noise, the lights, and folks picking up or dropping off their coats on Ethel's bed. This made it almost impossible for me to fall asleep. Only after the celebrations fizzled out, did I finally drift off. I expected my mother to slip in beside me sometime during the night. When I awoke in the morning, I knew she had not. *Where did she sleep?*

After the chores, breakfast and dishes, all much later than usual, I finally caught my mother sitting alone at the table drinking a cup of coffee.

"Why such a big party last night? Was it a special holiday here in Canada?" I asked her in German.

"What are you talking about? You're always talking!" she replied with her head in her hands.

And you don't talk enough!

"*Ja, Ja,* I know I should have told you before," she said. "Herr Kish and I became married yesterday. Didn't anyone tell you? Couldn't you figure it out yourself?"

Who was going to tell me? No one else speaks German! And why would I be asking if I had figured it out? Sometimes she just didn't make any sense.

It took a while for this information to sink into my "little head". When it finally did, a flash of realization hit me. I would now have a real father! *Ja, das ist sehr gut! Yes, this is very good!*

Though he looked exactly the opposite of the tall, blond, handsome father I had envisioned, this man appeared kind and gentle in the little time I had known him. I have had no dealings with men as fathers, except for my foster father on the farm who had always been stern but fair. However, there had been incidents at the *Lager* that had made me afraid of men. Some nights, through the thin wall that separated our units, I had heard a man's angry booming voice. The sound of a slap from a leather belt had followed, then the screams of a young girl. I'd guessed what was happening and had trembled. Covering my ears with my hands, I had hid under the bed covers. A loud voice from any a man still made me shake.

I had not heard my new father raise his voice nor seen him angry yet. Getting to know him would be difficult since I did not have a good grasp of either English or Hungarian which were the only two languages he spoke. I would have to be wary and study him from afar for a little while.

"Why did you marry him? I thought you were just going to work here?"

"Not now, Heli, I have a headache! Don't worry your little head about it."

Here we go again!

Another thought took shape. If he was my father, then Ethel had now become my sister! I had hoped that she would eventually regard me as such, and now she truly was. My Guardian Angel had answered my prayers and more. Even better, her whole family would now be mine. All those lovely people I met were now my extended family. One moment I had only my mother, then suddenly, I had a huge family.

When I tried to tell Ethel about this, she laughed and added, "Did you know that along with Joe, Bill, Helen, Alice, Margaret and I, there are two more brothers, Frank and Zoltan, in Ontario and one called John in British Columbia?"

Mutti had mentioned these names before, but she didn't know where they lived. Now I knew their names and places, but not where the places were. That meant that Herr Kish had nine children of this own and I was the tenth!

I guess I needn't call him Herr Kish any more since he is now my father. What shall I call him?

How formal were they here? Would it be "Father" as I had called my foster father, "Papa" or something entirely different. I listened to see how Ethel addressed him. It was "Dad". I hoped Ethel wouldn't mind if I called him that too. What if he didn't want to be called that? I ran to *Mutti* to find out what she thought. My mother looked surprised when I told her of my decision. My mother didn't know what to say which was surprising; she always had an opinion. And why did she look surprised? Had she forgotten that her decision to marry also affected me?

Eager to try out the new title and eager for his response, I caught him alone in the porch one day as he came in from the barn. I took his jacket, hung it up and helped him take off his boots.

"Tank you," he said.

"*Wilkommen*...Dad," I replied, emphasizing the last word.

He looked at me for a long time, then he smiled. He pointed at me and asked in English, "Can I then call you Iluska or Ilonka?"

Another name? I had been called Helene, Heli, Helen and now he wanted to give me yet another. I liked how he pronounced Iluska, "*ee-loosh-ka*", with the emphasis on the first syllable.

I pointed to myself, nodded and repeated, "Iluska". It turned out to be the Hungarian name for Helen.

His tone seemed genuinely kind and friendly, but I still didn't trust him and decided to hold back just a little longer.

***

Despite my initial joy about their marriage, I was in shock. Why hadn't my mother told me that I would have a father soon? Why did she tell me that she only came here to work? She still hadn't explained what we were doing at the *Lager* or why everyone seemed surprised to see me. She had blind-sided me again.

She had a lot of explaining to do, but I waited for the right time to approach her. She was always busy and catching her alone was almost impossible. Then one day, as I combed her hair—she loved having her hair combed—she seemed relaxed and content. I couldn't think of a better time to question her.

"Why did you marry Dad...I mean Herr Kish? You told me we were here to work."

She slouched down in the chair, put her head back and sighed. I assumed the sigh meant that I had upset her with my question, but to my surprise, she spoke as if though she was relieved to have it out.

"Yes, I know that was my original plan, but once here, I realized that without knowing the language or having any money, we could never survive on our own. Where would we stay? I couldn't live in the same house as Herr Kish and not be married. What would people say? Everyone said that things were bigger and better in America, and I wanted us to have a better life. I knew that the western countries sponsored thousands of people from the camps after the war. That is why I moved us to the *Lager*. Herr Kish had been a widower for quite some time, so he applied to the Canadian government to sponsor a Hungarian wife for him?"

I interrupted, "You are Hungarian?"*Another little thing she had never told me!*

"Yes, I was born in Hungary but fled to Austria before the Russians came through. That is why we were accepted at the *Lager* as displaced persons." She took a deep breath. "Do you remember the letters that my friend helped me with? Well, those were my correspondences with Herr Kish. There had been other women he had been considering for his wife, so I knew I had to try harder. I sent him photos of me and references from Frau Stöber. Not wanting to take any chances, I did not mention that I had a daughter. I didn't inform him about you until after the final arrangements went through. It didn't matter at the time because I had no intentions of marrying him, but he didn't know that. It looks like he was embarrassed that I had tricked him and had not told anyone about you. That is why everyone was so surprised when they saw you with me." She kept on talking. I wasn't going to interrupt her. "I know things didn't work out the way I planned, but that happens a lot in life. We just have to make the best of it. Besides, he is a kind man, there is lots of food on this farm, and we are safe here. I believe we will be just fine."

Another big sigh. Was that a sigh of resignation, disappointment or contentment? I was shocked at all the information she was spouting without any prodding on my part. *I* was certainly happier. I hoped *she* was happier too. The simple explanations had answered most of the questions that had been tumbling about in my "little head".

Comb her hair and she'll tell me everything! I'll have to remember that for the future.

I made one braid down her back, twirled it around into a bun at the back of her head and supported it with pins. Everything was in its place, including the "tumblings" in my brain.

Bombardier

A Trust Given

April to July—1954

My next most important move was to learn English as soon as possible because I would be starting school soon. My mother could not teach me; she did not know the language. My new father spoke English but not correctly. Ethel, on the other hand, aged sixteen and in grade eleven, knew excellent English.

I don't know whether she wanted to teach me or not, but I became her shadow. We began by using the English names for objects around the house and farm. Lots of gestures, facial expressions and drawings had to be used. When all else failed, we had to depend on my mother. By trial and error and constant gentle corrections by Ethel, I slowly learned some basic English.

Each day, I became more nervous about starting school. If anything went wrong, how would I be able to defend myself? The teachers in Austria had accused me of being restless. How would the new teachers react to me here? Because I couldn't understand or talk proper English, would they think I was stupid? How would I ever be able to make friends? My mind began tumbling again. Then I realized I was no longer on my own. I now had a sister that would stick up for me. I relaxed a little.

Preparing for school meant more than learning some basic words. My flimsy winter clothes needed to be replaced with warmer ones. With no time to go shopping, we had to make do with what we already had. Somebody found a pair of boy's underwear for me to put on under my wool stockings. They made my legs look like they were fat and wrinkled. In Austria, my ankle high shoes were enough to keep my feet warm and dry. Here, my shoes went into a pair of rubber galoshes that had adjustable straps at my calves to keep out the deep snow. Heavy wool mittens, replaced the gloves I wore in Austria. I didn't mind that, but I did object to the long string attached to them that looped around my neck and through the sleeves of my coat. Only babies wore those. *So now I am a baby?*

To my horror, both *Mutti* and Ethel insisted on wrapping a heavy wool kerchief around my face and neck. In Austria, only grandmothers wore these babushkas. *Now I'm an old woman?*

I might have been only eight years old, but I still had a sense of style! I turned to Ethel for rescue. Through my mother, she explained that should the bus break down, I would freeze to death if I wasn't dressed properly.

The first day of school in Canada arrived. Up early in the morning, face washed, my hair brushed and braided, our lunch made and packed, I was ready to put on my outer clothes. Ethel indicated that we still had to do the dishes before we left.

"*Mutti* do it," I suggested in English.

"No, Helen. It's *our* chore." She handed me the tea towel.

Before I had dried and put the final cup away, Ethel was already dressed and looking out the north window by the stove for the arrival of our school bus. She had explained that our school was seven miles away in the town of Cupar. As she waited, she gestured for me to put on what I called my "old woman's clothes". I hoped the children on the bus would not make too much fun of my terrible taste in fashion. With the roads unploughed and almost hidden, I also hoped the bus could reach us through all the snow.

A signal from Ethel indicated that the bus was heading into our driveway. As we slipped out the door, a monstrous, squawking beast came to a grinding halt in a cloud of snow right in front of us. It resembled a beetle on treads and skis. The porthole windows along each side could pass for its multiple eyes. Its disgusting yellow colour did nothing to improve its appearance.

"What is…?" was all I managed to get out.

"A Bombardier," Ethel shouted above the noise.

We stepped inside this monster. A distinct stench of diesel fumes, egg salad sandwiches and sardines hit my nostrils. Its dim interior revealed children crowded on either side of the bus facing inwards while more straddled the centre seat facing forward. All heads turned towards me. As I peered back, I realized that all the girls were dressed just like me, including the horrid babushkas. *I can't talk like them, but at least I'm dressed like them.*

Ethel directed me to a side seat and sat beside me. I knew immediately why she had insisted on these ugly but warm clothes. There was absolutely no heat in this vehicle! The deafening roar of the motor made introductions impossible. The vehicle jumped to life and leapt across the field like a rabbit, swerving wildly around fence posts and bounding over snowbanks. We were tossed around like pebbles in a baby's rattle.

Between the smell, the motion, and the nerves, I wasn't sure whether I would be able to keep my breakfast down. That would be a fine kettle of fish—sardines maybe! Throwing up at this point would not be a good way to make friends or good first impressions. Through gestures, I expressed my fears to Ethel.

"You wouldn't be first or the last one to have that happen, " she answered. "I've seen kids vomiting into the jacket hood of the kid in front of them."

Breakfast intact, I made it to my new school—a one story square building actually made of stone or brick. Registered as Helen Kish, I was very proud to have the same last name as Ethel.

I tried to explain to the teacher that I had almost completed grade three in Austria, but they still put me in with the grade one class! No longer so proud, I was confused and humiliated. I might not be very good at math, but I did know other things! As the odour of wet woolen mittens on the radiator filled the room, I sat at my desk and pouted. The teacher didn't let me do that for very long, and I became the centre of attention. After I was introduced, each classmate would give me a specific order like, "Hop to the board" or "Bring the eraser here". If my actions coincided correctly with the order, they cheered me on. Everyone, including me, had fun doing these exercises. Each day the students had to come up with harder and more complicated orders. Some I understood, some I didn't, but that didn't matter. The more mistakes I made, the more fun we all had. This was the first time I was not scolded for being incorrect.

My lessons did not end in the classroom. A different classmate was assigned each day to assist me during recesses and lunches. Slowly, but surely, my initial objections and hurt feelings were replaced with eagerness and gratitude. I enjoyed learning English and making friends —all due to a game invented by a clever and kind teacher. I had never associated school or teachers with fun or games. In Austria, school was a serious business. No one moved or spoke without permission, absolute attention had to be given to the teacher at all times, and memorized homework had to be repeated to perfection. My last year of school there had been filled with anxiety due to the harsh attitude of my teacher. She had left a bad taste in my mouth, but now I had tasted something new and sweet and it went down well.

The only things that still did not go down well with me were the ugly long johns under my stockings. Toasty and warm when we were out for recess or in the Bombardier, they were hot, itchy and unfashionable in the warm classroom. I became much happier once the weather warmed up and I no longer had to wear them.

When spring arrived, we could finally use the swings, slides and teeter totters at recess. Playground equipment was also new to me and swings were my favourite. One day, I was leaning over the swing seat on my tummy, swaying back and forth happily when hoots of laughter burst from behind me. Not wanting to miss anything but still leaning over the seat, I glanced back to see what had caused it. To my surprise, my friends were pointing and laughing at me!

"What?" I asked jumping up and turning towards them.

"You have funny looking panties!" one of them said, pointing at my bottom.

The group of three girls stood there with their eyes wide open, their hands muffling their giggles. To my great dismay, I realized that my skirt had been blown up by the wind to expose my underwear. My bloomers from Austria must have looked strange to them. Not only were they long-legged, but their colour was also odd. Made of brown flannel, they looked like I'd had a bathroom accident. Ashamed that anyone had seen my underwear and embarrassed by their teasing, I felt the heat rise in my face. There was nothing I could do about it. Their teasing had appeared more as act of surprise rather than unkindness, so I just joined in, also giggling, pretending that indeed, it was truly funny.

However, as soon as I arrived home, I found every single pair of those panties and purposely put a tear into them. Then, I showed them to my mother and indicated my desperate need for new ones. She agreed that no daughter of hers would go without proper underwear and promised me new Canadian ones. I figured I had been pretty smart in finding a solution to my problem. Ethel knew what I had done, understood, and said nothing, just chuckled. A trust had been given and a bond formed.

I remained in grade one until school closed for summer holidays.

Eventually, the one-roomed school houses scattered in rural Saskatchewan were closed. With schools then centralized in towns, many children had to board in or near them. The government realized that bus transportation was needed so that children could remain at home. This in turn forced them to improve the country roads. But the long winter months with much snow, proved to be another challenge. The roads were not routinely ploughed in the 1950's. This necessitated the use of snowmobiles as a supplementary means to get children to and from school. It was Joseph Armand Bombardier from Quebec who built this vehicle that floated on snow. With skis in front and treads in the back, it was used, in some provinces, not only to transport children to school, but also to carry freight, deliver mail and as an ambulance when necessary.

Holy Communion

July—1954

My first summer holidays in Canada on the farm! *Wunderbar!* But before I had no time to think about how I was going to spend it, I was whisked off to stay at Big Helen's farm. They lived closest to the Holy Trinity Hungarian Church where I was to receive catechism for my First Holy Communion. Despite the fact that I had photographs and papers to prove I had already received this Sacrament in Austria, they insisted on heaping more holiness on me. If it's free I was happy to receive any extra blessings.

Unable to understand English very well, I found the lessons boring, but my time at Helen and Frank Kovach's turned out to be wonderful. Like my foster mother, Big Helen was quick and generous with her hugs. She included me in every task, and every task became a game. We giggled and laughed like two girl friends.

While sitting at her table near the window one morning having a bowl of Cream of Wheat with cocoa and cream, Big Helen asked me, "What were you doing last night, roaming around the house? Were you not able to find the toilet?"

I understood most of what she said, but looked out the window trying to pretend I didn't. She asked again. This time I couldn't pretend any more.

"I not know why you saying for," I replied in my best English.

But I did know what she was talking about. It had happened before. I thought it would be best to confess.

"*Ja,* I do-ink it. No want to. Talk Ethel, please." I couldn't explain, but knew that Ethel would be able tell her.

When Big Helen would eventually speak with Ethel, she would discover that I had sleepwalked a great deal, almost as soon as I'd arrived in Canada. One time, I had awakened and found myself in the kitchen without knowing how I arrived there, and Ethel had gently directed me back to bed. Another time, she had told me that I had been crying in front of the closet in the middle of the night. Ethel had attempted to get to the root of it and had suggest, "Perhaps you are homesick. Have you been dreaming about Austria?"

I *had* been dreaming a great deal of my foster family and missing them terribly. Every time I thought of them, I noted a dull ache in my chest along with a great sense of guilt. I had not said any goodbyes and still had not written to them. *Mutti* had claimed she couldn't remember their address.

Big Helen must have read the distress on my face because she changed the subject. "Do you know why your name is also Helen?"

What does that have to do with what we are talking about?

"Well," she said, "God made me first, and I was named Helen. He looked at what He created and liked it a lot. He decided to use the same mould to make another fabulous Helen—you!" She saw me smile, giggled with delight and hugged me.

These people seem to know what I am thinking and feeling without words. My mother does not.

Two weeks later, Helen and Frank dropped me back home at the farm. *Mutti*, Big Helen, Frank and I stood outside the porch saying our goodbyes. I hugged Big Helen and thanked her with much enthusiasm. She returned the favour. *Mutti* was also being grateful and gave Helen some baking. Frank came up behind me, brought his arm around my neck and hugged my shoulders. He put his cheek on mine and whispered in my ear, "We'll miss you, Helen. We love you." Then he headed to his truck.

Out of nowhere, I heard my mother shriek at him in Hungarian, "*Gazember!* Bastard! Don't you touch my daughter!" Her face had become twisted; her voice rose as she pounced and waved her fist at him. "What did you do?" Then in clear English said, "I keels yoo!"

Both Helen and Frank stood paralyzed with their mouths open. Frank tried to defend himself in Hungarian. "You're crazy! Nothing is going on. I was just saying goodbye. We like that lovely girl!"

"She no lubblee girlee to yoo!" *Mutti* screeched back in English.

Then Big Helen turned to Frank and said, "Let's go Frank. Nothing you or I say will convince her otherwise." She shook her head sadly and led Frank away from my mother. But she came back to give me another hug. "You did nothing wrong, Helen, so don't let her upset you, okay?" They climbed into their truck and sped off.

For the next several days, *Mutti* ranted and raved and could not be consoled. Nothing Dad or I said satisfied her. She cursed and called Frank every horrible name she knew in Hungarian. When that wore out, she turned on me. What did he do to me? Did he touch me anywhere? She examined my underwear and my body. I did not understand what she was talking about or what she was looking for.

I was sad and angry because I thought I would probably never see Big Helen and Frank again. If I did, I would definitely have to apologize for my mother's actions.

Lessons Learned

August—1954

Upon my return from Big Helen's farm, I hoped that I was finally free to explore and enjoy the rest of my summer holidays, but Ethel decided otherwise. It was time to buckle down to some serious English lessons. I didn't like being stuck inside on a beautiful day, but was grateful to spend time with my new sister. Eager and excited to begin, I found the first few lessons great. Just as I had on the boat, I thought learning English was going to be a snap.

Ethel used the first grade reader, *Dick and Jane*, to introduce me to English. I knew how to read but was not familiar with the English sounds of the alphabet.

Deek voss vallkink.

Chain voss chompink.

Zee Shpot r-r-runnink.

My sister laughed so hard, she was bent over and had tears rolling down her cheeks. What was so funny? I had pronounced every consonant and vowel the way I had learned in Austria; I thought I was doing great.

When Ethel finally composed herself, she commented, "I really *do* have my work cut out for me. I promise you one thing, Helen. By the time I'm through with you, there will be no hint of a German accent in your English even if it kills us both"

Whatever she said, I knew she meant it. First, my fast-clipped rhythm had to be slowed down. I had to soften the harsh German consonants considerably—no "hissing S's" or "rolling R's" were allowed. Some of the consonants in English did not sound the same as in German. "W's" were not pronounced like "V's", and "V's" were not pronounced like "F's". The vowels were also different. The English "E" sounded like the German "I" and the "A" like the German "E". I did not need to capitalize every noun, or worry if it was masculine or feminine. In English there was no formal or familiar "you". That made things much easier. But it was not easy to recognize which and when certain letters were silent. I concluded that the English language rules made no sense. *Och mein Gott! This is harder than I thought. I don't want to do this any more.*

One day just as we were beginning our lesson I told Ethel so.

"Well, my dear, there is no choice," she said. "I know it's a lovely day outside, but this is more important. I don't want to be here any more than you. Come on now, no slackness or snivelling allowed.

"Vot you say?" I asked not understanding the last part.

"Never mind, I was just kidding. Let's carry on. The sooner we get started, the sooner we'll be finished and the sooner you can go and play, okay?"

I understood and liked the word "okay". So short, so simple and so nice.

We carried on—every word practised to perfection, every error corrected. Once I had read all the primer, Ethel introduced me to comic books. The visual images helped me understand the words more quickly. She started me off with familiar stories from *Grimm's Fairy Tales*, then progressed to *Treasure Island* and *Robinson Crusoe*. At first I just looked at the pictures and tried to imagine what the characters were saying.

Ethel had me read them out loud, constantly correcting my pronunciation. Because I couldn't get it right the first time, I didn't want to try any more. When I had attempted to repeat my times tables to the teacher in Austria, she had screamed at me every time I had an answer wrong. Now, I didn't want to try with Ethel either. I began to cry.

Ethel stopped, sat down facing me and talked very quietly. "Listen Helen. I don't know why you are crying, but I'm going to guess. It doesn't matter if you get it wrong as long as you learn from it and try again. To become good at something takes time, patience and mistakes. *Every* mistake or failure made in life makes you smarter and stronger. I will still love you no matter what. Now let's try that line again."

I did not fully understand her words, but I did understand her comforting tone. I felt sad that I had acted in such a bad manner; I should have known that she was on my side. If she could be patient, so could I. If she was willing to work hard, I would too. I found it unbelievable and humbling that Ethel, almost a stranger, would give up her time, take on this difficult task and receive no rewards so that I would be better prepared for the next school year.

Not only did she teach me English, but also not to be afraid to try or make a mistake, to always do my best, and that my best will not be achieved the first time around.

Not A Chore

Summer—1954

The time came when I was expected to start doing chores. Any job that involved working with animals *and* being outdoors could not possibly be boring or hard, so I was eager to get out there amongst them. But the chore that Ethel had lined up for me had nothing to do with either of those—it involved cleaning the house! This had been her duty every Saturday before I arrived, and now she insisted I help her with it.

Little by little she instructed me on what had to be done, beginning with dusting every flat surface in the house. This would be followed by a good rub of lemon oil on all the beautiful oak furniture to keep the wood from drying up.

As Ethel handed me a flannel dust rag, she grinned and said, "Hey, Helen, take a good look at this rag. Do you recognize it?"

At first I didn't know what she was talking about, but when she again pointed to the rag in my hand, I recognized it as the remnant of my brown bloomers that my friends at school had teased me about. I thought it the perfect punishment for an article that had caused me so much embarrassment. Ethel and I thought it to be most clever and funny, and it sent us into gales of laughter. My mother would not have found humour in this situation, but Ethel and I constantly giggled about something or other. We were sharing a secret behind my mother's back and enjoying it. I knew it to be unkind, but it felt good to finally have a little control.

She doesn't have to know everything!

When we finally settled down, we knew we still had to clean the linoleum-covered floors. Ethel mopped the bedroom and living/dining room while I swept the kitchen and porch. Once mopped or swept, the floors were ready for washing. With a bucket of soapy water and a rag, Ethel got down on her hands and knees to accomplish that. *I hope she doesn't expect me to do that.*

But she did. After she completed the other three larger rooms, she handed me a fresh bucket and gave me step by step instructions as to how to wash the small enclosed porch. Ethel made sure I reached under, over, and into every corner, rinsed my rag often and left the floor as dry as possible.

That little porch was dirtiest part of the house. Everyone entered with grimy footwear, encrusted overalls or jackets, and splashed the floor with their dirty water as they cleaned up at the washbasin. Without fail, the floor became covered with either mud, manure, gravel, grass, straw, seeds, weeds, water or any combination thereof. To prevent these from being carried onto the rest of floors in the house, the porch needed to be cleaned regularly. Ethel decided that I should be totally responsible for this chore. It would be my decision when and how to clean this area.

"Make sure you do the best that you can every time," Ethel reminded me. "Be proud of what you do and how you do it, no matter how unimportant the job may seem. Every task you do has your name on it."

"You mean a clean porch is called Helen?"

"Precisely!"

I think I can handle that.

What I couldn't handle was cleaning the outhouse! I had been so happy in Linz when we had running water with a tub, sink and a flushing toilet. I had used an outhouse on the farm in Austria, and never dreamed I would ever have to use one again. The one here in Canada had two holes, allowing two people to do their business at one time. *Who would want to do that?*

Of course it was stinky, so I never stayed in there longer than needed, especially in the winter when my bum could freeze to the seat. I also had nightmares about falling into its pit. Ethel called it "the hell hole", and she was now going to teach me how to clean it. This time she used an ordinary broom and, with one quick sweep, cleared the cobwebs from all the corners, swept the seat area, then lastly the floor. She moved with such speed, I thought she was the fairy godmother waving her wand. As I stood outside watching her do her magic, Ethel suddenly let out a screech and dashed past me with the broom still in her hand. She stopped a little ways from me, turned around and breathing heavily said, "Close the door will you, Helen?"

Her eyes were wide, and she was shaking. What had she seen in there that had frightened her so badly? Her reaction certainly frightened *me.*

"What's the matter?" I asked, hoping she hadn't seen some monster down in the hole.

"Those damn moths, they give me the heebie jeebies!"

What a strange expression!

"What are heebie jeebies?"

"I'm terrified of moths! I can't stand them!" she replied, still breathless and rubbing her arms.

My big brave sister is afraid of itty bitty moths! I laughed.

She became angry and said, "Don't you laugh at me, you little shit!"

That made me laugh even harder.

I had to ask her,"Now that you made such a good job of cleaning the outhouse, are you going to put your name on it?"

This time she howled and came after me with the broom.

***

Whenever Ethel and I did any kind of housework, the radio blared out what she called "Country music". *Mutti* did not like it and always asked her to turn it off. Ethel only turned the volume down.

"What country?" I asked. I explained as best I could that when I lived in Austria, many European countries had their own programs on the radio.

"Country in this case means "not the city". We live on a farm in the country, and this kind of music is created by country folk, for country folk. That was Hank Williams, and the woman singing now is Kitty Wells."

Mutti and I never owned a radio, but in Linz, Frau Stöber would sometimes have one on. From it had poured the soothing music that she called the classics. As I now listened to the instruments and voices of these country musicians, I found them grating and piercing to my ears. Eventually, a deep resonant male voice caught my attention, and I asked Ethel, "Who that singer?"

"You mean 'who *is* that singer', and by the way, you did pronounce your 'th' correctly. So you like Tennessee Ernie Ford?"

"Yes, very much." I replied. Ethel never allowed me to use "yea".

I began to have my own favourites: Eddie Fisher's *O My Pappa,* Rosemary Clooney's *This Ole House* and Patti Page's *Doggie in the Window*. Not only did they make me move in rhythm, but they also helped move along the boring task of cleaning.

Between the country music, there were songs that were repeated over and over. They had catchy tunes like "*Brylcreem, a little dab will do ya*" or "*You wonder where the yellow went when you brush your teeth with Pepsodent*".

"Why do they keep playing these same songs over and over? They don't do that with the other ones? Who are Brylcreem and Pepsodent?"

She laughed and explained that these were products that the companies wanted us to buy.

"Do *I* want to buy Brylcreem?"

"You make me laugh all the time, Helen," she replied, chuckling. "No, only men use it in their hair to make it shiny and keep it from flying around. And Pepsodent is a toothpaste."

"What is toothpaste?"

"It's a paste you use to brush your teeth. Come to think of it, I have never seen you brush your teeth. I think it's time you learned to do that too."

"Okay, but may I use Pepsodent?" Ethel was also strict about the correct use of "can" and "may".

It was the music, the chatter, but mostly the cherished company of my sister that made the tiresome housework less of a chore.

Secrets Shared

Fall—1954

Within the first few months of arriving in Canada, I had gained a new country and a large, loving family. I had learned basic English but was still fumbling with the unfamiliar rules of behaviour and the way things were done here.

That August, I turned nine. Birthdays were definitely celebrated differently here. In Austria, *Mutti* did make me a birthday cake and usually bought me clothes or other needed items and that was it. Here, too, she had baked a chocolate cake to be served with whipped cream. Then Ethel did something strange—she added nine candles, lit them, and sang a *Happy Birthday* song.

"Now, make a wish but don't tell anyone, then blow out the candles. This is your special day, and we are celebrating you."

She bought me a colouring book and crayons. I've never seen any of these before and delighted in the brilliant colours that the crayons produced—a far cry from the pale coloured pencils that I will now never use again. *Mutti* made sure I had some new Canadian-like clothes for school...finally. I believed that Ethel might have helped her pick them out. I had never had this much fuss made over me, but I loved it. In Austria, it was Christ's birthday that was most important, not an individual's.

When I blew out the candles, I wished wholeheartedly that I would be able to remain here for a long time. However, I could not understand why I couldn't tell anyone of my wish.

What good is it if no one knows about it. I think I can safely tell it to my Guardian Angel.

***

Everyday was filled with new experiences and learning. There was a rectangular wood box attached to the wall in the living room. It nearly knocked me off my feet with its loud ring. I finally realized it was a telephone, although it did not look like any I had ever seen before. I watched whenever anyone used it but could not understand why, when it rang, it was only answered sometimes and not other times. This phone did not ring the same way each time like the ones in Austria had done. One time it would give two long rings, other times three. Then there were also combinations of short and long rings. One day this phone rang, no one was about, so I answered it.

"Hello, hello?"

"Who is this?" asked two people almost at the same time.

"It's Heli."

"Get off the phone."

"Okay-ee," I replied and hung up.

If you don't want to speak to us, why did you phone?

Confused, I later explained to Ethel what had occurred.

She asked, "What did the ring sound like?"

"It sounded like a telephone," I answered, rather puzzled at her question.

She chuckled, then proceeded to explain. "It's called a party line, meaning that many different parties or families share the one telephone line. Each house has its own specific pattern of rings. You turn the crank on the wall phone to match that pattern. Through the specific combination, everyone on that particular party line knows who that ring is intended for. If it isn't your ring, then you don't answer, nor listen in. If you need to speak to anyone outside your party line, you need to go through the operator in Cupar."

"But you could listen in without them knowing, right?"

"Yes, you could, but it is considered bad manners. If you did listen to get some juicy gossip, it could backfire. They could be talking about you!"

***

Between the lessons, chores and explorations, the summer slipped by quickly. Soon, I would be attending my proper grade in school, and I was much more prepared than before. Thanks to Ethel, I had gained more confidence in my English. And with my new clothes, I would not have to worry about looking too different.

I was finally rid of my high ankle shoes. No one wore those here except babies. For the new ones, we went to a shoe store in Regina. A clerk made me put my feet into some sort of machine that showed the bones of my feet.

"Yes, these are the right fit for you," she declared.

I didn't care if they fit or not, I loved them. They were black, flat shoes with a band across the top of my feet. Armed with a new wardrobe and new language, I was eager to start school. Ethel was entering her last year in grade twelve, and I would be going into grade four. I was shocked and disappointed when she enrolled me into grade three.

"Why I go grade three? I now go grade four, no?"

I hadn't failed grade three in Austria and should now be heading into grade four.

Ethel smiled. "Yes, yes, I know, but you need to know all the grade three lessons in English. I know you will do well. You're a smart girl."

Being told I was smart by Ethel made me feel better. Besides, I remembered how much fun I had this spring in grade one. *I will make her proud of me!*

Grade three turned out to be great. I was still getting a great deal of attention from my classmates and my teacher Mrs. Lehan. Unfortunately, I did not get off on the right foot with her. One of my classmates had given me a stick of bubble gum, and unlike the ones in Austria, its taste and texture went on forever. So I continued to chew it forever—right into the classroom. I was cheerily chomping away when

Mrs. Lehan approached my desk, leaned over and whispered in my ear.

"You must not chew gum in the classroom, dear. Please place it in this tissue. Thank you."

My face heated up and my heart pounded! Expecting a slap, I buried my head in my neck. No blow came, and when I looked up again, Mrs Lehan had already returned to the front of the class and was smiling back at me. I couldn't believe her kindhearted reaction! *I'm going to remember her forever.*

Ever since I had started school in Canada, I had experienced nothing but kindness and patience from the teachers. I could now relax and concentrate on learning. My whole attitude towards school changed. Now, no more learning for the fear of it, but rather for the love of it. And, love it I did. If for some reason I had to miss school, I would become so sad that sometimes I would cry. One reason was because I did not wish to be home alone with my mother. But mostly, I did not want to fall behind in any classes. What if I missed something important? Then everyone would be ahead of me, and I would feel like a dunce.

As soon as I was able to read a little English, that's all I wanted to do. Books allowed me to travel without a passport, without a suitcase, without heaving seas, or clattering cold trains. They took me to places I had never seen nor may ever see. They allowed me into the minds of people or animals. I couldn't do that in the real world. They were sacred objects that transported me to a world of make believe and adventures. Reading also provided an escape for me—far away and free from the constant nattering of my mother. I was hooked and would read whenever I could and as late as I could. Often in full view of my mother, I would read way past my bedtime. *Mutti*, thinking it was homework, would not interfere or stop me.

Ethel, on the other hand, was wiser. "Let me see your homework, Helen."

I was caught like a fly in a spider's web! One quick glance and she knew what I was doing, but she must have caught the panic in my eyes because she smiled.

“I think that’s enough homework for one night. You can finish it tomorrow, okay?”

She kept my big secret from my mother, and I loved her for it.

Who Is Santa

Christmas—1954

Fall went by quickly, and winter began to close in. Sometime in the middle of November, Ethel and I were sitting at the dining room table. She was working on an art project for her school. Having no talent for any art, I watched in awe as she created a most stunning border in gold. I must have disturbed her concentration because she got up and returned with a thick magazine that had a picture of a jolly fat man in a red suit and white beard. She explained that soon it will be time for me to write to Santa.

"Who Santa and why I have to writing?" I asked.

"The correct way to say that is 'Who *is* Santa and why *do* I have to write to him'. I guess you don't really know who he is, do you? His full name is Santa Claus. He lives at the North Pole with his elves who make toys for good girl and boys. He also has reindeer that pull his sleigh in thc sky on Christmas Eve when he delivers his presents. So if you don't write to him, he will not know what you want for Christmas. Do you understand?"

"Yes, maybe. I knowing elves, but flying reindeer...I no know. Is not Christ Child who bring you at Christmas? *Mutti* say is no nice to ask for me."

Ethel chuckled. She always did that when she heard me speak or when she thought I had weird ideas. This time, I thought she had some weird ideas too. I've read enough fairy tales to know that anything was possible, but the idea of a stranger giving me gifts just because I asked for them, seemed highly unlikely.

Perhaps seeing that I didn't believe her, she asked, "So, what did *you* do in Austria for Christmas?"

I went into detail about what happened on the eve before December 6 when St. Nicholas and Krampus visited.

"I've heard of St. Nicholas," she said, "but who is *Krampus*?"

I explained he was the devil who punished bad children with a switching, and if they were really bad, he carried them away to his den in the woods.

This time it looked like she didn't believe *me.* Her eyes widened and she shook her head. "That's a stupid way to make children behave. Well, you won't have to worry about him any more. We do not have anyone like him around here. Our St. Nicholas or Santa Claus, as we call him, only comes on Christmas Eve to deliver your presents. Children can sometimes visit him in some stores of Regina. You can sit on his lap and tell him what you would like for Christmas, but we live too far away to do that. That is why you must write him."

"I not know how to write good yet," I complained.

"You mean you don't know how to right well," she corrected me.

"*Ja*, that is what I said."

"It doesn't matter if you don't write well. It matters only that you write, otherwise you will not get any presents." She leafed through the pages of the *Sears 1954 Christmas Book* in front of me. "Here, I want you to look through this catalogue and pick out your favourite toy."

She opened it to the toy section for girls. Its shiny, colourful pages almost blinded me. Never had I seen so many toys. There were more on the next page, and the next. I understood then why everyone wanted to come to America.

"See if there is anything in there that you like, then write and tell Santa." She smiled, and returned to her art work.

At first glance, I liked everything. I wanted them all. That would be greedy, so I would have to choose wisely. For the next few days, I returned to that catalogue any chance I had and carefully examined every page and every toy.

How can I choose from so many when I have never had a choice regarding anything?

What did I want? That was a whole new idea too. I had always been told what I wanted, and never had permission to ask for anything. Here and now, Ethel actually wanted me to choose what I liked and gave me permission to ask for it. I felt a pinch of guilt that passed quickly, and I became giddy with the thought of choosing by myself and for myself. Considering that I had to give up my doll before coming to Canada, I began to feel better about asking for one. But which one? Each doll was more beautiful than the next, but each was different.

With help from Ethel, I struggled over each description and detail and eventually eliminated all but one—Saucy Walker. Her face was beautifully moulded with lovely blue eyes, rosy cheeks and an open smiling mouth that revealed two small teeth. Her hair was real, not just painted, and she even had dimples on her elbows and hands. But the most incredible feature about her was her ability to walk while simultaneously turning her head from side to side. When she was laid down, her eyes closed. She looked and worked as real as Willi's train had. Even if I didn't believe in this "Santa Claus", I did believe in Ethel.

I really hope what she said is true because I am going to ask Santa for a Saucy Walker doll.

As I worked hard to write a proper later, I sometimes didn't know the English word that I needed. When I did, I probably spelled it wrong. Trying to explain to Santa who I was, where I came from, and that we were strangers was no easy task. I also had to explain that I knew it was bad manners to ask a stranger for a gift or brag about myself, but that my sister had said that it was okay. I had been a good girl by doing my homework, my chores and learning English. Then, most politely, I asked if he could leave the Saucy Walker doll under the tree. I made sure I never told him about the bad thoughts I sometimes had towards my mother. I signed my new name and reread the letter. I barely understood it myself and hoped Santa had an interpreter. When I gave the letter to Ethel to mail, she looked surprised, laughed again but looked pleased. "Good girl, Helen!"

I worried about that doll for weeks. What if this Santa wouldn't come through for me because he didn't know me? I could pray to the Christ Child, but He would only give me what I needed, not what I wanted. If they don't come through, then I would have to remind my mother of her promise of a doll "more beautiful than ever", but I would wait until after Christmas. *All I can do is wait patiently.*

***

Patience was not something I had learned well yet. I needed something to take my mind away from that doll. So when Ethel asked me to help her get the house ready for Christmas, I was happy to do so. She explained that there would be cleaning, baking and setting up the Christmas tree, and all that would have to be done on week nights and weekends.

"I thought the Christ Child set up the tree." I explained how Willi and I saw none of the goings on during Christmas and were told that the Christ Child did all that.

"Boy, you guys have such strange ideas in Austria. Here, everyone takes part in the preparation. You'll see. It will be fun."

Well, the cleaning wasn't fun. Every nook and cranny had to be polished and cleaned better than ever before. I guess if the Christ Child was going to visit us, it better be perfect. *I wonder if Santa needs that much perfection.*

Baking was definitely fun. At the *Lager*, my mother never let me help her in any cooking or baking preparations. Perhaps, the food was too expensive and precious to allow for mistakes that couldn't be eaten. Here, Ethel insisted that I help, so *Mutti* was outvoted. I'm not sure whether I was helpful or not, but between the three of us, we made lots of goodies—poppy seed and walnut rolls, prune squares, and Christmas cookies.

There was one item of baking that only *Mutti* had the skill for—strudel. No one else knew how to make and work the dough. I watched as she gently stretched it tissue thin until it draped over the edge of the dining room table without a single hole or tear appearing. With the cinnamon, apple and raison mixture placed along one edge, she lifted the table cloth and carefully let the weight of the apples roll over the dough until it ended up looking like one long, thick sausage. This was cut or bent to fit the baking pans. When it came out of the oven, it tasted crispy on the outside and hot and gooey on the inside! Then she would make another with carrots and raisin filling.

The familiar aroma took me back to the bakery in Linz.

***

A week or so before Christmas, I came home from school one day to find an evergreen tree standing in the living room in front of the window.

"It's a *Tannenbaum*!" I squealed with excitement. "Can we decorate it right now?"

"No, Helen. The tree has to acclimatize," my sister said.

"Why does it have to climb and where?"

Ethel burst out laughing. "You're so funny, Helen."

I thought it was a serious question and still did not understand. My sister saw my blank expression and finally explained, "It just means that it has to sit at room temperature for a while. Tomorrow is Saturday, we'll decorate it then, okay?"

"*Ja, das ist gut.*" I said as I inhaled its fresh pine scent. Again I was taken back to Austria, this time to the farm.

"Speak English!" she demanded.

"*Ja*, that is goot."

Usually on Saturdays I slept in and didn't get up until I heard that everyone had come back from chores. That Saturday, I wanted to get started early to decorate that tree, but I had to wait for them to prepare breakfast, eat it and clean up.

I kept pestering Ethel with "Now?"

She finally surrendered, went into the bedroom and pulled out a big box from the storage closet. She carried it into the living room and put it by the tree. Gleaming things came from that box—balls, streamers, garlands and tinsels. We began to decorate the room first. Long crêpe paper streamers were attached to the top corners of the room and brought together in the centre. There, we added a honeycombed crêpe paper bell. Christmas cards, folded over a string, hung on the walls.

The tree came next. Ethel was the only one tall and steady enough to climb a chair and place a large silver star on the top. I handed her the silver garland, and she held one end while I walked around the tree wrapping the shiny string lower and lower on its branches. Finally off the rickety chair, Ethel began to unwrap the individual decorations in the box. Small chenille Santas went up. Then came the thin glass decorations. Slowly and carefully we freed them from their wrappings and placed them on a chair within easy reach. They were delicate and pretty in their colours and shapes—concave balls, bells, cones and elongated ovals.

"You must handle those balls with extreme care, Helen. They are very fragile," Ethel warned me.

Her words had barely left her mouth, when I dropped one as I was handing it to her. The glass ball was not the only thing that shattered. *Now Ethel will never let me continue to help.* I started to cry.

"Ohhh, sweetie, don't cry. It's alright."

"You…you called me 'sweetie'!" I said between my sobs.

"Well, that wasn't my first choice. I wanted to strangle you at first."

"Will you still let me help?"

"Of course, you silly goose."

***

With all the commotion, time flew by and the countdown for Christmas began. I was a nervous wreck. Would I be granted my wish? I could not imagine why not. I had met all of Santa's standards, but I may have pushed my "need" to the Christ Child a little too far. If He interpreted this as "covet", then I would be doomed. *I have never desired anything more, but then, I had never desired before.*

Christmas Eve came but nothing seemed to be happening. No one sang carols; I had learned a few at school and wanted to practice them. No one made ready for mass, but most of all, no one opened presents. I began to suspect that everyone had forgotten it was Christmas Eve. I finally turned to my mother and asked in German, "Why aren't we opening our gifts or singing or going to mass?"

Mutti shrugged her shoulders. "I doesn't look like anyone sings in this family. As far as mass is concerned, the church is closed because of the snowed-in roads. And, I don't know when people open presents here, so you better ask Ethel."

I trudged over to my sister on the couch and plunked myself next to her.

"What is the matter, Helen? It's Christmas Eve and you should be happy."

"Why aren't we singing, or opening presents?"

"Is that why you've been moping about? To answer your question, we never really sing carols here, but we can certainly turn on the radio. I'm sure there will be plenty you can sing along with then."

She hasn't answered my most burning question. What about the presents?

I had noticed that wrapped gifts had begun to appear under the tree about three days ago. So what was the hold up? I looked up at Ethel. She was watching me intently, and she was laughing at me again!

Does she not realize this is a serious matter?

She finally spoke. "When did you open your presents in Austria?"

"Always Christmas Eve," I replied, hoping that would help.

"Well, we normally open ours on Christmas morning, but I'm sure you can open some now. Let's go ask your mother."

My mother's answer was "Yoo do it wat yoo like it."

In a burst of excitement, I ripped the paper off the gifts without saving and folding it. For the first time, I actually hoped to find something specific. I opened all the gifts with my name on it. They came from *Mutti*, Ethel and Dad. Most contained clothing items like mitts, socks, a sweater, and a skirt and blouse. I tried to look and sound happy and thank everyone. But the one present I was seeking and needed was not there. I could not hide my disappointment. First I sighed a little, then I cried a little.

My mother noticed my behaviour and was not pleased. "You must be grateful and gracious for anything you get, Heli, even if it's not what you like or hoped for." She quickly turned away from me. *Of course she's right, but it doesn't make it any easier.*

Ethel, who had been watching me all this time, now came over, put her hand on my shoulder and asked, "Now what's the matter, Helen?"

I could barely control my tears and blurted out, "I ask Santa and Christ Child for doll in book, they no give me! Not fair!"

"Now hold on a minute here. I don't know about the Christ Child, but Santa is busy delivering his gifts tonight. You won't get his gift until tomorrow morning, but you need to put out some milk and cookies for him."

"Why I need do that?

"Because after travelling all over the world, he might be hungry and thirsty. Let's find him some baking that he might like." She steered me towards the kitchen. We laid everything out, but I wasn't convinced of anything. How could this Santa take care of all the children in the world all in one night? We were living in the middle of nowhere; he could easily miss our place in this blinding white snow!

"Don't give up just yet, Helen. Santa has not disappointed anyone so far."

Ethel wouldn't have said that unless she believed it. If she believes, then I must too.

> *Mail order catalogues from Sears Roebuck & Co. and T. Eaton & Co. provided a selection of goods that were otherwise unobtainable to rural Canadians. Staples like sugar, flour, coffee, tea and salt were stocked and purchased in the small rural town stores. Other necessities could be*

bought there, but the selection was poor and the prices high. One could drive into a city nearby for a greater selection, but most farmers could not afford the time nor the gas to do this. Some people did not even own a vehicle.

The catalogues arrived in the spring, summer and fall with a special issue for Christmas. They contained the latest fashions, furnishings, household and sporting goods, tools and toys. The customer would let his heart do the talking and his fingers do the walking. Once a decision was made, the order form was filled and mailed. The parcel arrived by post about two weeks later and was returnable if necessary.

A Promise Kept

Christmas Day and After—1954

The next morning, still in my long flannel nightgown, I dashed straight into the living room to look under the tree. I detected one lonely wrapped present, large enough to possibly hold a doll. It had my name on it but not who it came from. With no one in the house, I stood on the ice cold floor in my bare feet deciding my next move. *Should I open it? Better wait!*

I suddenly started to shake. Was it the cold room or was it my excitement? I decided it was the cold room and rushed back under my warm feather quilt to wait for their return. They had better hurry, or I wouldn't be able to stop myself from opening that box! As I waited, I tried to imagine the many hours of joy I would receive from having a doll again. I remembered my first doll, Greta, and wondered if Eva was taking good care of her.

Oh, oh, shouldn't have done that. Now I'm homesick for all the lovely people I had left in Austria—especially my foster mother!

Thank goodness my thoughts were interrupted by the bang of the door. Everyone was back! I ran to greet them, again in only my nightgown and bare feet.

Before I could even open my mouth, my mother scolded me, "Get some clothes on, Heli. You will catch your death of cold!"

Reluctantly, I returned to the bedroom, grabbed some clothes and dressed in front of the oil burner. I could hear the clatter of the cast iron frying pan as it hit the top of the kitchen stove. Breakfast was already in the making as I entered the kitchen. I could smell and hear the sizzling bacon. I was always hungry, but this morning I had a different hunger.

Interrupting my mother when she was busy was never a wise decision, so I turned to Ethel. She was washing up after chores in the small basin in the porch. She saw me coming and greeted me with the biggest smile, "Merry Christmas, Helen. How are you today?"

I would be really wonderful if I had my doll!

But these thoughts were rude and selfish, so I replied, "Merry Christmas you too. I yam fine. I open present under tree, yes?"

She grabbed the towel from the rack, dried her hands, then turned to me with a big smile and said, "I think your mother would like you to have breakfast first." She dumped her used wash water into a slop pail and headed into the kitchen to help with the breakfast.

Disappointed, I grabbed the same wash bowl, carried it to the stove's reservoir and refilled it with fresh warm water. As I rinsed the sleep out of my eyes, the warm water calmed me down enough to sit through breakfast without fidgeting. I kept peeking at Ethel and *Mutti*, looking for some signal that it was time to open the present. Ethel caught me looking and giggled.

Doesn't anyone realize how important this is to me?

Finally after forever, Ethel beckoned me into the living room and handed me the package from under the tree. Once the paper was off, I could see that indeed it was Saucy Walker. *Oh, thank you, Santa! Thank you, Christ Child!* I opened the tab and slowly pulled her out. She was more beautiful than I had imagined! The blue of her eyes matched the colour of her dress and bonnet. She had two thick, brown braids that reached her shoulders. The hair wasn't real as I had expected, but it was better than the painted hair on my previous doll,

Greta. I clutched her close, jumped from the floor and danced around the room.

"So I gather that you don't like her. We'll have to send her back," Ethel said slowly and seriously.

I looked back at her in horror. Her face remained blank for a minute or so, then she burst out laughing.

Don't do that!

I didn't put my doll down all day except for meals. She was not as soft as "Greta" because she was made of hard moulded plastic, but she was certainly more realistic. I examined her delicately sculptured fingers and dimpled elbows and watched as her eyelids closed when I laid her down. But she didn't get up and walk like the catalogue had indicated. There was no button to turn her on. Now what? I had to get Ethel's help. The two of us figured it out, and before long, I had her walking on the table. She was made in such a way that if you pulled on her arm and leaned her sideways slightly, her opposing foot would come forward. Then you had to lean her the other way to move her other foot forward. I was content with that.

It had been a long time since I had been this happy, but who was responsible for this? I had thanked Santa Claus and the Christ child already. Maybe I also needed to thank my Guardian Angel. Perhaps even my mother or Ethel? Not wishing to offend anyone, I decided to thank each and every one of them.

I had not yet given her a name. As I had done before, I wanted to name her after my sister, Ethel, but there was already a duplicate name in this family. Seeing as she came from here, I decided to give her a Canadian name—Sally. Sally was the younger sister of Dick and Jane in my first year primer.

My doll became my new playmate. I spent hours fashioning her a new wardrobe with my skills of crocheting, knitting and hand sewing. Her bed was a shoebox which resembled the one I had slept in on the farm in Austria with its elevated sides.

***

When the Christmas holidays were over, school occupied my time again. Everyone talked about their presents that they had received for Christmas. I, too, was eager to share my story but still could not express myself clearly in English. A great deal of pointing and drawing had to be used. They had never heard about a Christ Child who gave presents, nor my Guardian Angel, so like them, I credited Santa Claus for my beautiful doll. Most nodded and smiled, but one girl took me aside and with an almost adult confidence, whispered in my ear, "There is no Santa Claus, Helen. Your parents buy you your presents."

What? My sister has lied to me!

That very same evening, I wondered how I was going to approach Ethel with this most serious accusation. Finally after supper when everything was put away, she headed towards the dining table to do her homework as she did every night. I sat down very close to her, watched as she licked her upper lip with her tongue whenever she was concentrating hard. I kept trying to make eye contact, but as soon as I did, I looked away. I couldn't find the words to ask her.

"What is it, Helen?" she finally asked.

"Is there really Santa Claus? Was him who brought my doll?" I blurted out.

"You mean 'was it *he* who brought the doll'?"

"Yes, that's what I said."

"No you didn't, but that's neither here or there. What you're asking me is whether there really is a Santa Claus or not, right?" She paused as I nodded, then continued, "That depends on who you ask. Some people believe there is, some don't."

"What you believe?"

"Sort of…kind of…well, not really. My sisters and I never heard of Santa Claus until we went to school and other children told us about him. We used to make tiny sheaves of wheat and hung them outside our window. These were for Jesus' donkey to nibble on when they passed by. When Jesus saw this, He was pleased, so He left us presents."

"The Christ Child in Austria left us presents, too."

She gave a little shrug. "I guess it doesn't matter who brought the presents, as long as we are grateful and thank them. You decide who to thank."

I had already covered all my bases by thanking everyone. Whoever was responsible had kept their promise.

Milking

March—1955

I had been unprepared for my first winter in Canada with its bitter cold, excessive amount of snow, and its wearisome length. In Austria, we considered ourselves lucky to get a white Christmas and felt fortunate if the temperatures were low enough to preserve the snow for more than a few days. Plenty of it fell in the mountains for skiing, and that was as it should be. Winter only lasted for about three months, so by the beginning of March, the scent of blooming trees and flowers filled the air.

Here, in the middle of March, there was no hint of any colours—green or otherwise. By late February and early March, Dad had started visiting the barn on a regular basis both day or night. Sometimes even *Mutti* went, but she wouldn't allow me to go with her.

"Why Dad go in the barn all night?" I asked my sister one morning.

She corrected my English then explained, "He is making sure that the baby calf or piglet is on the right road to its new world."

"You mean he telling stork where to go?"

She looked at me, patted my head and grinned. "Yes Helen, that is what he is doing."

I didn't get to see or help the stork, but eventually I did get to see all the babies he brought. At milking time, I ran ahead of everyone and was already petting the new calves before *Mutti,* Dad and Ethel entered the barn. My mother settled herself between the two cows in the first stall, Dad took a similar position in the second one and Ethel took the next one. Before long, I heard the regular splashing of the streams of milk as they filled the pail. *Swoosh-swoosh, swoosh-swoosh!* The aroma of fresh milk filled the barn. As usual, it was Ethel whom I studied with fascination as the milk hit the pail and foamed.

"Watch this, Helen," Ethel said as she aimed the teat straight at one of the cats gathered at my feet. The cat did not run away but positioned herself to accept the squirt right into her open mouth. Then one by one the other cats lined up.

"Can I try milk, please?" I asked Ethel, knowing that my mother would never allow it.

"The word is 'may', not 'can'," Ethel corrected.

Before I could repeat my request correctly, I heard my mother shouting in German from the first stall. "Don't you go near those cows, Heli. They'll trample you!" She repeated it in Hungarian for Ethel.

"She'll be okay. I'll watch her," Ethel called back as she got up to let me sit on an old upside down pail beside her cow called Bossie. Ethel stood near the head of the cow and began her instructions. "Grab one teat in each hand, tighten your thumb and pointing finger around the top, then close the rest of your fingers in order. At the same time, pull down on the teat to squeeze the milk out and make sure you aim for the pail. Open that hand and repeat with the other."

I grabbed the two teats closest to me. They were incredibly soft and warm. I did as Ethel had instructed and concentrated on surrounding one teat with my thumb and forefinger. They barely met! I closed the rest of my fingers and squeezed hard. Nothing happened! My hand only covered the upper half of the teat.

"Keep your fingers tight and pull down," Ethel suggested.

A tiny spurt of milk came out but missed the pail. This was harder than it looked, and I had used my stronger right hand. The cow turned and looked at me. I'm sure I detected a look of disgust. She swished her tail and thumped the back of my head with it. My forehead hit the animal's side, and I almost spilled the milk from the pail. A roar of laughter came from my sister, and between breaths, she managed to say, "You're lucky her tail is not wet from pee or poo!"

Oh Kaka! I give up. When I get older I'm going to show that cow, Bossie, who the boss really is.

When all the cows were finally done, everyone except me carried two full pails of milk to a granary nearby. They each emptied their pails into a contraption which had a large bowl on top, a handle on the side and two spouts leading to a different clean pail.

"Would you like to help separate the milk?" Ethel asked me.

"What you mean?"

"This machine is called a 'cream separator' and it does exactly what the name says. It separates the cream from the milk. Most of it will go into a large can which is picked up and sent to the creamery in Regina. Once it's delivered, they send us a 'cream cheque' which we'll cash to buy things at the store. Now come, I'll start it and then you can continue, okay?"

She had to pull hard on that handle to start this machine. As soon as it turned at a good speed, she handed it over to me. When she let go, the handle kept turning on its own! I tried to grab it, but it almost flung me against the wall. I finally caught the handle but wasn't sure whether *I* was turning it, or *it* was turning me? As usual, Ethel watched and laughed. I seemed to be an endless source of amusement for her.

"Get a grip on that handle and keep turning it. The faster you turn it, the thicker the cream."

Soon, thick cream poured out of one spout and the thinned milk out the other. So now I knew the origin of that luscious white liquid. I also knew its destination—into my bowl of porridge with brown sugar, into my Jello as whipped cream and into the *Paprikash* chicken gravy. There was another use for that cream—making butter, and it had become my chore. I would fill a quart jar half-full with fresh cream and shake the jar until a ball of butter formed and floated in the leftover buttermilk which I promptly gulped down.

I worked up a sweat turning the handle of the separator until all the milk in the big bowl had passed through.

"Come, help me feed the calves." Ethel handed me two pails that were about one third full and grabbed two more full ones of the separated milk. We headed to the calf enclosure at the back of the barn.

"*Bzo! Bzo*!" she called as we entered the pen. All the calves raced towards us and almost knocked us over in their eagerness. Ethel poured some milk into a trough and the calves rushed towards it. "Most of these calves already know how to drink from the trough. Only the very new young ones need to be taught. Pour some of the milk into this old bucket here."

I watched with fascination as she put her fingers into the mouth of the smallest calf, waited until it began to suckle, then placed her hand into the pail just under the surface of the milk. As the calf sucked on her fingers, it slurped up the fresh milk.

"Now you try it."

"It will bite my fingers off!" I cried in horror.

"No it won't. It doesn't have any teeth yet."

So I allowed the calf to suck on my fingers. It pulled on them so hard, I thought it was going to swallow my whole arm. I withdrew.

Phooey! It's all slimy!

"Cup your hand, then it can't suck your fingers in as far," Ethel suggested.

I tried again and found I had greater control. I then moved my hand with the calf attached under the surface of the milk. The calf suddenly snorted and butted the bucket. I almost lost my grip on the handle. I looked at Ethel for advice.

Again, she laughed hard and long. "You put your hand too far into the milk. You need to make sure the calf's nose is not under the surface. Try again."

This time I did it right because the little calf sucked up that milk with gusto. Every once in a while, it would butt again like it does at its mother's udder. I made sure I had a good grip on the pail this time.

"Once the calves learn to drink from the bucket, they don't need our fingers any more. They associate the call and the bucket with lunchtime."

"Why we not let calves drink from their mother like we let piggies do?"

"If we do that, there would not be enough milk left for us or the other animals," she explained. "Besides, we need the money from the sale of the cream."

I watched as some of the leftover milk went to the mama pig and her piglets, some into a dish for the cats and some into the dog bowl. I hoped *Mutti* had taken the rest of the milk and cream to the house for us. I loved milk and cream and butter!

chickens & geese

CHICKS

April—1955

Near the end of April, my other new sister, Alice Kallichuk, and her husband Walter drove into our yard and dropped off a large, shallow cardboard box. Strange sounds and movements came from the one-inch holes in the sides. Dad had built an enclosure by the wood stove in the kitchen and now lifted the box into it. He opened the top of the box. Out of it poured an army of baby chicks chirping loudly and hopping over each other.

I couldn't contain my excitement and reached down to capture one of these yellow fluff balls. As I held it in my hand, its cries became louder, and its tiny claws dug into my palm. Dad told me to cup my other hand over it. As I did, the little thing stopped chirping, sat down and closed its eyes.

"It thinks it's under its mother's wing and now feels safe," Dad explained.

The chicks remained in the enclosure and entertained us with their songs and games during the day, but when the fire went out for the night, we had to replace them into their lidded box where they could huddle to keep warm. As the weather improved outside, they were moved to a mud hut north of the house. There, they were allowed to freely scrounge outside all day but were herded back in for the night. Once they were large enough, we had to carry each and every one to the regular chicken coop every night until they learned to return to their new home on their own.

Curious, I had to ask, "How come we buy baby chickens when we have mama hens here that have their babies?" I loved to watch these mother hens as they cooed and clucked around the yard with their babies in tow. At the slightest danger, her voice changed and the little ones would scurry under her protective wing.

Ethel, as usual, did the explaining. "Well, we normally remove the eggs as soon as they lay them in their nests in the chicken coop. If the eggs are not taken away, the hens become clucks or brood hens. Once in a while, a hen will lay her eggs where we don't find it, like the barn or haystack, and that's why we have the occasional clucks. We don't want them to do that because it takes them away from our egg production. We need the eggs for ourselves and to sell" She took a breath, then she let out a little laugh. "Did you know that these hens will also raise turkey or duck eggs. We just have to put these eggs under them, and the cluck think they are her own chicks. I once saw a brood hen go into a tizzy when some of her babies went into the water. She didn't realize they were ducklings. Was that ever funny!"

I wonder if that is the situation with my mother and me, and maybe that's why she is always in a tizzy.

Teamwork

May—1955

The weather had warmed considerably, and I needed to be outdoors. Outside was also where Dad spent most of his time. We had been getting along just fine throughout the winter, but had never spent time alone together. I began to follow and watch him from a distance. Early one Saturday, after the chores, I noticed he was harnessing both horses in the barn. Always excited to be near those magical creatures, I wanted to be part of whatever was going on.

"Where are you going with them, Dad?"

"It looks like a nice cool day to pick stones on the field," he explained in English.

"Pick stones? I can understand picking strawberries or flowers, but why would you want pick ugly stones? What are they good for?"

He looked rather small as he squeezed out from between those two enormous beasts. As he threw the reins over the back of Jolan he explained, "Every year, just before seeding, we need to remove any large stones that can break our machinery."

"How come you have to pick them every year? Once you pick them, are they not gone forever?"

"Nope, every year new ones come."

"Come from where? Does the stork bring babies to the stones, too?"

Dad laughed and laughed, and once he had control he explained in

Hungarian,"When winter comes, the ground freezes. As it freezes, it pushes the soil up, along with any stones within it. When it thaws in the spring, the soil settles around and under the stones. In this way, the stones underground appear to grow on the surface every spring."

At least that's the way I understood what he said. No matter, I just wanted to be with him and the horses. "May I come with you and help?" I asked, remembering to use "may" instead of "can".

"Yea, I sure could use some help, but you better ask your mother. We'll never hear the end of it if you don't. Go, I'll wait for you."

I ran to the house, found *Mutti* in the kitchen and begged for permission to pick stones with Dad.

"You're never that happy to help *me* in the house," she complained in German, then switched to English. "Yoo doo it wat yoo like it." She waved me off.

It was true. I did not like being in the house because I was never comfortable working along side my mother. She would tell me what to do, not ask me. *Mutti* never complimented me when I did well, only complained when I did poorly. But, of course, I could not explain that to her because I was taught that children never spoke back to their parents.

She rarely granted my wishes so when she said "yes", I couldn't believe my ears and I dashed back to the barn before she could change her mind.

The horses were harnessed and ready to be backed up from their stall.

"I see you're smiling, so she must have said, 'yes'. Good! Now just move back a little. The horses are a bit excited." With some gentle clucking and pulling of the reins, he led them outside and hitched them to what looked like a heavy wooden flat sleigh.

"May I ride on this thing?"

"It's called a stone boat. It's a little too jerky, so you'll have to sit and hold tight."

I sat on the sleigh, Dad walked beside it guiding the horses with the reins. The screech of the metal at the bottom of the runners as they scraped against the gravel in the yard made my teeth ache. I wondered which was the greater danger—deafness or toppling. We headed past the house and west to the field.

Once we hit the soft soil, the ruckus stopped, and the sleigh moved more smoothly and quietly. There, Dad stopped the horses and beckoned for me to follow him. "Okay, Iluska, it's time to work." He pointed to a particular sized rock. "We need to pick every stone that is as big or bigger than this one. You get the smaller ones, I'll get the big ones, and we'll put them all on the stone boat."

We picked all the ones near the boat, moved the horses to the next patch of land and repeated the gathering. In between the work, I would stop, catch my breath and look around. This field seemed endless in comparison to the one my foster *Vater* had owned in Austria. I could turn in a complete circle and never see the edge of the field. I closed my eyes, sensed the cool breeze drying the sweat on my body, smelled the dank odour of the wet spring soil and heard the horses nicker. Occasionally, when the sun peeked through, I felt its heat penetrate my thin jacket.

What a great place this is!

Dad did not push me to get back to work. I could see he, too, had stopped to wipe his face with the ever-present red handkerchief he had in the pocket of his overalls. We caught each other's eye and both smiled.

"You, okay?" he asked.

"Yes, Dad."

Then we set back to work. I had no idea how heavy some of those stones could be. Sometimes I think I picked the ones that were smaller than Dad had indicated. I was afraid that this would be a good reason for him to be upset with me, but he did not. Nor did he raise his voice or criticize me for my mistakes or my slowness. That was definitely a good sign. He did, however, tell me jokes that I did not understand, but I laughed anyway. He also told stories.

"Iluska, do you know why a marriage is like a team of horses?"

"No, why?"

"Watch how the stone boat moves forward. It moves forward because Jolan and Gitzka are pulling in one direction at the same time. What do you thing would happen if only Jolan was pulling or if they were pulling in different directions?"

"The stone boat would not move?" I answered, proud that I could figure that out without having any farm experience.

"*Igen!* Yes! The same thing goes for a husband and wife. If they don't work together, like a team of horses, their marriage goes nowhere. Remember that when you get married someday."

I like this story but don't think I will ever pull a stone boat with my husband.

We carried on until Dad was satisfied there were no stones left that could do any damage. He then guided the horses to the edge of the field towards the fence. I couldn't believe the strength of these animals. The sleigh had seemed heavy enough, but now it held a large number of heavy boulders. My admiration for these beast only grew. So did it also grow for my Dad.

By the end of it, horses and humans were hot, thirsty and hungry. We headed back. Dad dropped me off at the house while he watered and unhooked the horses. One look from my mother and I knew she wasn't impressed.

"That was hard work. How come you're smiling? You wouldn't have to work so hard if you were in the house with me. I hope you've learned your lesson."

You want me to stay in the house within easy reach of your wooden spoon and your sharp tongue? Never! I simply replied, "*Ja, Mutti.*"

"Now wash up good. You look like something the cat dragged in."

I didn't care what I looked like. The day and the work had been exhilarating! I was definitely going to try to spend more time with Dad. We had begun to communicate and had enjoyed each other's company. *He and I make a good team!*

Before mechanization, farmers required strong, but gentle, complying horses to help them with heavy work such as cultivating, seeding, haying, harvesting, hauling grain, wood and other heavy loads, and also for transportation. With their heavy muscled necks, short backs, wide girth and powerful hindquarters, these loyal companions worked tirelessly both summer and winter. More than once, these intelligent animals made their way through blinding winter storms to bring their owners home safe and sound.

The Power of a Pea

June—1955

Now that Ethel had become my legal and bosom sister, I wanted to know more about her past. So I chose one morning when we were washing the many individual conical plates from the cream separator. This task would take us forever, so there would be plenty of time for all my questions. I hesitated because I had been taught never to ask personal questions of people. If they offered first, then it was alright, but I was never to put the person on the spot. However, I thought that she and I had become close enough, and that I should know more about my new family.

"Where is your mother?" I blurted out, rather bluntly.

Her eyes widened, she frowned, then turned abruptly towards me. "Where is this coming from?"

Not cxpccting that reaction, I tried to soften my voice. "I'm sorry, I shouldn't have asked—it was rude of me. I didn't have a father and you didn't have a mother, so I thought that we had something in common."

"Hmm, I guess you're right. Well, my mother passed when I was the same age as you are now."

"That must have been awful for you. I don't miss my real Dad because I never knew him, but you must miss your mother very much.

Does that means you have been alone with Dad for all that time?"

"Oh no, most of my brothers and sisters were still home at the time. But by the time you came, they had all married and moved out except me. I lived alone with Dad for about three years. Brother Bill would come and go and only stay long enough to help Dad with the crops."

I was amazed. "You mean you had to take care of the house, the cooking, the washing and the chores and go to school at the same time?"

"Yes, but I would only do that during the weekends and summer holidays. We didn't have a bus or Bombardier until the year before you came. So during the school week, I had to board at Rudy Hauk's place nearer to Cupar. From there, we kids were hauled to school like cargo at the back of a truck. In the winter they used a van."

I tried to imagine myself doing all that work at the age of thirteen. My opinion of her rose even higher—if that was even possible.

***

A couple of weeks later, however, my feeling towards her slipped slightly. On this particular day, our parents had gone into Cupar. I had been looking forward to a glorious day without my mother and with just Ethel. Everything went fine until lunch time. I sat at the kitchen table eating the leftover pork chops, mashed potatoes and peas that Ethel had warmed for me. I gulped down the meat and potatoes but those peas tasted something awful. No matter how hard I tried, they would just stick in the back of my throat and wouldn't go down. I had to spit them out and left the rest on the plate. I was ready to leave the table.

"You can't go until you finish your peas, Helen," she chided.

Why is she being so stubborn and forcing me to eat these horrible green things.

It wasn't so much their taste as their texture that I disliked. They rolled around my plate as though they were alive and mocking me. I killed them with my fork and squashed them, but I had nothing left on my plate to bury them under.

"Just stick those things into your chipmunk cheeks already. They're not going to kill you."

I could see her jaw set firm. Any vegetables I ever had in Austria were either hidden in soups or stews, thus I had never developed a taste for them. After being being forced to eat too many cooked vegetables in the hospital in the *Lager*, I had a hatred for them, unlike the raw, fresh vegetables from the garden that I loved.

I will surely choke if I have to swallow these, but I don't want Ethel to be angry at me. What should I do?

I chose not to eat the peas! As a result, I sat at that table for quite some time. War had silently been declared. The longer I sat, the more agitated Ethel became. It was the first time we had clashed, and I did not like this feeling, but I disliked the texture of those peas even more. Neither one of us yielded. I would never have dared to be this headstrong with my mother. I guess I did not consider my life in danger with Ethel. Our pigheadedness was well matched.

"Why are you being so stubborn?" She pulled me off the chair and dragged me into a corner. "Now you stay here until you apologize. You're not the boss around here, you know...and neither is your mother!"

***

Before long, school was out for summer again, and I had high hopes for a lovely vacation with no catechism or tutoring. Aside from a few chores, I would have the whole summer to myself, and I planned to be as free and happy as a lark. The first indication of trouble began when I caught Ethel packing her clothes into a suitcase and some boxes.

"Who are you going to visit?" I asked.

"No one, Helen. I am moving into Regina to work at a bank."

"Moving! Am I going with you?"

"So sorry, Helen, but I have finished grade twelve, and now I need to start a career of my own."

"What is a career?"

"It means I will be working at a job and making money. It also means I won't be living here any more."

"You mean you're leaving ... leaving me?"

"Yes, Helen, and I'm truly sorry, kiddo, but I will come to visit you once in a while, okay?"

It was not "okay." No Ethel—just me, my mother and Dad! Who would help me with all the chores? I would probably have more now with Ethel gone. Who would help me with my homework? Who would answer the thousands of questions I always had? Who would I share my love of books with? And most importantly, who could I turn to when I became upset?

I had never realized she had become a warm fuzzy blanket that I wrapped around me whenever I felt overwhelmed, upset or just in need of a hug. Despite my protests, pleas and blubbering, she left. For weeks after, I was lost. I had depended on her to initiate our assigned tasks, and I would just follow her lead willingly. Now, *Mutti* had to nag me to do this or that—neither of which I wanted to do, least of all by myself. With Ethel, each chore had been a game that I enjoyed and from which I had learned. As we had worked, she would tell me funny stories from her childhood that kept me laughing every day.

I hope someday I will have stories to tell too.

I almost wished school was still on, then I would have something to occupy my mind and time. As it was, even the increased chores did nothing to ease my loneliness for her. I caught myself wandering around aimlessly as though a part of me had been removed and not enough pieces remained for me to function. Though I was not the one who had left, I felt like the one displaced.

I missed everything about her. The ever-ready smirk or chuckle when I used the wrong English word, the way she threw her head back in laughter at my strange ideas or interpretation of things, and even the way her tongue would lick her upper lip when she concentrated really hard. I missed the words not spoken, her reassuring smiles, her raised brow, and the way her eyes opened wide with surprise. But most of all, I missed her presence, for when she was near, I felt safe, worthy and confident. She had stirred familiar feelings that I once had when I was with my foster family. It seemed that the more you loved someone, the more painful the parting.

Why hadn't she found a job at a bank in Cupar where I could've seen her more often? I wondered if the real reason she went away was because I had made her angry for not eating those awful peas!

Have I underestimated the power of the pea?

On My Own

Summer—1955

I threw myself into the increased workload to ease my guilt and lessen my loneliness. All the house cleaning became my responsibility. Three large rooms plus the porch claimed my time every Saturday.

Screens and windows were now open to allow the fresh breezes through the house. Unfortunately, along with the fresh air came the sand picked up by the constant winds that whipped across our yard or clouds of dust that wafted in after a vehicle had passed on the gravel road. Without an invitation, this dirt made itself at home on any flat surface. It took several trips outside to shake the dust rag or mop to forcibly return it to its rightful place. The beautiful oak china cabinet, table and chairs and chiffonier also cried out for their weekly drink of lemon oil. When I finally applied it, I was sure I could hear the wood gulp, the same way I guzzled down the cold water from the well on a hot day. I knew what it was like to be thirsty.

Washing and waxing the worn linoleum floor was the main cause of my misery. Both required me to be on my hands and knees. Once washed, the exact amount of paste wax had to be applied evenly. With flannel cloth beneath my hands and knees, I wiggled on the floor like a drunken beetle to make it shine. Eventually, the floor resembled a rich carpet—alive with colour and depth.

At the end, breathing hard and sweating, I studied my work and felt very satisfied. The floors and furniture shone, and the smell of clean filled my senses. Now I understood what Ethel meant about the feeling you get when you do a job well. She would be proud.

The other household chores that I inherited were setting the table, clearing the table, and worst of all, washing the dishes which included those numerous, detestable plates from the cream separator. Three times a day, every day, every week for the whole summer! *I hate housework! Thank goodness Mutti does not allow me to cook or iron clothes. She says it is too dangerous for me. Sometimes, she is so smart!*

Any outdoor chores were welcome. I helped feed and water the chickens, pigs, calves, cats and one dog. I gathered eggs daily, but not without receiving a severe pecking from the sitting hens as I reached under them. My mother insisted that I pull weeds and slugs in the garden but quickly changed her mind when she realized I did not know the difference between a weed and a vegetable. Most of the time, I was at her beck and call to help with this or that. Her constant demands did not allow me to wander too far from the house. I would have preferred to be left on my own more often.

The only time I would scamper to the house freely and willingly was when a travelling salesman arrived. Not many strangers came into our yard, but in the summer, in the middle of a week, it was always exciting to receive them with their wares. Puppy, Dad's dog, would make a specific barking sound to announce a stranger.

The two salesmen that came most often were from J.R. Watkins and Fuller Brush Company. Clean, well-groomed and dressed in their fancy suits and ties, they made me feel frumpy and dirty, which I probably was. But once they opened their big black cases, it was like going shopping without ever leaving your home. *Mutti* usually did not want me around strange men, but for these she needed me as an interpreter.

From the Watkins man she purchased most of the spices, like cinnamon, paprika or cloves, plus vanilla extract. But the products they were most noted for were the red liniment and their first-aid salve.

Useful for both man and beast, Dad used the liniment on himself and his horses to relieve sore muscles. The Petro-Carbo First Aid Salve, a disinfectant and moisturizer, was rubbed onto the cows' teats and on our chapped hands. The only product I was interested in was the thick gooey syrup called Watkins Beverage Base which produced a most delicious orange drink when mixed with cold water from the well. From the Fuller Brush dealer, we bought clothes brushes, shoe brushes and hair brushes.

During the salesman's time in our house, he was treated to coffee and baking. In return, he presented us with a sample of one of his products, or some trade-marked item like a letter opener. To me the salesmen represented another world outside the one I was familiar with. They provided me with an adventure, much like my books, except they were real.

Playmate

Summer—1955

Although my mother kept me close, she did allow me to wander over to Mary Ann's or Lenny's place about a quarter of a mile east of our farm. Up a hill and on the left lived Lenny and his sister Susie with their mom and dad, Alice and Walter Kallichuk. Alice, being Ethel's sister, was now mine also. Mary Ann lived right across the road from them with her parents, Joe and Doraphine Kish. Joe was my new Dad's oldest son whom I now considered my new brother. Ethel had explained earlier that I had become an auntie to Lenny, Susie and Mary Ann.

How strange that my nieces and nephews were only a few years younger than I.

I could not develop a friendship with Lenny like I had with Willi. Lenny was not quite five years-old and wanted nothing to do with a girl. His sister, Susie, was still a baby. So really, I had only one option —four-year-old Mary Ann. I believed that I was *her* only option too.

I had first played with Mary Ann during *Mutti's* wedding reception. We'd had difficulty communicating in English, but a lot of acting and antics on my part did the job. Mary Ann laughed at me, but the message went through. Every girl understands the gentle motion of rocking a baby or the delicate tipping of a tea cup to your lips. We got along well.

Today, I needed the company of a girl friend. My mother and father had no time for play, and I didn't even want to spend time alone with wonderful me. It was time to seek out Mary Ann. I scooped up my doll, Sally, and with my mother's permission, headed out down the road.

"Sally," I said. "I know you are a walking doll, and it is a lovely day, but I'm going to carry you, otherwise it will take us forever to get to Mary Ann's place." She agreed.

The warm breeze carried a slight hint of mint that must have come from plants near the slough just up the gravel road. As I passed it, a sudden racket on my right startled me. From the cattails at the edge of the water, a whir of wings and panicked quacking came from two wild ducks taking flight. One of them had an emerald green head with a white band around its neck. The other was a plain light brown. I recognized their colours, but did not know what they were called. In Austria, I had never really seen many wild creatures, but here, there were plenty.

As I strolled along slowly, I remembered mother's parting words, "Look out for the cars." I don't know what she was worried about? Hardly any vehicles used this road. Even if one did come, I would be able to hear its tires long before they ever reached me. Not worried about being run over by a car, I was more concerned with choking to death on the dust they created as they sped by.

I carried on, remembering the last time Mary Ann and I had seen each other at her house last winter. There, I had seen several small pieces of fur stretched out on boards and had asked what they were. Doraphine had explained that they were muskrat pelts that Joe trapped and sold to be made into coats.

Does that mean that my mother's fur coat is made from real animals?

I preferred playing at Mary Ann's home, rather than mine. I never fully relaxed at home, no matter what I did, and playing with Mary Ann was no exception. *Mutti* would constantly interfere with our games, telling us what we were doing wrong, whereas Mary Ann's mother joined in the fun.

At the top of the hill, I made a right hand turn into her yard. As I neared the door, I could smell cinnamon. Not only was the smell inviting but so were Doraphine and Mary Ann. We giggled and hugged.

"Let's have tea," Mary Ann said as she pulled out her toy-sized tea set and placed it on her own little table by the sofa. The set, with its flowered tea pot and four matching cups and saucers, looked like real china. Her mother brewed us some real tea and cut some fresh cinnamon buns into bite size pieces. We poured the cooled, weak tea into our tiny cups which held only enough tea for one sip. Smiling and laughing, Doraphine took part in our play by pretending to be the waitress that served us.

Why can't my mother be more like that?

Mary Ann and I chatted as we ate and drank. Even though my English had improved considerably, it still was not adequate enough to get in a good gossip session. I did, however, know the words for please, thank you and sorry—all essential for correct manners. My mother taught me to use these words generously. She told me that good manners made you appear grateful and gracious and that meant good breeding—whatever that was. I just wanted to make sure Mary Ann knew that I was grateful. She was such a good little hostess.

After tea, we were ready to play outside. We had barely cleared the steps and were looking towards the barn when a huge cow lumbered towards us, her head high and her udder swinging to and fro. We screamed and ran back into the house.

"There's a big cow outside who wants to kill us," Mary Ann cried to her mother.

Doraphine looked out the door, saw the cow and laughed. "That's Jóska! She's my pet cow. She won't hurt you."

This cow is a girl, and "Jóska" translates as "Joseph", which happens to be both my Dad's name and Mary Ann's dad's name. Why would she give a cow a boy's name?

Her mother, still laughing, came back in the kitchen, grabbed some old bread and what seemed to be broken egg shells. She opened the door and offered it to the cow. It was obvious, they knew each other and had gone through this routine before. As we watched in fascination, the cow gulped it down and demanded more. I couldn't believe my eyes. *Since when do cows eat bread and eggs?*

Doraphine finally shooed her away so that we could get out. Mary Ann and I wanted to explore the barn. We entered its dark interior and stood in the centre waiting for our eyes to adjust. I felt something rub against my ankle.

"*Ach*, what the heck is that?" I wanted to use the other word starting with "h", but Ethel had told me that is wasn't a nice word for a little girl, but that "heck" was okay to use. *Everyone else around me uses the other "h" word. Why can't I?*

Then I heard the mewing and knew we would be fine. A horde of kittens had gathered at our feet, rubbing and scratching us to get our attentions. One was black and white, two had grey stripes, two more were multicolored and one was the prettiest orange. I was thrilled. Mary Ann seemed to love animals as much as I did. We cradled and stroked their silky soft bodies, kissed and crooned over their cute little faces for at least an hour. By the time we left, each one had a name.

Doraphine met us as we headed back to the house. With a big smile on her face she said, "Come with me, you guys. I have a big surprise for you!"

We followed her north of the house to an abandoned red truck that the sun had bleached to orange. The bottom part was completely gone, and only the hollowed-out cab remained. The doors were also missing, and inside, we saw the outline of Mary Ann's dog, Trixie, lying on an old black coat.

What's the big surprise?

"Is Trixie sick?" I asked Doraphine.

"No," she said. "Look again."

Then I saw them—four squirming tiny new puppies snuggled up to Trixie's belly. Mary Ann and I gasped and attempted to reach for the babies. Doraphine cut us off by placing her arm across the opening and said, “We must give them at least a week before we handle them, okay?”

We were disappointed, but we obeyed, although not without grumbling.

As we walked away, I was unaware that I was thinking out loud and said, “I sure wish I could have a dog of my own.”

Oh dear! I’m becoming just like my mother—letting my mind talk out loud! Have I caught the germ from her?

Doraphine interupted, “You are welcome to have one of Trixie's puppies when it gets old enough. It will be your birthday present. Would you like that?”

“Oh, *Ja...* I mean yes.” I clapped my hands with joy. But then I thought about my mother. “*Mutti* will never let me have a dog.”

“Sometimes I just don’t understand Lisi,” she said as she shook her head. “I’ll tell you what, Helen. I’ll talk to her when the puppy is ready to be taken. It will be some time near your birthday. Meanwhile, ask your father to convince her.”

“Okay” I replied. In my heart, I still didn’t feel confident enough in him, or me, to ask such a great favour. We had started a good connection when I had helped him pick stones, but I still barely knew him.

I sure could use his help. A dog would be a wonderful playmate.

Birthday Gift

August—1955

July was done. Soon it will be my tenth birthday. Mary Ann's was very close to mine—hers was on the third of August, mine on the tenth. Doraphine insisted that we should celebrate them together on her daughter's birthday. I thought it was a great idea, but when I told *Mutti,* she thought otherwise.

"You would be interfering with Mary Ann's day. It's her birthday, not yours. I'll take care of my own daughter's birthday! I won't let you to go if you're going to celebrate your birthdays together."

I didn't know what to make of that and couldn't really come up with an argument. All I knew was that I wanted to be there for Mary Ann's birthday. I simply replied, "If you won't let me go, I have to let Doraphine know."

It was *Mutti* who phoned Doraphine, and I heard her speaking yet another language, Romanian, the same one she used to communicate with Ethel's boyfriend, Steve. I didn't know where she'd learned it. She could speak three languages—German, Hungarian and Romanian—and was now trying to learn English. *Sometimes she appears so smart, other times she makes no sense at all—like now!* When she got off the phone, she switched to German and muttered angrily to no one in particular, "No one is going to tell me how to raise my child!"

Oh, oh. Bad news for me?

But, she turned towards me and said, "You can go, just remember it is not *your* birthday!"

How can her mind say one thing, and her lips another? I didn't care what her mind said as long as her lips said the right thing. And this time they did.

The party turned out to include only Mary Ann and me—the two celebrities of the day. Her mother had decorated the house with streamers and balloons. We sang "Happy Birthday" to each other and blew out the candles together. This time my wish was that my mother would let me have that sweet puppy.

As we were munching down the cake, we discovered that Doraphine had placed money in the batter, and now we were cashing in. I found a quarter in my piece, and Mary Ann found a dime. A quarter! I could buy more goodies and drinks the next time we went to town. I felt a bit guilty that I found more money than Mary Ann, seeing that it was her birthday. But she, being only four, knew nothing about money.

Maybe with this extra money I can buy her a treat. Yes, that's what I will do.

I had not told my mother that we had celebrated together, so the following week I had my birthday party and invited Mary Ann and Doraphine. When it was time to blow out my candles, I knew exactly what I wanted to wish for this time. To have my hair cut before I started school this fall. I realized that I have made two wishes for one birthday. Was that too greedy? No, not really. I was just making up for all the previous birthdays when I had no wishes. I hoped both will come true.

"Eat, leelee girlee," *Mutti* urged Mary Ann. We didn't need urging. The chocolate cake slid down our throats just fine with the help of mounds of whipped cream. With no money hidden in this cake, we did not have to worry about swallowing any coins. Doraphine and *Mutti* chatted in Romanian while drinking coffee and also having some cake. Mary Ann and I had coffee too but with more cream than coffee.

I watched Doraphine and *Mutti* talking but could not understand what they were saying. My mother suddenly become agitated. Her voice rose, her words tumbled out more quickly. Mary Ann's mother tried to calm her but could not. Once my mother started, there was no stopping her. Doraphine shook her head and said no more. Mary Ann and I did not play together that day, and they left soon after.

They had barely stepped out the door when my mother turned to me in anger. “Why did you ask Doraphine for a dog?”

“I didn’t ask her,” I replied. “She offered.”

“Either way, you can’t have one. We already have a dog.”

I was grateful to Doraphine for asking my mother, but she did not realize that I had not spoken to Dad yet. Now for sure everything hinged on him. I raced to find Dad quickly before her mind became set. Thank goodness he wasn’t out on the field but was already heading for the house with his old dog, strangely named Puppy, at his heels. I met him at the granary, and in my broken English and even more fractured Hungarian, I begged him for a puppy that was ready for me at Doraphine’s place. I explained how my mother had already laid down the law of “No!”

He smiled and scratched his head then replied in English, “I don’t know, Iluska. You know what your mother is like. Once she makes up her mind, even the devil can’t sway her!”

“Kerém szépen. Please, I’m begging you!”

“Have you chosen which puppy yet? Is it ready to be picked up?”

“Yes, and yes.” I knew exactly which one.

His lips clamped together, his brows furrowed.

Oh, no! Is he angry at me?

His next words took me by surprise. “Don’t worry, Iluska, you will have your puppy.”

Together we headed to the house. I kept quiet, while Dad did the persuading. I mustered up all the Hungarian I knew and listened carefully. *Mutti* had been at the stove stirring onions in the frying pan. She turned, the wooden spoon still in her hand. Dad brought up the subject. My mother shook that big spoon at him, splattering a little of whatever was on it onto the floor.

"We have Puppy already. We don't need another dog."

"Puppy is getting old. We need a younger dog around," Dad responded calmly as he sat down at the kitchen table and lit a cigarette. That was *Mutti's* signal to pour him some coffee. She put out a cup and saucer for him and filled it with old coffee from the big pot on the stove. This action was totally automatic, and so was her response, "I already told Doraphine and Heli that we don't want a dog. Are you going to make a fool of me now?"

Dad, with his cigarette in one hand and the other pouring the coffee from his cup to his saucer, kept his voice low. "She is all alone here, you know. It will be good company for her." He slurped the coffee from the saucer and took another puff from his cigarette.

Mutti's voice rose. "She is not alone. She has us."

I groaned, but Dad did not give up. "Let the girl have her own dog. It's her birthday for God's sake! I'm sure she will feed it and take good care of it."

Yes, Dad, keep it up!

Clearly agitated, my mother returned to the stove and with her back to us said, "Well, it better not interfere with her chores or it will go back!"

Go back? That means it needs to be here for it to go back!

Dad turned to me and winked. "Tomorrow, you bring that puppy home, okay?"

More than okay—we were both winners. He had won against my mother, and I had my dog. I don't know which one of us had the bigger smile. He had become my hero, and I loved him for it. He may not have looked like the father I had imagined, but he sure had the heart that I needed.

I have just received the best birthday gift ever!

Getting Married

August—1955

That same day, I had another birthday present. Steve and Ethel's car drove into our driveway. I hadn't seen Ethel nor heard from her since she left in the beginning of July. A whole month and a half had passed without her. I was a bit nervous, fearing she would remember only how stubborn I had been about eating my peas and forget about all the other good time we had had together. She appeared to be very happy when she stepped out of the car. *Mutti* was in the house, but I was on the bench under the living room window. When our eyes met, she came directly towards me, smiled and gave me a big hug. I almost cried with relief.

"How *are* you Helen?" She sounded concerned.

Then Steve came towards me and also gave me a hug. I liked Steve. His voice was so gentle and kind. He made you feel like no one else mattered except you. I also liked his ready smile and laugh. Today, he seemed happier than ever.

Ethel and Steve held hands as they entered the house. I followed. She greeted my mother coolly, but Steve shook *Mutti's* hand with a smile. The four of us sat down at the table. *Mutti* served coffee and brought out the left-over birthday cake. Ethel smiled wished me a happy birthday and gave me my birthday presents. As I carefully opened the beautifully wrapped gifts, she asked me what my mother had given me. We had to be careful what we said to each other because, just as I was understanding Hungarian better, *Mutti* was also understanding more English.

"I got some hankies and a new sweater."

"How thrilling! Do you like the presents I brought you?"

"I do! I love every single gift you ever gave me!"

Previously, she had bought me the book *Heidi* and now, *Black Beauty.* This time, she hit two nails on the head—I loved books and I loved horses! Along with that, she also gave me a colouring book of Elizabeth Taylor, with an even larger box of crayons than before—64 in all! I didn't know so many brilliant colours existed. I gave Ethel a big hug and kiss and thanked her repeatedly.

How does she always know what I like?

I guess my mother bought me gifts that I needed. She wouldn't even have known or thought about the kinds of gifts Ethel bought me. Besides, I *did* need those clothes. They just weren't as exciting as Ethel's gifts.

Perhaps I have to learn to be more grateful and gracious!

Steve and Ethel had a piece of my birthday cake and drank their coffee. Ethel seemed tense and did not say much to my mother. Steve chatted with her cheerfully in Romanian. All of a sudden, the look on my mother's face changed and their conversation became agitated. I felt a knot of dread in my stomach. Her sudden changes in mood were becoming alarming to me.

Ethel became angry. She glared at my mother and said between gritted teeth, "You witch, you have nothing say about this. You can't tell me what I can or can't do! Where is Dad?"

I had seen her fighting with my mother before but had never been this near to the scene of the battle! My heart began to race. I heard *Mutti* reply in Hungarian that he had gone to get the cows for milking.

Ethel jumped up and grabbed Steve's arm. "Jesus Christ, Steve, let's get out of here! We'll go and talk to Dad."

They left the house and hurried towards Dad who was almost near the barn with the cows by this time. I had followed them through the screen door. My mother swept past me and almost bowled me over. Picking up a wooden stick that always leaned against the bench beside the door, she waved it in the air and chased after Steve and Ethel. At the same time, I could hear her screaming at the top of her lungs, “No way! Over my dead body! I won’t allow this!” She had become unravelled like a ball of string.

What is going on here? Why the sudden change of mood? What did Steve say that changed everything?

I did not dare follow them. When my mother was in this state, I did not want to be anywhere near her, so I waited patiently on the bench. Soon Steve and Ethel returned, with *Mutti* close behind still screaming and threatening them. With a quick look in my direction and a hasty “Sorry!” from Ethel, they jumped into their car and sped off, the gravel in the driveway spitting behind them.

I wanted so badly to knowwhat had happened but knew better than to approach *Mutti.* Her “state” went on forever. Every morning and all day long, she would begin anew and rant at Dad in Hungarian.

“How could you let them do this?”

“What could I do?” asked Dad. “They’ve already made up their minds!”

“But he’s not a Hungarian or a Catholic!” she argued. “Those Romanians are nothing but gypsies and heathens!”

Dad sighed. “The Romanian Church is very similar to the Roman Catholic church. Besides, he seems like a very good man. He’s nice and has a good job. I will not stand in their way if they want to get married!”

Och mein Gott! Steve and Ethel are getting married?

Mutti clenched her fists. “You should forbid it!

“*Elég már!* Enough already!” He marched from the house. But it was not enough. She reminded me of a dog with a bone that wouldn’t let go of it until every morsel of marrow was sucked out. She continued to rant and rave for several days and nights. Dad would leave the house early and often beckoned me to do the same.

Sometimes retreat was our only option. I had never seen her quite like this before. But then, no one had ever gone against her wishes or orders. I did sometimes, a little bit, but I always eventually surrendered. This was one time she was not going to get her way, and she was not happy.

I was definitely not happy! Furious at her for causing my sister such grief, I wanted to defend Ethel, but it was not in my training. Children did not question the action of their parents. I also felt I needed to apologize to Ethel for my mother's bad behaviour. Constantly at me about good manners, for some reason, my mother didn't feel they applied to her.

Several days later, she was still chewing on the bone, but the intensity had burned itself out. I really needed to know if I had interpreted their "discussions" correctly about Steve and Ethel getting married. I simply asked my mother, "So, when are they getting married?"

She was shocked that I knew but said, "They want to get married in November, but not if I can help it." Her voice sounded agitated again.

Oh, oh. Did I disturb the hornet's nest?

She was getting nowhere with Dad, so now she turned to me in anger and said, "I will never allow you to marry any man if he isn't a Hungarian or a Catholic. Do you hear me?"

"*Ja*, *Mutti*," I replied. Finally she had an answer she wanted to hear, so she stopped her tirade. I let out a sigh of relief and shrugged my shoulders. *I can make that promise, I'm never going to get married anyway.*

Joined At the Hip

August—1955

The following day, I ran over to Mary Ann's place eager to claim my prize. Ever since I knew that the puppies existed, I had taken every opportunity to go over and play with them. Mary Ann's mother had finally given us permission to touch them, but no lifting was allowed. We had stroked them gently and assured their mother, Trixie, that we meant no harm. As they had grown older and stronger, Doraphine had given us instructions on how to hold them and for how long. Their fuzzy coats and baby fat had made them so soft and cuddly. The smell of milk came from their warm breaths as we had kissed their cold noses. Two were solid black including their eyes and noses, while the other two had some white on them. The only other colour was pink—pink tongues and pink toes.

Today, Doraphine questioned me relentlessly as to whether my mother had given her permission. I assured her that she had. She pressed for more. "Are you absolutely sure? I don't want any more trouble from your mother." I nodded vigorously and she smiled. "Alright then. Have you made up your mind as to which one you want yet, Helen?"

"Yes, that one." I pointed to the pup with a white muzzle. The white continued down his neck and chest making him appear as though he wore a white shirt. All he needed was a bow tie! He had always come bounding up to meet me when I arrived, wiggled into my arms, licked my face and generally made a total fool of himself. I loved him.

"Well, you can have him," said Doraphine. "He is now old enough to leave his mother."

Mary Ann asked, "What are you going to call him?"

I didn't know very many dog names except "Lassie" from the movie I had seen in Linz. I didn't even know what kind of dog he was, so I asked Doraphine.

"Trixie is a border collie," she said. "They're supposed to be very smart dogs."

I just couldn't think of any fantastic name and came up with "Coalie". He was a collie and his coat was black as coal.

That's not the best name, but once I know him better, I'll give him a proper name more suited to his character.

On August 11, Coalie became my dog. As I coaxed and called his name, he followed me home. We were both so excited. As predicted, he was an intelligent dog. I finally had someone I could boss around for a change, not unkindly though. Coalie loved any orders I gave him and caught on quickly—eager to obey without complaint.

Perhaps this is what I should do with my mother—obey without complaint. No, no. I don't think so!

When I was unhappy, so was he. His head dropped and his tail drooped. Sticking close to my side, he would constantly look up at me as if to say, *"I am here, don't worry."* I couldn't resist him and would kneel down, hug his neck and bury my face in his coat. It was his signal to lick me. I would giggle, and before long, I felt better.

When I smiled or laughed, he knew I was happy; he'd jump around me, almost tripping me in his excitement. He became my dear friend. I learned that he liked food as much as I, so if I had a sandwich or a cookie, I would try to eat it outside so that I could share it with him.

Dad claimed Coalie and I were joined at the hip.

I believe I will never be lonely again.

Moving Comics

August—1955

About a week and a half before school started that September, Alice and Walter came to drive us into Cupar for shopping. Having no vehicle of our own, we relied on them to drive us to wherever we needed to go or to pick things up for us.

Walter drove, Lenny sat in the middle and Alice sat in front with Susie on her lap. Dad, *Mutti* and I sat in the back. Saturday evenings, after the chores, were really the only times we went into town for shopping. My mother had gathered a crate of fresh eggs to take to Harry's Store in exchange for flour, sugar, spices, tea, coffee, or fruit, or sometimes even an article of clothing. When we arrived and parked, Dad and Walter went to the beer parlour in the hotel at the end of the street. Alice, with her kids in tow, headed to the hardware store. *Mutti* agreed that we would all meet at the café later.

The bell above the door rang as my mother and I entered Harry's Store. The smell of the oiled floor boards mingled with sharp odour of over-ripe bananas. Today, Sam Moscovich, Harry's brother, worked behind the counter. I never would have guessed they were brothers. Harry appeared tall, thin and white haired, while Sam was short, chubby and balding. Both were always kind and funny.

Sam called out as we entered, "Hello, Mrs. Kish, how are you today? I see you brought your lovely daughter with you. Harry, come see who's here."

I blushed but was thrilled by this small compliment. Harry must have been at the back of the store for he came up from behind me, pulled my braids and pinched my cheek. Again I blushed. He went to the counter and brought back a candy. "This is for you, sweet girl. Enjoy."

"Thank you very much, Mr. Moscovich," I blurted out, further embarrassed by all the attention.

My mother, on the other hand, lapped it up. I was sure she thought that if they liked me, then she must have done a good job. Any compliment meant for me bounced directly in her direction. *I'll let her share my compliment, but I won't share my candy.*

As she carried on with her grocery shopping, I looked around the store. High, dusty shelves loaded with even dustier cans of food covered two opposite walls. The back of the room looked like a clothing shop. Men's, women's and children's apparel hung on racks, while a free-standing shelf held everything from hosiery to hankies. I had never been shopping with my mother in Austria, so this place was exciting. A one stop shop! I figured this was probably where my mother had bought my birthday gifts. Today, along with her other supplies, *Mutti* bought large boxes of peaches, pears and plums, plus more than the usual amount of sugar.

Who is going to eat all that? They will surely rot before we could eat them all!

After the exchange of eggs, some cash and the groceries, which we would pick up just before we left town, we went next door to the Cupar Rexall Drug Hall. I knew that the owner and druggist was the dad of one of my school mates, Kent Stuart. He also had an older brother named George.

As *Mutti* had her prescription filled at the back drug counter, I looked at the cards, gifts, and other items that filled the shelves. So much to see, but I made sure not to touch anything. I wandered over to the cosmetic counter and looked at all the barrettes and hair bands. I still wore my hair in braids although I had begged my mother to cut it, so that I could be like everyone else. So far, she would not hear of it.

I also spied a bottle of Evening in Paris perfume. Was the smell as pretty as the blue bottle it came in? The lady behind the counter let me smell an opened bottle. It had a lovely scent, but I knew that I couldn't afford it, and my mother wouldn't consider buying me such a frivolous thing.

"That is just cheap perfume. When you get older, you can buy the good stuff like I have." She had come up behind me without me hearing her. I had to agree with her. She *did* have the loveliest perfume ever. I knew that she had brought it over from Austria.

She then picked up some Milk of Magnesia, Mercurochrome and band-aids for cuts and scrapes. I was always getting injured, and I remembered how badly the Mercurochrome stung when applied to my wounds. But I thought it was pretty interesting how it turned my skin a shiny, brilliant pink. All my friends considered that blotch of pink a badge of courage. I must have been very courageous.

Other items I recognized were Dodd's Kidney Pills that Dad took and the vile tasting cod liver oil pills that my mother made me take during the winter. Even though they were swallowed whole, their fishy flavour would present itself over and over throughout the rest of the day. They might have kept me healthy, but they sure put me off any fish meals. *Mutti* paid with cash and as we left, everyone waved us goodbye.

I love these people, everyone is always so friendly whether we know them or not. It seems as though everyone knows about us, but we don't know them yet.

Just two doors down was the Cupar Café. *Mutti* and I entered and found Alice and the children already seated at a booth just right of the door. Alice was drinking coffee, and Lenny was gulping down a vanilla ice cream float with Orange Crush. Susie, now about a year old and sitting on her mother's knee, was banging her spoon on the table, demanding some of Lenny's float.

My mother gave me some money and said, "Go to the counter and ask the lady to get me a cup of coffee. Get yourself a soft drink."

I swivelled around on the stool by the counter as I waited for the waitress. My eyes were drawn to a strange clock plugged into the wall on my right—a black cat, sitting on its haunches with a clock as his tummy. Its huge yellow eyes moved left and right with each tick-tock. A tail, hanging below the clock, also twitched in time. I was so fascinated, I did not notice the waitress trying to get my attention.

Finally I heard her say, "What can I get for you?"

I ordered my mother's coffee and added, "I would like a bottle of Zoop.

She looked at me strangely and asked, "What kind of soup would you like? We have tomato or chicken noodle today."

"No, not soup. I want Zoop, the soft drink."

She still looked puzzled. "You're Helen Kish aren't you?"

I nodded, wondering what that had to do with anything.

She beckoned me with her hand. "Come to the cooler and you can pick your own."

I looked into the large cooler that was full of ice and water and immediately found what I was looking for. I pulled out the green bottle.

"That's pronounced 'Seven Up'," she explained and giggled.

What stupid language would make a word with a number?

I had assumed the 7 was a "Z". The "up"' in German is pronounced "oop", so that's how I came up with Zoop. Made sense to me. So now I had to be careful not to be side swiped by numbers in this strange language.

I returned to the booth and enjoyed my "Zoop." As Alice and *Mutti* talked in Hungarian, I caught and recognized the word "movie." I understood enough to make out that Lenny and I would be going to a show in town. My heart gave a flutter at the possibility of watching a movie. I had only seen one in Linz called "Lassie Come Home." I had cried my heart out throughout that show. It was wonderful!

I normally always spoke to my mother in German, but because Alice didn't speak it, I knew it was impolite, so I used my broken

Hungarian. "Am I seeing a movie? Which one? Where? When?"

Alice was either laughing at me or my bad Hungarian, and before my mother could answer, said in English, "You and Lenny are going to see Snow White and the Seven Dwarfs. Would you like that?"

Of course I want to see that, especially since I had once starred as one of the dwarves. I know the story well.

I finished my drink and took my quarter to buy treats for the show. What to choose? I liked the caramelized popcorn called Cracker Jack, but chose the pink sugared one called Lucky Elephant because I had learned from experience that it contained the better prizes.

While *Mutti*, Alice and Susie remained at the café, Lenny and I walked around the corner at the end of the street to the Cupar Recreation Hall. As soon as we arrived, we paid our ten cents for our ticket and parted. He found his friends, I joined some of mine, and waited anxiously for the movie to begin.

This was the first time I had been in this building. A huge stage covered by curtains completely filled the front of the hall. Plaques with names like Vimy Ridge, Passchendaele, Somme, Dieppe and Ypres surrounded three sides of the stage. I reminded myself to ask someone about these names later.

I opened my popcorn and searched for my prize at the bottom. This time it was a painted tin whistle. I was happy. But not as happy as when the movie began. I expected real people with little children as dwarfs, but these characters resembled a moving, talking, singing comic book. *What is this?* I turned to my companions and asked. They told me that it was called a "cartoon". I was spellbound by the enchanting scenery, the simple beauty of Snow White, the handsome prince and even the cruel witch. Not accustomed to the telling of a story through song, I became captivated by Snow White's voice which was almost as exquisite as my mother's. My heart also sang. But it was the Seven Dwarfs that delighted me the most. Cute and extremely funny, each had their own personality. I wondered which dwarf I had represented in the play at kindergarten? Probably Bashful. I sure hoped I hadn't been Dopey.

With the movie over, we met everyone back at the café. Dad and Walter had returned from the beer parlour and were acting silly. *Mutti* didn't look impressed. They had picked up the groceries from Harry's and had put them in the car. Without asking, I went straight to the counter to buy my treats for the week. The popcorn had cost ten cents, the movie also ten cents, so I still had five cents left. I remembered that I had promised to buy something for Mary Ann with the quarter I had found in her birthday cake. I could buy candy that looked like cigarettes or a licorice cigar, but realized that Jawbreakers were the better choice. For five cents, I was able to buy twenty five of them, enough to last me through the week until next Saturday. These hard, black round candies couldn't be chewed. That's why they were called Jawbreakers. As I sucked on one, the top layer dissolved and a new colour and flavour would come through. These, to me, were the perfect sweet—many new flavours that lasted a long time for a cheap price.

Alice grabbed the sleeping Susie in her arms, and we piled back into the car and headed home. Hopefully, each received what we desired or required. I received both.

Cupar is a town located approximately 45 km northwest of Fort Qu'Appelle on Hwy #22. Prior to the 1900's, Scottish, English and Irish settled there. After them, many Eastern Europeans came from Bukovina, now split between Romania and Ukraine. Many were Hungarians, but some were Romanians. It became a village in 1905, and received its name from a Canadian Pacific Railway official who came from the town of Cupar in Fife, Scotland.

Preserving

Early Fall—1955

Before school started, I discovered the reason why *Mutti* had brought all that fruit at Harry's; she planned to preserve them. That meant only one thing—I had to help her! Before we started, we both tied our hair back with a kerchief, put on an apron, and scrubbed our hands with a nail brush. Even though the screen door remained bolted, the sweet scent of the fruit attracted more flies than usual. We had to change the fly paper often and make regular rounds with the fly swatter.

Mutti washed, peeled and cored the pears, peaches, and plums. Cherries, she said, would be done at another time. She prepared the syrup and heated the water in the canner. I washed and rinsed the glass sealers, the glass lids and counted out the rubber rings. The slippery fruit went into the jars, the silky syrup followed and the jars were sealed. As the fire roared, the water in the large canner roiled and boiled. Gently and carefully, each jar was lowered into it until it was full. It took several batches and all day until all of the fruit was processed. Even though my mother had chosen a cooler day, the heat from the stove and the steam from the canner made it unbearably hot and tedious work.

I don't have many days left before school starts, and this is not the way I want to spend them!

Ethel had taught me that when I had to do something I didn't like, don't complain, just get to work and get it done. The sooner you get it done, the less you suffer. I didn't understand it then, but I did now and found it good advice. As I worked, I didn't want to suffer, so I just turned my mind back to the movie Snow White. I remembered how the dwarfs had sung as they worked. They had claimed it made the work go faster. Faster was what I needed now. I began to sing *Row Your Boat*. I didn't even get past two lines when my mother begged me to stop.

"You shouldn't sing if you can't carry a tune. You sound like a cat in heat!"

I didn't know what that meant, but I understood that she disapproved, and it made me angry. Before I could stop myself, I lashed out, "Well, if I had a voice like yours, I would sing all the time. I never hear you sing."

Uh-oh. I've talked back. She'll be furious!

But instead, she became quiet and sad, then answered, "I belonged to a singing troupe that toured all over Hungary, Romania and Austria before the war. I sang a great deal and loved it. But no one sang when the bombs fell, and no one sang after. Singing is for fun and has no place at work. If our boss would catch us singing at work, he would consider you lazy and probably crazy. Fun is fun and work is work."

Why can't we have both at the same time?

From that lecture, I suspected that she considered "fun" to be one of the seven deadly sins.

I had to sacrifice two more of my precious free days. The vegetables from the garden also had to be preserved. Peas, beans, and tomatoes went through the same process as the fruits. Cucumbers and beets were changed into pickles and relish. Rhubarb and currants were boiled down into jams. Carrots, potatoes and parsnips went directly into the root cellar through a trap door on the outside of the house, and they were left on the earth floor in a corner and covered with an old blanket to keep them moist and dark. All the jars of preserves also had to be stored in the cool dark root cellar.

This cellar was simply a dug out earthen hole beneath the living room and was accessed through a pull-up trap door. It was now open as *Mutti* balanced herself on the narrow, steep steps. I had carried all the sealed jars of vegetables from the kitchen and, as I handed her the last one, I also climbed down into the dark and dank space. It was not very large and the ceiling was so low that my mother had to bend her head. The strong smell of fermenting sauerkraut filled my nose. I liked the fried sauerkraut with apples and caraway seeds, but I didn't like it at this stage. My eyes finally adjusted and I could make out long, large shelves along one wall completely filled with colourful jars of the fruit and vegetable preserves.

"Now we can have fruits and vegetables throughout the winter," *Mutti* said proudly.

I agreed. They looked pretty, and I knew they would look and taste even better in the middle of the long cold winter. I had eaten some of them last winter, but I had not realized the amount of time it took to prepare this food that would be gulped down in three minutes flat.

***

A little after my adventure into town, Mary Ann and I spent some more time together. I presented her with ten of my Jawbreakers, and she was delighted. However, Doraphine explained that there had been plenty more money in the cake besides the ones we had found that day, and those were now in Mary Ann's piggy bank.

Too late. I couldn't very well take back my gift; it wouldn't be right. And anyway, what Doraphine and Mary Ann had given me was worth much more than my measly ten Jawbreakers. *I need to preserve their friendship and my promise to Mary Ann.*

> *Canning food in glass jars was one method of preserving food without electricity. Boiling the sealed jars, killed any micro-organism that may spoil the food or make its ingestion unsafe. All such preserved food kept better and longer when protected from light and heat. Before canning, root cellars were relied on heavily for fruits and vegetable storage through the winter. Earthen floors were best,*

because they were cool and slightly moist. By combining both methods, folks had a variety of fruits and vegetable at their fingertips throughout the long winter when fresh ones were unavailable at the stores in town.

Forgive and Forget

Fall—1955

Before I knew it, summer holidays were over and school had started again. I was more than ready to get out of the house and be with my friends again. This year, however, there would be no Ethel. I was heading into grade four and on my own but felt I was going to be alright. I knew my way around the elementary school and had made friends with some of the children last year. Our new teacher, Mrs. Demorest appeared to be as kind as Mrs. Lehan had been.

At school, I became familiar with the morning ritual of saying the Lord's Prayer, although I still could not recite it in English, but I did say it in German. "*Unser Vater, der du bist im Himmel...*" We also sang *God Save the Queen* at the end of each school day.

The only thing I feared and often had nightmares about was being left behind by the bus after school. Ethel had always made sure I was on it before it took off. Peter Eros, the driver, promised he would keep an eye out for me, but eventually it was my friends I really trusted.

Most of the girls on the school bus were not in my class, but they still accepted me as their friend. Irene Kramer was one grade above me and always greeted me kindly. There were three girls, all one grade below me, who became my friends both on the bus and in the school yard. They were Goldie Kayter, Shirley Eros and her cousin Linda Eros. Without realizing it, these friends allowed me to practice my

English and learn some of the Canadian ways. I never made friends with any of the boys on the bus because my mother had warned me not to talk to boys. Again, I could not understand why.

This year I also made a new friend at school. Her name was Sherry Stan, and we spent most of our recesses together. One day we had a big fight and, from there on, we went our separate ways. Mrs. Demorest, our teacher, must have detected the change in our behaviour because one day she asked us to stay remain behind during recess. We stood at her desk, not sure what this was all about. Are we going to be rewarded or punished?

"So tell me, girls, what seems to be the problem here. I noticed you two are not talking and playing together any more. Are you fighting and, if so, why?"

Neither one of us could remember why we had a fight or what had started it. We just knew that neither of us was going to take the blame or give in.

As we shrugged our shoulders, Mrs. Demorest smiled and said, "There you have it. You don't even remember the fight. Can you remember the fun you had together?"

We both nodded and looked at each other. Certainly, we could remember that.

"Now don't you girls think you're being silly? Why don't you both say you're sorry. Remember it takes more courage to forgive and forget than to fight. I also know that both of you are brave girls. So what do you say? Give each other a hug and go play."

We couldn't come up with any real arguments against that reasoning, so we did as we were told. It felt so good to be friends again!

***

I wondered how Ethel was doing. Did she miss me as much as I missed her? Soon she would marry Steve and will live happily ever after. I hoped *Mutti* wouldn't interfere with their plans. *She is starting to sound like the wicked step-mother in my fairy tales.*

As the wedding neared—supposedly on November 19—my mother

again began to rage against their marriage. She mumbled and grumbled, but Dad would have none of it. Being the coward than I was, I agreed with him but in secret. But *Mutti* was not accustomed to not getting her way. An uneasy feeling began to grow in my heart.

What am I going to wear to the wedding? I guess my winter "Sunday dress" will have to do, although a new outfit would really be nice. I knew better than to ask for a dress directly, so I approached my mother in another way. "What are you going to wear to the wedding?"

"Nothing."

"You mean you're going to go naked?"

"*Ne légy bolond.* Don't be crazy. I'm not going and neither are you!"

"What? How can you do this?

"I can do anything I want."

I could see there would be no further discussion. I must find Dad immediately and plead my case. *It's not fair! I don't care if she doesn't go, but I sure want to!*

As soon as I stepped out the door, Coalie nuzzled me to play. "Sorry, Coalie, not now," I said. In response, his ears and tail drooped. "Thanks, Coalie, you're such a good friend. I love you too."

I didn't know where Dad was but could hear some clanging in his blacksmith shop. It was a small, ramshackle wood building that leaned rather heavily to one side and looked like it could collapse at any moment. I had never been inside. As I peered through the partially open door, I could hear someone move inside.

"Dad, are you in there? May I come in? I need to talk to you."

I couldn't see him, but I heard his "Okay" from somewhere in the shop. I squeezed through the door with Coalie right behind me.

Now I knew why they called it a blacksmith shop. *Everything* was black! Heavy soot covered the walls, the low ceiling, the benches, and even the window panes. I could only make out the white of Dad's eyes because his face and hands were covered with black smudge.Dirty coveralls and skull cap disguised the rest of him. He blended into the dark background like the green frogs in the grass. My eyesight may have been poor, but my nose prickled from a very strong scent.

"What *is* that smell?"

"It's used motor oil. We put it on the ground in here," Dad replied.

The dirt floor was compacted like a smooth paved road. "Why would you do that, Dad?"

"We can't have a wood floor because of the forge, and we also can't have fine dust in the air. Both would catch fire from the open flames and sparks."

He was such a wise man, and he was going to need the wisdom of King Solomon to solve my problem. He had successfully come through for me once before when I wanted Coalie. Hopefully, he can sway my stubborn mother again. Between English and Hungarian I tried desperately to explain that *Mutti* had refused to go to Ethel's wedding and had included me.

He shook his head from side to side, smirked and said, "We'll see about that. I'll talk to your mother tonight, okay?"

I let out a sigh of relief. The inside of my heart had been like this shop—dark with not a trace of light. Now, Dad had wiped away the soot from the windows of my heart and allowed a ray of hope inside.

I was now free to study this strange place. I recognized nothing, so I pointed to different objects and asked about their name and purpose. He introduced me to the forge, the anvil, the bellows and what they did. He knew everything. And now *I* knew everything.

"Can I help, Dad?" I asked, eager to show him that I was thankful for his help with my mother.

"You can help straighten some old nails." He handed me a tin can full of bent, rusted ones. He demonstrated how to hold the bent nail down on the wood bench, tap it gently until it stuck in the wood, then pound the bent part with a hammer. When I tried, most of the nails went flying through the air and disappeared into the dark floor or hit Coalie lying on the floor. He jumped up and left before more headed his way. Eventually I did master the craft. I realized that I loved using tools and was curious about how things worked.

Not long after, we heard *Mutti* calling us in for lunch. Dad removed his hat and coveralls and we headed towards the house. Coalie sidled up to me as soon as we left the shop, his beautiful white chest covered in soot. I giggled. When my mother laid eyes on me, she did not giggle; she barked at me.

"*Och mein Gott!* What have you done to yourself? Where have you been? You are as black as a chimney sweep!"

She and I were still using German instead of Hungarian or English. And yes, I was a mess. From the mirror in the porch, I could barely make out my complexion and clearly saw my sooty clothes and hands.

"I was in the shop with Dad," I replied with pride, looking at Dad for support.

He didn't respond. I realized he wouldn't have understood what we had said in German. Luckily, my mother turned to him for an explanation in Hungarian. She seemed upset with him, but he just shook his head and waved her off. *Wish I could do that.*

"I forbid you to ever go into that shop again. Now wash up and set the table," was her answer. With her order given, she turned away.

After lunch, as I cleaned up the kitchen and did the dishes, I felt sorry for myself. Everything fun was forbidden—the rubble in Linz, the bomb shelters in the *Lager*, the ship episode, and now it was the shop. And only God knows what was next. I wish I could forbid her from forbidding!

But what of Dad's promise? He had not said a word about it at lunch. Was he still going to help me get to Ethel's wedding? He had said he was going to speak to her tonight. I guess I just have to learn to be more patient.

The evening came and went. The subject had not been brought up. What was he waiting for—a better time? There was never a better time with my mother. Hasn't he learned that yet? I went to bed and despaired.

The following morning, I was hopeful again. As I was waiting for the school bus by the kitchen window, Dad approached and whispered in my ear, "I will speak to her today. By the time you come home, we will have an answer."

"Please, please make it happen!"

I left for school with a glad heart. He has challenged her before and had been victorious. Surely he will be again. He was my hero! My mind turned to more important things, like what dress would I wear to the wedding.

After school when I got off the bus, I covered the usual quarter mile to the farm house in half the time. Huffing and puffing I entered the house and saw Dad and *Mutti* at the table. I looked at my mother's face, then my father's, seeking the answer. Their silence was the loudest I have ever heard. I looked at Dad again.

He returned my look, shook his head sadly and said in English, "Sorry, Iluska. I couldn't convince her to let you go the Ethel's wedding. I'm surprised I can make *her* go. You'll be staying with Lenny and Susie at their grandmother's house in town."

What! She gets to go and not me? She doesn't even like Ethel!

Heartbroken, I couldn't even speak. No is no, it didn't matter the reason. I ran to the bedroom and hurled myself onto the bed—good school clothes and all. First I sobbed and sobbed. When no more tears would come, I became angry. What had I ever done to deserve this? I did my homework. I did my chores. I did as I was told. And what did she do to me—forbid me from going to Ethel's wedding. What more did she want from me?

"Heli, it's time to do your chores!"

That's what she wanted from me! Work, work and more work with total obedience. She was only happy when she could boss someone around. Well, it looked like she just added another one to her list—Dad! *And I thought men were supposed to wear the pants in the house.*

I got up, washed my face and went about my chores. Coalie heard all my complaints and as I knelt down to hug him, he licked my face, nuzzled his cold nose into my neck and whimpered as if to say, *"Don't worry, I'm here."* Holding back my tears, I hugged him harder, kissing his cold black nose.

As my pity party went into full swing, a solution entered my mind —run away! Then they'd be sorry! That would make one less person for her to boss around. I knew of a few abandoned buildings that Coalie and I could stay in. If not, there were always haystacks around that we can take shelter in. We'd have each other for comfort, and Coalie could protect me from wild animals. I would take some food and water and be okay. But it would be the food and water that would be a problem—I would not be able to take enough for both of us to last for any meaningful time. Maybe people would feed us in exchange for work. But then again, everyone knew my parents and would surely send us back home. It was hopeless. We would never survive out there on empty tummies.

I went about my chores and tried to avoid my parents. I was still so angry that I couldn't look either of them in the eye. Dad was trying to get my attention, but I ignored him. My mother had forbidden me to do a lot of things, but this one was going to be a hard one for me to forgive. That's when Mrs. Demorest's words entered my mind. *"It's more courageous to forgive and forget than to fight*".

I wasn't ready to forgive, or forget. I wanted to fight for the right to go, or at least try. If I knew why she wouldn't let me go, maybe I could argue against what I was sure would be ridiculous reasons. I planned my attack—in the kitchen just before supper. I figured it was a safe place and time since Dad would soon be coming in and could prevent her from becoming too angry and going over the edge again.

"Why won't you let me go the Ethel's wedding? You know how much I love her. I'll mind my manners and won't embarrass you or Dad. *Bitte*, please *Mutti,* let me go with you."

She turned to me and looked surprised that I would even ask. "That will never happen. No girl of mine is going to be exposed to strange men who have been drinking. This will be an adult party and no place for children. You'll be safe and sound with Lenny and Susie at their grandmother's house."

My mind became trapped in the web of a terrible thought—*I wonder if this forbidding had not so much to do with the men at the wedding, but is more about forbidding me to love Ethel!*

There went my grand, courageous attempt to stand up to my mother! I couldn't think of an objection. My mind and heart shut down. I surrendered. It felt good not to feel anything—much more peaceful!

WALKING TO CALIFORNIA

December—1955

November 19 came and went. The wedding was over. Still in a daze, I could not come to terms with what my mother had done. But there was no sense in crying over spilt milk. I once heard one of my teacher's use that expression and liked it. I could not undo what had already been done. So, to overcome my grey mood, the grey skies and the grey walls, I decided to decorate the house for Christmas. I brought out all the shiny tinsels, balls and streamers and pretended that Ethel was helping me.

Where was she? It had been over a month since her wedding, but I hadn't seen her since that terrible day in August when my mother had unravelled. Ethel certainly wouldn't have told my mother her whereabouts, but Dad should know..

One day, with my mother out of the house, I decided to seek him out and ask my many questions. "Do you know how and where Steve and Ethel are? How come we haven't seen them? Are they going to be here for Christmas?"

He was sitting at the dining room table smoking his pipe and reading the Hungarian newspaper. I did not like the smoke from his cigarettes and neither did *Mutti*. She called them his "coffin nails". Every time he lit one up she would say, "There you go again, putting another nail in your coffin." I didn't know what she meant, but Dad always laughed silently, his eyes crinkling and his shoulders shaking.

The aroma of his pipe tobacco, however, I loved. It reminded me of the cherries I picked in Austria—sweet and fragrant. He laid his pipe down in the ashtray, placed the paper on the table and smiled. "You know, Iluska, Steve and Ethel are very happy, but they've gone to California on their honeymoon."

"What's a honeymoon?"

"A honeymoon is a place where couples go after they're married," he explained.

"You and *Mutti* didn't go on the moon."

Dad shook his head, laughed again, but made no comment.

So I asked him the next question. "Where is California?"

"I don't know. All I know is that it's in the States. Maybe when you're in school, you can look it up on the map, yes?" He picked up his newspaper. "Anyway, they won't be back until spring."

Convinced that I would not survive without her until spring, I was now more determined than ever to find and walk to California. *Won't they be surprised!*

***

Christmas passed without much excitement. I had gone to the trusty Sears catalogue and showed Dad what I would like for Christmas. It was a toy hand-operated sewing machine that would allow me to sew clothes for my doll, Sally. I also showed my mother which clothes I would like for her to order for me from the catalogue. Without Ethel's guidance, she wouldn't have known the latest trend, and I would have ended up with some old woman's clothes. I no longer believed that the Christ Child or Santa Claus brought these presents and made sure I thanked both my parents for my gifts. Christmas without Ethel had been no Christmas at all. There had been no "joy to the world".

As soon as I returned to school after the Christmas holidays, I asked Mrs. Demorest if she could help me find California on a map. She reached above the blackboard and pulled down what looked like a huge blind, but it was really a map of North America. Not familiar with maps, I had her show me where we lived and where California was located.

As I was studying it, she asked, "Why are you interested in California? Were you reading something about it. I could get more information for you, if you like."

"No, I only need to know the direction and how far Coalie and I will have to walk to visit my sister Ethel in California."

I was still peering at the map when I heard my teacher give a slight giggle. I turned to face her and was met with the kindest smile I have ever seen.

"Are you missing your sister, Helen?" she asked.

"Yes, that's why I want to visit her," I replied. "Is it very far?"

"Too far to walk, my dear," she replied gently.

I couldn't walk to California, and I couldn't phone Ethel to come home. The full weight of that finally hit me. I dreaded the thought of spending the whole winter, indoors, alone with my mother. Was it going to be same as our last winter at the *Lager*? Then I realized I now had Dad and Coalie to share this weight.

I hope they're up to it.

Winter Blues

Early 1956

The new year promised nothing to relieve my misery. Dad shook his head when he heard on the radio that the temperature would drop to -30 degrees Fahrenheit the next day. I didn't understand the actual number, but I knew it would be fiercely cold—too cold to play outdoors. Every night, when he listened to the weather, he would shake his head. He did this until the middle of March.

Meanwhile outside, the snow kept piling higher and higher. It began with large, lazy flakes wafting down with no wind to chase them. Then a stiff rush of air came from nowhere and plastered the snow against the side of the buildings, piled it up in the yard so high that it made it almost impossible for Dad to get to the barn and henhouse for his chores. I was still in awe at the great amount of this white stuff.

Inside, as the wind howled, the frost grew thicker in the upper corners of the bedroom. The wood by the stove had to be replenished twice a day. At night, the oil heater tried to warm all three big rooms but was unsuccessful. In the morning, as Dad restarted the wood stove, he also had to chip at the layer of ice in the drinking water that was now stored in the kitchen. *Mutti* and I did not abandon our warm beds until Dad announced that the kitchen was toasty warm. All our windows, except in the kitchen, frosted up so thickly we could not see out, and daylight could barely pierce through. As I studied the fern patterns on them, I could feel the cold breeze on my body as it penetrated the single pane of glass.

One particularly cold day, Ethel's predictions about the Bombardier came true. On our way to school, it broke down in the middle of a field. All the children dragged ourselves out, bent against the bitter wind and trudged through knee-deep drifts towards the nearest farmhouse. By the time we entered the blessed warmth of that kitchen, we were wet, cold and in pain. My boots had filled with snow, and my toes and fingers hurt.

How come they feel like they are on fire when they are frozen?

We did not make it to school that day and were eventually driven home. It was a grand adventure, but I cried. I did not want to go home.

Luckily for me, Dad was also in the same predicament—stuck in the house with my mother. With not as much work to be done outdoors in the wintertime, he was a prisoner too. Whenever my mother began her lectures on either one of us, the other attempted to deflect her attention. Sometimes it worked, sometimes it didn't, but we both understood and shared our misery.

One Sunday afternoon, all three of us sat at the kitchen table. The fire in the stove roared louder than the wind outside. Dad was rolling cigarettes with a packet of Zig Zag papers and a can of Vogue beside him. A while back, he had allowed me to practise rolling one, but I had bungled it terribly. We had laughed and laughed.

But right now *Mutti* and I had just finished a game of cards and I had won. I celebrated my victory with a resounding, "Yee Ha!" I had just recently learned that expression from one of the comics I read.

Mutti glared at me and said in clear English, "Godammit, you cheetink!"

I was stunned. She just had to spoil my victory! I looked at Dad for help.

He shook his head, grimaced and replied in English, "Don't be silly, Lisi. She doesn't know how to cheat. Here, have a game with me, then."

I didn't take part in the next game, but watched in astonishment as

Dad won the round and went "Yee Ha!" like me.

My mother left the table mumbling. Dad winked at me. I giggled with my hands over my mouth. I still liked this man, even if he had let me down regarding Ethel's wedding.

The winter days were boring and endless. I didn't have to do any outdoor chores, except bring in wood for the fire and gather the few eggs from the chicken coop.

I still wanted to go outside to play with Coalie. He had grown a heavy fur coat for the winter and looked very handsome. I made sure he received more food and checked to see where he could survive these horrendously cold nights. Puppy always squeezed between the small space where the barn doors met and spent the night in the barn. I wasn't sure if Coalie would go there, so I took him to the straw stack beside the barn. There, I dug out a hole on the south side large enough for him to curl up and be out of the wind. I directed him inside, and he seemed happy but was out in a second to follow me around. I did check occasionally to see if he used it. He had. One less worry for me.

Travelling in the winter on the prairies was not recommended. Mostly because the roads did not get ploughed very often and getting stuck in the wide open prairie far from any help could cost lives. Even if the roads had been cleared, the bitter cold weather sometimes prevented the vehicles from starting. If started, they could stall anywhere along the way. Some of the vehicles still had no heaters, making it very uncomfortable for its passengers. Sometimes, people had no choice but to use their sleds and horses instead of their vehicles in the winter. Horses always started and never stalled. They also found their way home in a blizzard without help.

Thriftiness

Midwinter—1956

We discarded nothing. Everything was converted to something else. Sheets became tea towels or pillow cases. Thinned towels turned into face cloths or dish cloths. A threadbare collar was removed, reversed and sewn back on. Buttons, zippers or snaps had to be removed from old garments to be saved and re-used for lost or broken ones. The wool from old torn sweaters was unravelled and re-knitted into scarves, mitts, or hats. Clothes that could no longer be worn in public became our work wear around the farm. It did not matter whether they fit or matched, it only mattered that they covered the essentials. When we returned from anywhere, our "good" clothes were exchanged for our "work" clothes. Any materials not suitable for anything else were either converted to rags or rugs.

Mutti and I both had more time on our hands now. Time to catch up on indoor chores like sewing, mending and darning. My mother used the Singer treadle sewing machine under the window in the living room, while I used my toy hand-cranked one. I spent my time knitting and crotcheting as I had been taught in my second grade at the *Lager*. I could not believe that my mother did not know how to do this.

But *Mutti* did know how to mend holes in socks and decided it was time I learned how to darn. She brought out a beautifully painted mushroom-shaped tool which she had brought from Austria. This, she placed into the sock over the hole. She then threaded the wool unto a large-eyed blunt needle.

"If you have wool of the same colour or one close to it, then use it," she explained. "But it's not the colour that is important, it's the thickness. Too thin and the patch won't last. Too thick will make it uncomfortable on the foot."

With a thimble on my right middle finger, I was ready as she handed me the sock. She demonstrated how to stitch around the outer edge of the hole to reinforce it and catch any loops of the knitted sock. Taking it back, she sewed a few parallel strands of wool across the hole, then returned it to me to finish. Again, she took it back to show me how to now weave in and out in the opposite direction through the first strands, to create a new patch of fabric over the hole. I carried on where she left off. When done, I was very proud of my fist attempt. The hole was gone and the sock usable again.

Looking at her for a nod of approval, she only said, "*Gut*, now you will make a good wife."

Wife? That's not the reason I wanted to learn how to darn. Darn the darning!

As with the socks, anything around the house that could be fixed, was fixed. The unmatched broken dishes were glued together. There were no "sets" of anything, just a mish-mash of patterns and shapes. Cups with no handles became drinking glasses or vases. Dad could solder any leaking aluminum pot or pan. The only pans that never needed soldering were the cast iron frying pans. Rickety chairs, couches or beds were stabilized with nails and screws, but there was nothing Dad could do about the squeaking bed springs.

Empty tin cans were especially valuable. Dad used them to store nails, nuts and bolts and other smaller articles in his blacksmith shop. In the house, we punched holes in their bottoms for drainage and filled them with seedlings or flowers.

I think I stole every box that ever entered our house. Ethel had taught me that there was a place for everything, and everything had its place. In order for me to achieve that, I chose small cardboard boxes or their lids to separate my smaller items of clothing like socks, hankies or panties in my dresser drawer. That way, they didn't get all jumbled up. I liked things neat. Pretty cookie or candy tins became jewelry boxes, sewing or crochet kits. I hoarded anything that even resembled a box, even if I had no use for it at the time. That went for every article on the farm. We never threw anything out in case you might need it in the future.

Food was definitely never wasted! My mother would make me finish every bit of food on my plate.

"During the war," she would state, "people would have given their lives to eat what you just left on your plate."

After that, I was careful not let my eyes get bigger than my tummy. I also had no choice in what was served. The first time my mother had served fried pork with sauerkraut and potatoes at lunch, I wouldn't touch the sauerkraut.

"If you're not going to eat it, then leave the table," she ordered.

Relieved not to have to eat it and happy there was no lecture about the hungry people in the war, I scooted out the door. As the afternoon wore on, I became increasingly hungry but was determined to hold out until supper. Supper finally came. Darned if she didn't serve that same left-over sauerkraut! By this time, I had no choice but to taste it. It was surprisingly delicious!

What a sneaky way to make me eat something I thought I hated.

Any leftover food went into soups or stews. After sitting for a day or two, the flavours blended well and sometimes tasted better than when they were fresh. Other left over meat went into sandwiches. Slightly over-ripe fruit became a compote. Dry, old bread became bread pudding or french toast. Any foods too old were passed on to the dogs or the hogs. Peelings, rotting vegetables or fruit, sour milk, egg shells, even rotten eggs went into the slop pail and later fed to the hogs.

Saving and re-using all these items made sense to me. But there was one saved article I objected to re-using—newspapers or catalogues for toilet paper. Even in the *Lager*, we had proper toilet paper, now this? Not only was it uncomfortable, it did not work well. I looked forward to Christmas in order to get the soft tissue papers that were wrapped around the Christmas oranges. Most welcomed present ever!

> *Re-using, reducing and recycling in the old days was called frugality or thriftiness. It was not always a choice but a necessity. Sometimes, the required products were not always available. Even when they were, folks still hesitated to buy. To spend money on something new, when one merely had to convert something they already possessed, was considered a sinful waste of money. Most people purchased a new product only when they could not make it themselves or when they truly could not manage without it. Other times they simply bartered and exchanged both services and products with others.*

Hopeful

Spring—1956

Somehow, I survived that dreadful winter with my wits intact. I hoped that not all the winters would be this long and severe. I could only leave the house a few times. When the weather and *Mutti* permitted, I played with Mary Ann or went sledding by the west slough. Instead of a sled, I used either a flattened cardboard box or sat on a shovel with the handle between my legs, facing downhill. This technique often resulted with a blow to my head from the handle. Of course Coalie loved it. He would bound beside me up the hill and down the hill. Most of the time though, it had been too cold to be outside.

Spring finally arrived. I could tell because Dad was busy directing the stork to the barn again. All the deliveries seemed to have been made without a hitch. But one Saturday morning, Dad entered the kitchen carrying something in a blanket. He placed the blanket, and whatever was inside it, in a large cardboard box near the stove.

As I crowded behind him to see, he said, "We need to take care of this little one until it becomes stronger. Will you help me with that?" It was the most pitiful, pinkest piglet I have ever seen. Barely breathing, it just lay there.

"Is it going to die?" I asked before I realized I didn't really want to know.

"We won't know that until tomorrow morning. We have to keep it warm and fed, then it might be okay."

Throughout that morning, we took turns checking on it and attempting to make it interested in milk from a make-shift bottle. The little thing did not respond! It was breathing but not moving too much. Agonizing over the possibility of it dying, I decided to do everything I could to prevent that.

"Don't get too attached to it," *Mutti* warned.

I promised I wouldn't.

I decided to call him Trooper. I knew that a trooper was a warrior from my western story comic books. Warriors fight and that's what this little guy was going to have to do. I continued to shove the nipple into his snout leaving a drop or two of milk there. Holding him in his blanket, I rubbed his head and body like Dad had shown me and crooned in his ear. This went on for the rest of the afternoon—rubbing, feeding, crooning. When I put him down, I made sure to cover him and place the box close to the stove. Dad had promised that if he's warm and fed, he should survive. By the end of the day, Trooper had begun to suckle a little. I became excited!

My mother warned me again. "Heli, remember what I said. Don't be too hopeful." I went to bed that night, hopeful. I prayed to my Guardian Angel to let little Trooper live.

The following morning, as soon as I woke, I ran to the stove, looked in the box and there was Trooper...sitting on his haunches and squealing for his next meal. This time, he suckled and squealed with vigour. This he did the next day and the next. Soon his shrieking filled the air whenever anyone approached. He was now strong enough to be returned to his mother where he would then be able to fight for its rightful place at the dinner table.

Thank you, Guardian Angel, for letting me be hopeful and successful!

***

I didn't have the opportunity to get into the barn until about the beginning of April. I was anxious to see all the babies and congratulate all the mamas. This time when I entered on my own, the smell in the barn was not as strong as it had been the last winter. Due to the warmer temperatures, the doors had been left open more often. The air was dry, the manure less pungent, but the smell of milk was still strong.

No longer afraid of the big cows, I carefully checked all the hiding spaces under the mangers for baby kittens. Sure enough, I found one mama cat with her litter. As I picked one up and cuddled it, the mewing broke my heart. A baby missing and crying for its mother! I understood that feeling and immediately returned it to its place.

I walked to the back enclosure to see if I could spot Trooper. There he was, still smaller than the rest. I hadn't noticed the notch in his left ear before. I wondered how that happened. He didn't seem to be aware of his size or his injury and jostled and grunted as vigorously as the others. I had done a good job there.

My attention now turned to the new calves. They had all come running to the railing as soon as I had leaned over to look for Trooper. There were six of them, all still pretty small.

Tonight, I'll probably be helping them drink out of a pail like Ethel used to do.

I looked around, said hello to all the mama cows and even squeezed my way between them to pat Jolan and Gitzka, just the way Ethel had shown me the very first time. I made sure to bring a cut-up apple for them this time. I threw Gitzka her share because I couldn't reach her, but I wanted to make sure Yolan took hers from my open hand. Her warm breath, her bristly whiskers and her soft lips made me giggle. Though I couldn't hold them, or be too close to them, the horses—of all the animals on this farm—stirred something in me that no other did. I could not understand why.

As I headed towards the double door at the front of the barn, a waft of air hit the top of my head. I looked up at a pair of barn swallows taking turns swooping down on me. I knew that they were devoted parents protecting their young in their mud nest on the rafters. I moved out of their way so as not to upset them but remained close enough to watch. They looked like the same elegant birds I had seen in Austria. When the sun hit their blue-black heads and back, it reflected the colours of the rainbow. They looked so delicate with their cinnamon buff bellies and split tails. Most of all, I envied their swift but controlled dives. How come they never crashed into anything? Compared to them, I was a big bumbling ox that had once actually trampled through a closed screen door. Walls and door frames constantly stepped into my path, trying to trip me up.

I hope someday to become as graceful as a delicate swallow.

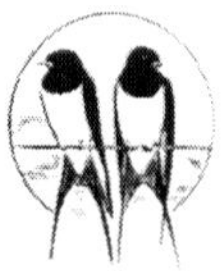

Mending Fences

Spring—1956

Early one Saturday, as we had nearly finished our breakfast, I heard Dad ask my mother for something in Hungarian. I understood most of it but not the particulars. *Mutti* turned to me and translated it into German. "Dad has to go and fix some fences in the pasture before we let the cows out. I want you to help him. Dress warm because it is a bit cool out there today. Make sure you do as you're told."

If it meant working outside and with Dad, I was happy! Right after we had eaten our fill of bacon, eggs, fried potatoes and coffee with generous amounts of thick cream, we headed out.

Hurray! I don't have to clear the table or do the dishes!

Dad harnessed the horses to the hay rack already filled with pre-cut fence posts. Coalie bounded around, eager to be part of any activity. Even old Puppy took part, although at a slower pace. Happy to be working with Dad and the horses again, I went directly to the front to say hello to them. They had become more familiar with me after my many treats through the winter. With their ears forward and their noses reaching toward me, I assumed they were happy to see me too.

Is it really me they want to see or are they just expecting a treat?

I didn't care. I never tired of touching their incredibly soft noses and breathing in their special smell. They snorted a greeting, their nostrils and lips quivering. I loved that sound.

Onto the hay rack, Dad also added a five gallon pail of water with a lid, an ordinary hammer, a sledge hammer, a crow bar and a straight heavy iron bar. A roll of new wire and two sets of work gloves went in last. We jumped on to the rack and headed out to the pasture west of the house. Old Puppy followed for a little while but then turned back. Coalie kept circling the wagon with his tongue hanging out, tail wagging and happy as a jay bird. It was indeed a great day for being outside—clear blue sky with only a few puffy white clouds. A cool but light wind felt refreshing. I stumbled up to the front of the rack to watch the horses—their large rumps moving in rhythm, tails swishing and the harness jingling. It always fascinated me how they could twitch one particular muscle to rid themselves of any horse flies that landed. Sure wish I could do that. By the time I felt their bite, they had already flown off with a major chunk of my body.

Dad steered the horses along the fence line and stopped them at the first leaning post with a drooping wire. He did not tie them to anything How did they know to remain there?

He climbed off, put on his gloves and removed the U-shaped staples which separated the barbed wire from the rotting post. The old post was thrown unto the wagon to be later used for firewood. Grabbing the straight bar, he plunged it into the ground near to where the old post had been, added some water to the hole and continued to shove the iron bar as far down as he could. I thought the pail of water belonged to us and the horses if we should got thirsty.

"Why are you doing that?" I asked.

Unlike my mother, Dad always seemed happy to answer my questions with patience. "It's to make the dry earth softer for the bar to go in easier and faster."

The straight bar dug deeper and deeper as he rocked it to and fro to widen the hole. When he felt it was deep enough, he placed a new post in that hole and pounded it in with the heavy sledge hammer. Somehow or other, he never missed the mark. Any space around the bottom of post was trampled in with earth. He then grabbed the drooping bottom wire, put it on the crow bar and began to stretch it against the post, one third up from the bottom until it was tight.

"Come here, Iluska., I want you to hold this crowbar tight until I staple this wire to the inside of the post."

I put on the other pair of gloves that were way too large for me and put my full weight on that crowbar to keep it from moving. We repeated this action for the wire that went near the top. Dad kept reminding me to be careful because the barbs could do some serious damage. I already had several scars on my body from trying to go under or between these fences. No reminder was necessary. We continued along the edge of the fence until every post became upright and every wire looked tight. This was harder work than I had expected. Huffing and puffing, I threw off my jacket and kerchief, reminding myself to put them on before we head back. As usual, my mother had made me dress too warmly. I hoped those cows appreciated our efforts. This fence would prevent them from being hit by vehicles or getting into any crops that may make them sick. Keeping our cattle on our side of the fence also made us good neighbours.

All the tools were gathered and loaded back on the hay rack, and we were about to board when Dad motioned for me to follow him.

"I have a surprise for you. I noticed this when I was checking the fences earlier on, and I want you to see this. You must be very quiet and move slowly. Order Coalie to stay."

I did, and he did. I followed Dad to a patch of tall grass just a little away from the fence line. He pointed into the clump and moved aside for me to see. I looked, but couldn't see a thing and whispered, "What?"

"Look again."

Sure enough, three baby bunnies huddled so tightly and still were almost invisible in the dry brown grass that surrounded them. I drew in my breath and looked long and hard at those precious little furry things. If Dad had not tapped my shoulder, I would still have been there. He moved away and whispered for me to follow. I had the impression that he was saying something like "see but let it be". When we were back near the rack, I couldn't contain my excitement any more. I jumped up and down and squealed with delight.

"Thank you, thank you," I kept repeating. It had been a such a thrill to see those adorable bunnies! Thanking him didn't seem enough. I hugged him.

He looked surprised, but he also smiled broadly. "*Yoi, kislányom.* Oh, my little girl!"

We made it back to the house by two o'clock where lunch awaited us. I liked this arrangement—work outside and come in to a meal I didn't have to prepare and clean up after. Now that I had worked outside with Dad a few times, I preferred to do a man's work rather than a woman's. Even though it required more strength, it was more interesting and challenging. Housework on the other hand remained the same mindless task day after day. All the neighbours noticed and complimented my Dad on his beautiful crops or healthy herd of cows, while no one ever commented that the house, clothes and dishes were clean. Not to mention the tons of other work done by a woman that went unnoticed. I wanted to be a man.

***

Not long after, on a beautiful cloudless day near the end of April, I was in the main yard near the house when I noticed a woman opening our driveway gate for a car.

Ethel!

I was so excited that I ran straight for them and was almost knocked down by the car. They finally stopped in front of the house and got out. I was on her like flea on a dog.

She's back! She's back!

Coalie caught my excitement and wiggled his way towards her. Anyone I loved, he wanted to love.

"Let me go, chipmunk. We have some presents for you."

What does she mean? Doesn't she know she is my present!

Ever since she left for the first time to Regina and the second time for California, I had been blaming myself for her absence. I had to set things right. We all moved inside to the kitchen around the table. Dad had seen their car and had also joined us. Ethel handed me her belated Christmas present—a brand new Roy Rogers and Dale Evans lunch box that also contained a thermos, the latest prized possession in our school. The other gift was a Rita Hayworth paper doll with cut-out clothes. I loved them both! As I hugged her and thanked her, I whispered in her ear, asking if we could talk alone. She agreed but told me to wait for a while. They continued to visit with *Mutti* and Dad, chatting in Hungarian or Romanian. After a little while, Ethel signalled me that she was ready. She led the way by grabbing her coat and handing me mine.

Mutti saw us and asked, "Where are you going? What are you two plotting now? You can discuss anything right in here."

I could see the annoyance in Ethel's face. "Never mind, we'll be right back," she retorted.

"I'm just showing Ethel the new babies in the barn." I lied.

My mother accepted that explanation.

We headed out towards the barn and entered its warm interior. We stopped in the middle aisle and, before I could put my thought into words, Ethel interrupted. "What is it Helen? Are you alright? I hope she hasn't been too hard on you?" She looked at me with worried expression.

"No, no. This has nothing to do with her. This has to do with you and me. I never did say sorry for not eating those peas or not going to your wedding. Can you forgive me?"

"What peas? Oh yea, that day. Are you still fretting about that?"

"Yes, isn't that why you left, because of me?"

She hugged me. "You are the silliest goose ever! I never left because of you! I left because I needed a job. Then I didn't return because Steve and I were married." Letting go of me, she looked down to make sure she hadn't stepped into anything nasty with her new penny loafers. She then continued. "We had been engaged since March last year. I couldn't wear my ring to school because a girl doesn't normally get engaged until she is finished school."

I couldn't take my eyes off her face. It was so nice to see her.

"I'm glad we have a chance to talk. But why were you gone for so long? I was going to visit you in California, but I found out it was too far to walk."

Ethel chuckled. It was good to hear that chuckle again. "We stayed at Steve's sister's place in California. Steve needed to recuperate from his asthma in the dry desert. He is feeling much better now. I promise if we ever leave for a long time again, I will tell you, alright?"

"Yes, thank you." I was so happy that I'd had a chance to mend *my* fences, too.

"I do have a secret to tell you, though, Helen, but you must promise never to tell your mother."

The only other person around is Coalie, and I don't think he will tell my mother.

I was always excited and felt special when she shared a secret with me. "What is it?"

"Even if I had not gotten a job or married Steve, I still would have left," she said. "Your mother has made my life a living hell since she came. She really lived up the name of a wicked stepmother. I had been on my own for three years and had taken care of things. Then your mother comes along and thinks she can boss me around."

She stopped to catch her breath, then continued. "Can you believe that she locked me out of the house when I came home after a date with Steve! I actually had to climb through the kitchen window to get in. Then, she yelled at me for three days for doing that. She drove me crazy. I had to get out! I'm sure you must have been somewhat aware of it, no?"

I knew my mother was driving *me* crazy, but didn't think that my brave Ethel would be affected. She at least could talk back to her. But now that she mentioned it, I did remember hearing them argue frequently in Hungarian. I also remembered Ethel crying more than once behind the sheet curtain that separated her bed. I guess, Ethel didn't stand a chance against my mother either.

All I could say was, "I'm so sorry that *Mutti* made you so

unhappy, Ethel."

"Well, she still makes me crazy. I hate her, but I love you. I promise that Steve and I will try to visit you often. You, on the other hand, have to promise to call me if it gets too bad, okay? We are living in Dysart now, not very far away."

"Yes, yes." As long as we were not totally separated, I was happy. We hugged each other, and I let out a sigh of relief. I was so glad it hadn't been my fault for her leaving.

I guess not everything is about me!

front of farm house, Mutti, Dad & I - July 1954

Helen, Frank, Ethel, Steve, Walter, Alice, Pauline, Dad, Mutti
Lenny,Susie and me - 1956

Ethel Kish- 1954

Ethel & Steve - 1955

Steve & Ethel Sulea - 1955

Alice, Walter & Lenny Kallichuk

Walter, Lenny & Susie Kallichuk

Susie, Lenny and Allyson 1959

"big" Helen and Frank Kovach

"big" Helen & Frank Kovach

Mary Ann, Coalie & I - 1956

Mary Ann & I - 1956

Joe & Doraphine Kish - 1950

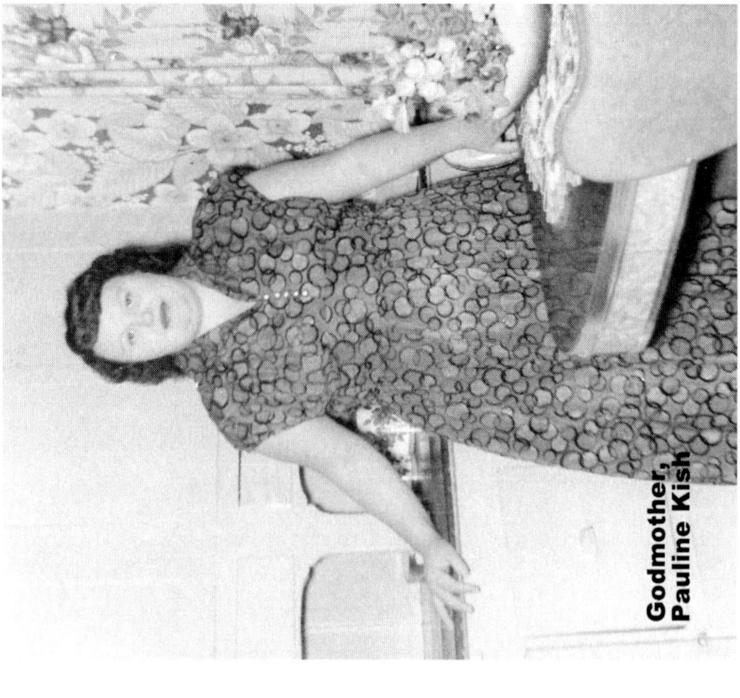

Godmother,
Pauline Kish

Bill Kish

Confirmation class - 1957

Ernie

godmother Pauline and i

My Biological Father - 1944

Mutti & Dad's Wedding day
April 20, 1954

Mud On My Soul

Easter—1956

Sundays were the best days of the week. No work was allowed except that which was absolutely necessary. At least that's what God commanded and He was smart. With the snow gone and Easter near, we prepared for the first mass of the year in our little church in the country. Almost everyone had received new clothes at Christmas specifically meant for wearing to church. Both *Mutti* and I had bought our dresses from the Sears catalogue and Dad had a new crisp white shirt.

Saturday before Easter, as with every Saturday since I arrived here, I had to clean and polish everyone's shoes. "Good grooming includes clean shoes" was one of my mother's many rules. First, any dust or dirt had to be washed off before I applied the correct colour of shoe cream with a small brush. I could just about hear the dry leather slurping up the cream the way my dad slurped up his coffee. Time had to be allowed for the slurping—time for the polish to soak into the leather. Then the fun part began. With my left hand tucked inside the shoe and my right hand holding a soft clean brush, I applied vigorous strokes to the top and sides of the shoe until it shone like new. Changing a dirty, dusty, old pair of shoes into shiny, almost-new ones, made me feel like a magician. I became so proud of my job that I didn't want anyone wearing them because then the magic spell would be lifted.

Easter Sunday arrived. No getting up late, no yummy bacon and eggs—no food or drink at all! Holy Communion required fasting. But the chores were still absolutely necessary.

Don't the animals know it is Sunday?

No chores for me today though. My parents didn't have the time or patience for my dawdling ways. I was ordered to get ready and remain as clean as I could until we were ready to leave. Staying clean had not been an easy task for me at the best of times, but I could lie on the couch and read a book. I had been in the middle of *The Adventures of Huckleberry Finn* by Mark Twain and now continued reading it. I liked the story of the young boy's adventures. I had concluded that boys had more exciting times than girls.

The sound of the screen door slamming indicated that *Mutti* and Dad were back from the barn. They still had to get cleaned up and dressed, so I continued reading. From the bedroom, I overheard my mother's fussing and my Dad's cussing.

"Godammit! I hate this monkey suit. It's too hot and the tie is choking me!"

"Here, let me help you with that. You have to wear one. I won't have my husband go to church looking like a hobo. People will think I don't know how to take care of my man. And stop swearing on a Sunday! God will surely punish you"

Finally, all three of us were ready. Clean, spruced up and wearing "eau de moth balls", we waited for Alice and Walter to give us a ride to church. The temperature outside had risen considerably by the time we arrived at the small church that stood on a knoll overlooking a field, joined by a cemetery and surrounded by a fence. This building, too, was made of wood, but at least it had been painted white with black trim. *Maybe that's what our buildings on the farm need—paint.*

Many people had also arrived early in order to go to confession before mass, but as I watched them chatting, I believed the real reason they were early was to catch up on all the latest gossip. Men and women immediately separated into their individual groups. The men, all dressed in their good suits, ties and hats, kept tugging at their shirt collars. Was it the heat or, like Dad, were they uncomfortable wearing their fancy suits? Their deep raised voices argued about politics, crops, machinery or their animals.

While the men twitched and squirmed in their suits, we ladies preened and pranced in our new frocks. Sundays gave us an excuse to dress up and look pretty, even if it was only for the Lord. Anyway, that's what my mother said. Most of us wore one new item—dress, hat, shoes, or jewellery—and everyone noted and complimented on it.

Unfortunately, women were not allowed into the church without covering their heads, bare arms and bare legs. So along with the lovely dress, a full slip and stockings were required. Wearing nylons meant wearing a girdle. My sister, Ethel, had mentioned how nice a girdle made a woman look but complained that on a warm day, like today, it made you feel like you were wearing a tea cozy.

Most of the ladies huddled in the shade or sought out any breeze that came their way. I liked the look of the silk stockings with the black seams running down the back of the leg but was glad I didn't have to wear them or that awful girdle yet. I overheard the ladies exchange cooking tips and opinions on the latest styles. They also grumbled about how they couldn't get their husbands to do this or that. I wanted to share that I had the same problem with my mother, but I really did not know these women well enough.

I headed inside because I also had to go to confession. No one received the Eucharist without confession. As I stood in line, as usual, I became nervous. I began to feel guilty even though I couldn't come up with any mortal sin that required confession. Then I remembered that all my sins involved my mother. I had lied to her and had unkind thoughts towards her. That will have to do for now. As I waited for my turn, I wondered why I had to confess to God. He already knew what I had done. I made my confession, did five Hail Marys for my penance, and returned outside to join *Mutti* and Alice.

Why do I have to ask for God's forgiveness. I should ask my mother for forgiveness. On the other hand, I prefer to speak to God—He won't spank me or nag me for days.

Soon everyone started moving up the stairs to the double doors of the church. As the men entered, they removed their hats, while the women made sure they had their hats or kerchiefs on. I tied a light kerchief under my chin, but it made me feel warm immediately. Once inside, the men and women parted like the Red Sea. The men and boys filled the pews on the right, while the women and small children filled the left. My mother, Alice and I genuflected, crossed ourselves and sat in the third row. I was lucky and ended up sitting on the other side of Alice, away from my mother. Dad and Walter sat across the centre aisle.

I had been in this church before, but hadn't paid much attention to its details. As I peered around this time, I became aware how different it looked from the huge cathedral I had attended in Linz. I remembered the lofty, stone-structured ceiling richly decorated in gold, and the tall, narrow stained glass windows throwing their light on large, heavily carved pews. Ancient marble statues had looked down upon us. This church, on the other hand, had a low ceiling, a small interior and plain windows. It did have statues of Jesus, Mary and Joseph, but they were made of plaster and were already showing signs of peeling paint

A commotion at the back of the church indicated that the High Mass had begun. Altar boys, followed by the priest, led the procession towards the front. Incense filled the air! Normally I liked its smell, but today there appeared to be too much. Some folks closest to the aisle were coughing and clearing their throats. Someone had thankfully opened the back door to let the smoke out and allow some cool breezes in. God bless that man!

I knew that the service would be sung in Latin; In Linz, I had always followed it with my German prayer book. Alice picked up a missal from the slot at the back of the pew, and so did I, thinking it would be in English. It was unreadable. Leaning towards Alice, I whispered to her, "Where is the English prayer book?"

She smiled and whispered back, "There are none. They are all in Hungarian."

Oh swell! Now I have to learn to read Hungarian! I'm barely able to read English!

Thank goodness we could change our positions from sitting to standing to kneeling, or I would surely have dozed off. And now the sermon—it was in Hungarian too! Not only that, but the priest's voice never changed in pitch, tone or volume. *It is putting me to sleep!*

I tried hard to concentrate but couldn't distinguish the rumble from the pulpit from the grumble in my tummy. Escaping into my world of fantasy, I wanted to build a raft like Huckleberry Finn and drift down our slough to Zanzibar or perhaps as far as Shangri-La. Both destinations sounded more exciting than where I was now. What adventures and treasures would await me there?

The ringing of a small bell from the altar cut into my dreams. Something important was going to happen. We would soon be receiving the Holy Communion. The pews emptied and everyone lined up in the centre aisle. I reached the altar, knelt, and placed my hands under the silk cloth hanging over its railing. Watching from the corner of my eye, I saw Father Barton and an altar boy coming near. I recognized the boy as Gary Kayter, the brother of my good friend, Goldie; both rode the school bus with me. As Father and Gary approached, I raised my head, opened my mouth and placed my tongue on my lower lip. Gary moved a gold plate with a handle under my chin, and Father gently placed the Host on my tongue. I knew the purpose of the cloth, the plate and the tongue was to prevent the Eucharist, or the body of Christ, from being accidentally touched or dropped.

Back in my pew, I took care not to crunch down on the wafer but let it melt in my mouth. It did not fill my tummy, but it filled my soul. I imagined a bright clean light coming from my heart. It felt so good, I promised myself that I will never allow the dark stain of sin to enter me again.

As others took their turn at Communion, I went back to my day dream—back to my raft building. *Now let me see, what will I need? Wood, nails and poles.*

Again, my thoughts were interrupted by the priest's loud sing-song prayer.

"*Dominus vobiscum.*" (May the Lord be with you.) *I hope He will be with me on my dangerous river journey, but will this service ever end?*

"*Per ómnia saecula saeculorum.*" (For ever and ever.) *I hope not!*

"*Miserére nobis.*" (Have mercy on us.) *And He does. It is finally over! Now I can go home, have a lovely dinner and build my raft.*

When we arrived home, we would normally have changed out of our Sunday best and put on our dirty, ragged work clothes, but not today because we had a Sunday guest. It was our turn to treat the priest to dinner. Dad removed his suit jacket and tie, and loosened the top button of his stiff white collar. *Mutti* and I stayed in our good dresses and put on bib aprons.

Dinners on our farm were actually our noon meals. And on Sundays, the dinners were always the same and the best. Today was no exception. Everyone raved about my mother's chicken soup with golden globes of oil floating on top. Into that went thinly cut fresh homemade egg noodles that melted in your mouth. She had prepared everything the day before, and now as it was heated, it filled the whole house with its delicious aroma.

Dad and Father Barton slurped down the soup with relish. My father insisted on getting the boiled chicken feet and the one parsnip that flavoured the soup pot. No one ever bothered to fight him for those two treasures. But, today, both of them were first offered to Father Barton. He declined.

The second course included fried *Paprikás* chicken swimming in a thick cream sauce, *Knödel*, or dumplings and carrots. Dad and Father Barton gulped down their chicken and cleaned their plate of any left-over gravy with freshly baked bread. When I removed their plates, they looked like they had not even been used.

Finally, with coffee came dessert—cherry flavoured Jell-O covered in mounds of fresh whipped cream. A large piece of chocolate cake made from scratch was also offered. Only Father Barton and Dad sat and ate at the dining room table. *Mutti* and I were at their service.

"More soup, Father Barton? Here, have another piece of chicken!" *Mutti* had done the coaxing; I had done the serving.

I considered this arrangement rather unfair. Both my mother and I had been fasting just as long as Dad and the priest. As I fetched more food from the kitchen, I had to be particularly careful not to drool on it.

After the two men had finished their meal, they remained at the dining table chatting and drinking *Manischewitz* wine leisurely. Dad had once explained that this was a Jewish wine. I didn't really know what Jewish was, but I knew it was the opposite of Catholic, so I asked *Mutti*, "Why do we serve Jewish wine to a Catholic priest?"

"Don't ask such silly questions, Heli. It is none of your business."

Whenever she didn't know the answer to my question, she would tell me "it's none of my business", or "not to worry my little head". *She'll never admit she doesn't know nor indicate that maybe I have asked a good question!*

Dad sucked on his pipe while Father Barton lit a cigarette. Both leaned back with a sigh. That gave my mother and I a chance to eat whatever had been left over. We were both glad to do that in the kitchen, seeing as the living room became filled with blue smoke. My tummy finally became as full as my soul.

I stayed around waiting for *Mutti* to put the food away, so I could start washing the dishes. For some reason or other, this time, she shooed me out of the house. Maybe, she was trying to show Father Barton what a good housewife she was. Whatever the reason, it was unexpected free time for me—more time to build my raft.

I scrounged around the farmyard and found plenty of old planks of wood that I carried to the edge of the slough in the corral north of the barn. Now, I needed the tools to build it. Dad kept his crooked nails and hammer in the blacksmith shop—the same one my mother had forbidden me to enter again. I could not get to Zanzibar without the raft, and the raft could not be built without those tools. If I went into the shop, I would disobey my mother. That would be a sin and put a splotch on my clean white soul too soon after my confession. There appeared to be only one solution—run in, grab what I need and get out. The faster I was in and out, the smaller the sin, the smaller the splotch on my soul. Yes, that would be acceptable to both God and me.

Back at the slough's edge I began to build my raft just like the picture I had seen in the book that morning. Coalie urged me on and the raft came together. I stomped on it a few times to test its strength. It felt sturdy, but I realized that I would not be able to take Coalie because he would upset the raft. I ordered him to stay. He sat at the edge of the slough and whimpered while I boosted the raft into the water. It floated! I had already gathered a good strong pole with which to push the raft. I was anxious to begin my journey to Zanzibar and Shangri-la. I was glad I still had my Sunday dress on—it wouldn't do to arrive at such exotic places in my rags.

I grabbed my pole, stood on the raft and pushed off the shore. Coalie began to bark anxiously and jumped around the edge of the water. I felt a slight wobble, so I set my feet farther apart. Another push with the pole, and…a sudden gust of wind hit my chest, and I toppled backwards. I hit the water. It was not deep but was icy cold and took my breath away. I crawled onto the grass and tried to catch my breath. Coalie licked my face and barked as if to say, *"What do you think you are doing?*"

What *was* I doing? I didn't even know how to swim! Had that gust of wind on my chest actually been the brush of my Guardian Angel's wing? *Has she just saved me from drowning?*

"Thank you, Guardian Angel," I said aloud between chattering teeth. "Now can you please come with me and help me explain my ruined dress to my mother? No? I guess you've done your share of saving me for one day."

I didn't die from drowning, but I would surely die when *Mutti* sees my ruined Sunday dress. If I told her that I had been rafting, she would kill me twice. I better not tell her the whole truth, just the part about falling in the mud. Anyone can slip and fall—especially a klutz like me. That meant that I had to lie. And that meant I was going to have to sin again!

Not only was there mud on my good dress, but now there will be mud on my soul. *At this rate, I shall have to go to confession every day!*

Seed Of Hope

May—1956

Spring at last! The cows were put out to pasture while their calves remained in the corral just north of the barn, until they learned to nibble on the fresh grass and no longer required milk from the pail. Then they joined their mothers in the meadow.

The mama pig and her piglets, along with Trooper, were moved outside to a fenced-in pen east of the barn. They grunted with pleasure as they rooted in the soil. Because roots were not enough to fatten them, Dad also gave them ground up oats and barley called chop mixed with separated milk, plus all our kitchen and garden leftovers.

With all of the animals now out of the barn, Dad decided to give it a good spring cleaning and asked me to help. Though cleaning out the manure in the barn was a stinky job, I somehow did not mind its odour. By the time I finished clearing up the table and doing the breakfast dishes, Dad had the horses hitched to the stone boat and was already piling on the manure from the barn.

As I approached, he called out to me, "Could you grab that pitchfork, Iluska? There's a pile of clean straw in the last stall. Spread a thin layer of it into the cleaned stalls. Not too much though, yea?"

I noticed that he always asked, never ordered. When the last pitchfork of manure went on the stone boat, Dad took the reins and clucked at the horses. They lurched forward. *Hey, wait for me!*

I ran to catch up to him. "Where are you taking this?

"To a big manure pile near the garden where we're going to dump this."

The horses strained to overcome the drag of the sled on the ground, but they didn't have to go far to get to the garden. One large pile already existed, and Dad started another. I considered it my job to entertain Jolan and Gitzka while he cleared the stone boat. On the way back to the barn, I wondered why the manure was piled near the garden, so I asked Dad.

"Did you see the other pile of manure there?" he answered. "Well, that has sat there for quite some time. In the fall, it will be spread into the garden soil to fertilize it."

"What's fertilize?"

"The manure becomes food for the plants in the garden. It makes them grow big and strong."

"What? Do you mean that the plants eat the cow poop to grow, then we eat the vegetables so we can grow."

He laughed. "Well, I never thought about it that way, but yea, something like that."

Yuk! No wonder I don't like vegetables, including peas.

***

I couldn't get out of it. This time I was trapped. No amount of acting like a dunce worked. I had to help my mother plant the garden.

Mutti had ordered Dad to plough up the garden as soon as the soil had thawed. The garden plot was located south of the house and had a slight slope. It was surrounded by a row of *ribizli* or currant shrubs inside a wire fence. These currants appeared to be the only fruit around —no apple, plum or cherry trees in sight, unlike Austria. No wonder *Mutti* had to buy all that fruit for canning. What would those currents taste like?

My mother had tomato, cucumber, green pepper and cabbage plants already growing on the windowsills in the house. It was time they went into the garden. She had cut the seed potatoes allowing for at least one "eye" for each section. The peas, carrots, corn, beets, lettuce, turnips and parsnips came in packets of seeds. Onions and garlic were planted as bulbs. We didn't have to plant any dill for pickles nor poppy seeds for the yummy poppy seed roll that my mother baked. She explained that those seeds came out on their own every year.

Good, less work for us.

My mother and I began early in the morning, right after chores and breakfast. We marked the rows with lengths of string tied to sticks. She made a furrow with the hoe, put in the seeds and showed me how to cover them with the surrounding earth.

I remembered what Dad and I had talked about earlier—that there was cow poo in there. I sure didn't want to put my hands into that! But when I studied the ground carefully, there was no sign of any manure. I knelt down, grabbed some of that soil in my hand and pulled it over the seed in the furrow. It felt cool, crumbly and looked almost black. It didn't feel like poo, and it didn't smell like poo. Its smell reminded me of the forest in Austria—sweet, musty, and fresh—like mushrooms. With the warm sun on my back and the cool earth beneath my knees, I closed my eyes and enjoyed the moment. *Mutti* seemed occupied and hadn't bugged me yet. When we did finally come together, she let me plant a few seedlings so that I would recognize them later. *Why does she want me to recognize them?*

I became hot, tired and cramped and looked for my mother for relief. I stood up and wiped my brow with my arm. "Are we almost done? How big is this garden anyway?"

She neared and rested on her hoe. "I don't know, the measurements here are different from the ones we used in Europe. Dad said it was about an acre. Anyway, let's stop and rest for a while. I need a drink of water."

She was right; the measurements were different. I had learned about decimetres, centimetres, metres, and kilometres in the *Lager* school. The same went for grams, and the only thing I had to do to change one to another, was to either multiply or divide by ten, a hundred or a thousand. Easy! Here, they taught me about inches, feet, yards and miles. Then ounces, quarts, gallons. But there seemed to be no easy way to switch from one to the other. It all had to be memorized.

We walked to the house, had our drink of water and headed back to carry on for a while longer. After a while, I stood up and looked around. Less than half the garden was planted.

My God, we'll never finish.

"Are we going to have to plant the whole garden?" I asked, not really wanting to hear the truth.

"No, this huge garden was made to feed the large family that Mr. Kish once had, but now there are only three of us. That's enough for today, Heli. We'll plant the potatoes and corn tomorrow"

I got up, eager for the rest. She came over and did something I had not seen her do too often. She smiled and then laughed at me.

"You should see yourself, you're a mess!"

I didn't dare say it, but thought, *you don't exactly look or smell like the Queen of Sheba either*. She acted relaxed, content and actually happy. What brought this about? Was it the beautiful weather? Was she glad that I was working with her and not with Dad? Or was it the satisfying feeling that I too felt at having done a good day's work? The reason didn't matter. The result did.

Has she planted a little seed of hope with her good mood? Will it grow and last for a while?

Eden

Summer—1956

I didn't know how I felt about school being let out this summer. On one hand, I was glad for a break from learning, but on the other hand, it meant more work for me at home. Aside from weeding the garden, I had also been given the added task of bringing the cows home from the pasture for milking every afternoon before supper.

At first, I had not been thrilled. Would they cooperate? What if they decided to charge and trample me? After all, I was just a fly in their eye. Sometimes the pasture that they grazed in was a good two miles from the farm. Would I be able to walk four miles every day?

The first few times I had to herd them, they were in the pasture not far from the house. To ease my fears, I pretended to be Heidi herding her goats like in the book. To my surprise, the cows accepted me as boss, or was it Coalie's presence that made the difference? Each cow entered their individual stall without coaxing. I guessed that they felt the need to be milked as much as I felt the need to be boss.

One day Dad informed me that the cows had moved to the far pasture. I groaned. He instructed me to go south until I hit a fence line, then turn east and they would either be in the next field or the one after that. That was as good as I got for directions. I definitely wanted Coalie with me this time, as a companion and a guide. If we found the cattle, they knew their way home, and I would simply follow them.

Should we not find them, then I would likely be lost and would have to depend on Coalie to guide me back. As usual, he was by my side and in a few moments bolted ahead of me.

I had decided to go barefoot for summer. I found shoes unbearable in the heat, and sandals always let the stones in. The bottom of my feet had become quite calloused and hardened; I thought nothing could hurt them, but I had never crossed a field of stubble. The stiff shafts were too tall to affect the bottom of my feet, but their sharp ends turned my ankles into hamburger. I shuffled to prevent further pain, and that seemed to work, so I carried on.

No sooner had I solved *that* problem, when another arose. Dried thistles! No matter how tough my soles were, they were no match for those tiny, but painful daggers that found all the tender spots on my feet. Once attached, they gave me no peace, only pain. They had to be removed. But they were so small, so invisible, that I could not find them. I called Coalie over so that I could lean on him for balance as I stood on one foot and pulled the arrows out. With a sigh of relief, I put my foot down, only to step unto another nest of stingers! I hopped and screeched like a mad magpie. Coalie cocked his head to one side, then the other, whimpering as if to say, *"What's the matter?"* It took me another fifteen minutes to sit, seek, and pluck out those varmints.

I have to keep going, but next time I will wear those darn shoes. Now where are those stupid cows!

My eyes scoured the field ahead trying to find some brown lumps among all the green but no luck. What I *did* find was a clump of tall trees. Coalie and I ran for their cover from the heat. Even now at four thirty, the air still felt sticky. As soon as we entered the shade, we felt the blessed coolness and plopped ourselves down on a patch of grass. We both lay there with our tongues hanging out and panting.

We'll just stay long enough to cool off a bit.

The ground felt wonderfully cold against my back as I closed my eyes and listened to the chatter of the poplar leaves high above me. A light breeze rustled the grass heads nearby. I heard the distinct drone of a bee as it buzzed by, then silence as it found its nectar. To my left, but farther away, I caught the lilting song of a meadowlark, which I liked it even better than a robin's song. This was interrupted by the not-so-sweet sound of quarrelling blackbirds from the nearby slough. I opened my eyes, looked up and caught a patch of blue between the swaying branches. As I tried to imagine a special cloud formation, I heard them —mosquitoes—buzzing near my ear, circling. Once they found the landing strip on my big forehead, I knew they would call their friends over for dinner.

"Come on, Coalie. Time to go!"

We finally located the cows and started them for home. On our way back, my mind returned to my mother and how her pleasant, joyous mood, which had begun in the garden, had been short lived. She had fallen back to her usual harsh words and lengthy angry outbursts. She had me walking on eggshells again.

Now dreading to go home, I could not forget the feeling I had in the shade of those cathedral-like trees. There, no one nattered at me or made demands. No unkindness, or blame was dished out. Only nature, Coalie, and I existed. It felt like the Garden of Eden where animals, plants, and humans lived in peace and joy. I believed it was also where God dwelt.

"Eden" was what I called that place in the field. Each time we passed it on our way to get the cows, Coalie and I would stop and lie still. I would also go there whenever I needed some peace and quiet. If the weather or time did not permit, I would close my eyes and pretend I was lying under the trees with God's creatures.

Braids Bobbed

Summer—1956

My summer holidays rolled by quickly. I read as much as I could, but without the school library, reading material became scarce. Thank goodness for the *Children's Digest* that Ethel had subscribed for me earlier. This magazine had everything I needed to keep me busy—stories, comics, science, sports, and even world happenings. It was from there that I first read about Mowgli, a boy who had been brought up by wild creatures of the jungle, and just like me, he believed he could talk and understand the animals. *The Jungle Book* became my favourite read.

The science section of this magazine would sometimes have instructions on making toys from common, simple items. I made a toy parachute using only string, a hanky and a rock by attaching the strings to the four corners of a hanky and tying a rock to the other ends. When I tossed it up in the air, the hanky ballooned out and wafted down beautifully. The key to its success though, depended on the right weight of the rock.

A great deal of my time had also been spent with Mary Ann and her mother picking wild strawberries in the meadow not too far from the house. Growing close to the ground and being very tiny, made them difficult to pick. We knelt in the dirt and plucked them, but they never made it into our bowls. We were worried that the ants and the bees would want to steal them, so we hid them in our mouths. Only Doraphine went home with a full bucket of berries.

On another rather warm day, we went picking Saskatoon berries. Being at eye level on a bush, they had been much easier to pick than the strawberries. Mary Ann and I found them too sour to eat without sugar, so this outing was not as much fun—all work with no reward. As we were picking, it had begun to drizzle.

Oh good! I don't want to do this any more anyway. What a good excuse to go home.

I headed towards the path to the house, but Doraphine called me back. "Helen, we're not done. You're not going to dissolve or rust you know." She giggled as she added "Besides you're only going to get wet on top."

What? Not get out of the rain? Ever since I could remember, I have been taught to obey all the rules so you don't embarrass yourself or anyone else. If it rains, you go inside. Right?

Wrong! I discovered that rain could be fun. I breathed in the fresh moist air that smelled divine and stopped fretting. Off came our shoes, and we let the soft mud squish between our toes. Soon the mist turned to drops that became larger and larger. Mary Ann and I turned our faces to the sky to catch the rain in our open mouths, but it only plopped into our eyes, blinding us. Our hair plastered itself against our skulls, and our clothes hung on us the way they did on the scarecrow in the garden. We roared with laughter at the state of each other.

We continued picking the berries until Doraphine felt we had enough for some pies. Or maybe she thought we were beginning to rust a little around the edges. Either way, we emptied our bowls into Doraphine's pail, placed them on our heads and marched home like soldiers.

Mary Ann's mother made every effort to dry and clean me up before she sent me home. *Mutti* would never have understand or approved. I didn't care because I had learned that not everyone lived by the same rules and breaking them could sometimes be fun.

***

One of my other goals this summer had been to convince my

mother to cut my hair. No one else in school had long hair in braids like mine. I had turned eleven that August and would be going into grade five—old enough to look more grownup. I had been hounding my mother all summer, and each time she had refused.

One day when *Mutti* and I happened to be in Harry's Store, I noticed some pretty barrettes.

"I want to cut my hair so I can wear these." I reminded her again.

She replied in English. "No, no cut!"

Harry Moscovich must have overheard our conversation because he added his bit. "You're not going to cut that beautiful hair of yours, are you?"

"Tankee yoo, Harry, I tellink she no cuttink," my mother replied.

Gee, thanks for nothing, Harry.

Suddenly he changed his tune. "But if you really do want to cut your hair, my wife, Mona is a hairdresser. She would love to meet you, Helen. I have been telling her about you."

I couldn't believe that Harry had switched over to my side. My mother tried desperately to argue her point in English, but before long, she gave up, and a date was set for the cut.

Mutti and I arrived at Mona Moscovich's house a week later. She met us at her front door and welcomed us in with a big smile. She was a small, very pretty woman with her well-groomed hair and makeup; she looked much younger than her husband. I looked around, stunned. Her home had all the modern furniture and appliances. Everything was new, clean and bright, but it was the floors that caught my attention. They shone like a mirror. Mona ushered us through the living room, then the kitchen, where my mother handed her the two dozen eggs as payment. As Mona led us down to her basement, I noticed there was no earth or dirt, only more gleaming linoleum, and one part of it was dedicated to her hairdressing shop. She directed my mother to a couch and asked if she would like a cup of coffee. *Mutti* understood and nodded yes.

"Helen, you have a seat here on this chair. Would you like something to drink too? Yes, good. I'll be right back."

She headed back up the stairs and returned with two coffees and an Orange Crush for me. She gave my mother her coffee, then turned to me. "So, Helen, in what kind of style would you like your hair cut?"

Style? I didn't have a clue. I never, ever had a cut nor been to a hairdresser. Mona showed me a few pictures of hair-dos, and I chose the shortest one with the curly hair. It reminded me of Ethel's hair when I had first met her. Mona showed the chosen style to my mother and asked, "Okay?"

"Ja dat ist goot," *Mutti* replied, but was shaking her head in a "no" all the while.

Mona let out my braids, combed out my hair and tied an elastic at the back of my neck. "My, but you have beautiful thick hair, Helen. Are you ready to lose it?"

"Yes, please." *So ready to look normal.*

She took a large pair of scissors and began cutting just above the elastic. The cut tail of hair came off, and Mona handed it to my mother who wrapped it in a kerchief. Meanwhile, my head bobbed forward, and all the loose straight hair left on my head flew forward into my face. I looked in the mirror and laughed. My hair was flat on top and flat on the sides. My head felt so light, I thought it would roll off my shoulders. I hoped Mona would not leave my hair like that. I did not like it. She then guided me to the sink and washed my short hair. Now I knew why my mother loved it when I worked with her hair. *It feels wonderful!*

With me back in the chair, she began the styling cut. Before long, Mona whipped the towel off my shoulders, brushed off any stray hairs and began rolling it in curlers that had brushes poking through a wired mesh. I had never seen these before. Once all my hair was set in curlers, she led me over to another chair that had a hood over it. She sat me down and turned it on. Hot air pelted my shoulders, and I jumped. With her hand on my shoulder, Mona assured me it was only a dryer for my hair. The noise of the dryer did not allow me to hear what Mona and *Mutti* were discussing, or if they even understood each other. I just hoped my mother minded her manners.

I came out of the dryer pink and well done. Mona removed the rollers, brushed my hair, then put some kind of spray on it. I had closed my eyes during all this, afraid that I may not like it. If I didn't, Mona would not be able to glue all that hair back.

"It's done. You can look now, Helen."

I opened my eyes and looked in the mirror. Who was that person? *It's me! It's me!* I did not look like a little girl any more but older, almost pretty. Maybe *Mutti* would take me more seriously now. I jumped out of the chair and hugged Mona. "Thank you, thank you."

"You're very welcome, Helen. Just remember to come back for trims. Otherwise the style won't stay, okay?"

My mother and I walked back to Main Street to pick up Dad from the beer parlour. We had been unable to find anyone to take us into town today, so Dad had harnessed the horses and driven us in with the grain wagon. Now heading back home, it was a good thing that the horses were aware of the ditches and knew their way home because Dad didn't.

That beautiful hairdo only lasted for two days, then I had to wash and curl it. I did not have curlers like Mona's, so I had to curl my hair Ethel's way—with bobby pins. Having watched her often enough, I knew what to do. Using the narrow handle of the comb, I separated a strand of hair, curled it around my middle finger, pushed the strand down flat against my scalp and secured it with a bobby pin. It took me quite a while to get it right, but the results were pleasing. The problem was that the curls lasted only one day. So now, every night, I had to wash and curl my hair and sleep with the bobby pins poking into my skull. If I didn't do that, my hair looked like rats had gnawed at it during the night.

Mutti knew nothing about short hair and couldn't help me. She merely said, "I told you not to cut your hair!"

I secretly wished I could have a perm. I considered applying sugar water to keep the curls for longer, like we had done in Austria. But here on the farm, the local flies and bees would surely invite all their relatives for a party in my hair. The end result was that I now had to spend more time and energy on my hair.

What have I done? I better be more careful what I wish for in the future.

"DP"

October—1956

I was eager to start grade five. Aside from wanting everyone to see my new hairdo, I also longed for the company of children my own age. I could only chat with myself and Coalie before we ran out of things to talk about. Spending time outdoors working with Dad had been fine, but being with *Mutti* indoors, was not. She had fallen back to her old habit of being unkind and nasty to me and everyone around her. Occasionally I would argue back, but most of the times that only made things worse, and other times, I did not have the courage.

My mood brightened when the bus finally arrived that first day of grade five. My classmates and I met in the school yard by the flagpole where Mr. Hughes, the custodian, hoisted the Union Jack. *Flags can be given names*?

Some of my classmates did a double take when they saw me, but most liked my new hair style.

Mrs. Irene Ermel would be my new teacher. New people always made me nervous. Would she be as kind as the last two, or would she be more like the ones I had in Austria? We followed her into the "big school" which was not far from the elementary one. This was the same two-story building from which Ethel had graduated. Between my new haircut and the "big school", I felt really grown up.

My anxiety about Mrs. Ermel was quickly put to rest by her actions and her kind voice. She was so wise. She taught us how Canada had been discovered, and how men from Europe like Cartier, de Champlain and even the Vikings sailed across the ocean to gain control of this young land. How could it be considered "young"? I assumed that the whole world was the same age. She called this subject "History". This was Canada's life story, and I became fascinated. Mrs. Ermel also knew about the workings of a water pump, like the kind we had on the farm. I always needed to know the why, how, where, when and what of things. This teacher answered a lot of my questions about how things around me worked.

School is so much fun!

***

I really enjoyed being back with all my friends until one day in late October. I went outside at recess trying to catch up with them. Out of the corner of my eye, I noticed two girls, not within my group, pointing and laughing at me.

No one else is near. It has to be me they are laughing at. Why?

Thinking back to my underwear incident in grade three, I looked myself over but found nothing wrong. Maybe they thought my new haircut funny. I went up to them. "How come you're laughing at me?"

"You're a dirty Dee Pee-ee! You're a dirty Dee Pee-ee!" they shouted in a sing-song fashion.

Again I looked at myself. There was nothing on me that was dirty. My mother made sure of that. She always insisted that even though clothes may be patched or worn, they should never be dirty. Whatever they were saying had nothing to do with my cleanliness.

So, I asked them, "What's a Dee Pee?"

"I don't know, but my dad said you are one," one of the girls replied.

I walked away feeling hurt, but not knowing why. I could tell by their tone that "Dee Pee" did not mean something nice. I had to ask someone, but I couldn't wait until tonight to ask my parents. I decided to ask Mrs. Ermel. Running back into the school, I found her in the Teacher's Room, and asked if I could speak to her. I explained that it was of the *utmost importance*. This was a term I picked up from one of the books I had read. It worked, because Mrs. Ermel came at once and ushered me into a private room.

At first she chuckled as she said, "So what is it that is of 'utmost importance'?" But when she saw my face, her kind voice almost brought me to tears. "You look troubled, Helen. Something has happened. Tell me about it."

I explained what had happened, but that I didn't understand what they had meant by "Dee Pee", never mind a dirty one.

She put her arm around my shoulders. "Oh dear, dear me. Don't you worry about that. Those girls were extremely unkind and I will certainly have a talk with them."

That really hadn't answered my question, so I asked her directly, "What is a Dee Pee?"

She thought for a moment before speaking. "The letters stand for displaced person. A displaced person is anyone who has been forced out of their home or country by some bad circumstances. Right now, there are many Hungarian refugees coming to Canada. I don't know why they were forced out of their homeland, but they are most welcome here in Cupar." She held my face in her hands and looked directly into my eyes. "There are some people, Helen, who, when they don't understand something, become afraid. When they are afraid, they become unkind. Do you understand?"

I nodded "yes", but I didn't understand at all. First of all, I was not dirty. Second of all, they certainly needn't be afraid of me. I was the biggest coward ever. They might have a reason to be afraid of my mother mind you, as she wasn't always kind. She *had* come from Hungary, but that was long ago. And, I had heard the meaning of that word before. It had been explained to me at the *Lager*, but I hadn't understood it then either.

From 1945 and on, the Hungarians were under the rule of Moscow. All their wealth and freedoms were taken from them by the Russians. On October 23, 1956, students and workers took to the streets of Budapest (the capital of Hungary) and demanded personal freedom, more food, removal of the secret police, and removal of Russian control etc. It became known as the Hungarian Revolution. On November 4, Soviet tanks went into that city to restore order. They acted with immense brutality even killing wounded people as a warning to others who were still protesting. Approximately 30,000 people were killed. To escape the expected Soviet reprisals, approximately 200,000 fled to the west leaving all their possessions behind.

The Morning Of the Killing

Fall—1956

Kook-a-roo, kookoo! Kook-a-roo, kookoo! It's half past eight and you're too late!

That darn rooster. He's at it again like an alarm clock with no shut off button! If I had my way, he would be in the pot by now.

It was a Saturday in late October, and almost every morning since spring, that rooster has been squawking and strutting his stuff under my window. More importantly, how come I was still in bed, and why hadn't *Mutti* awakened me to do chores this morning? Jumping out of bed, I slipped into my ragged work clothes and strode into the kitchen. No one was about. I grabbed the loaf of bread from the bread box, cut a slice and slapped some butter and rhubarb jam on it. Still munching on my sandwich, I put on a jacket and headed towards the barn. There was always something going on there.

As I neared the barn, a most horrendous sound filled the air. It wasn't coming from within the barn, but rather from east of it where the pigs were housed. Was a wild animal killing one of our pigs? The high-pitched squeals ripped through the air again and again! I stuffed the rest of the bread into my mouth and ran to see what was going on.

Mutti stood just outside the pig pen but did not notice as I approached. I came up behind her and followed her gaze to whatever had taken her attention. In the pen, a pig was running around and around, its shrill agonizing scream hurting my ears. As it neared, I saw blood spurting from a cut in its neck. It finally collapsed to the ground, and all became still.

My mother suddenly noticed me beside her, grabbed my arm and shouted, "Get out of here! I didn't want you to see this. That's why I let you sleep in this morning."

It was too late! My eyes had seen it all except the actual blow that had come from the large knife that now hung loosely in my father's hand. It was still dripping with blood! That image did not match at all with the Dad I knew. Then another thought came to my mind—Trooper! I looked hard for the notch in the ear that would identify him, but found none. *Thank goodness!*

I had watched many chickens being butchered and had never thought too much about it. Dad would catch them, stretch their necks and chop their heads off. He would then release them and let them run around without their heads until they bled out. It was gruesome, but at least there wasn't much blood, and those chickens died silently. I forgot they couldn't make sounds without a head, unlike this butchering.

The pig's ear-splitting screams still echoed in my brain. Blood was everywhere. I even tasted its scent in my mouth—like metal. My stomach lurched—my bread, butter and jam reversed their course.

Mutti told me to get back to the house and that she would be there soon. I stumbled to my bedroom and threw myself down on my bed, still reeling from that horrendous scene.

***

I knew there would be much work ahead preserving that meat. I had helped a few times before but had not connected the meat with the animal. Never had I witnessed the actual killing or the cutting of the meat which was done in the granary by Dad and my brother, Bill. I had only seen it as it came into the house in pieces. This time I kept seeing, smelling and tasting the horrible death scene over and over. For the first time, I welcomed *Mutti's* nattering that distracted me enough to be able to function.

I covered my hair, put on an apron and washed my hands thoroughly. The first parts that came in from the granary were the thick slabs of fat. I watched my mother dice this into small square bits, place them into a large pot and render it down until it became a clear liquid which was poured into wide-mouthed containers, covered and stored in the root cellar. Once cooled and hardened, it became lard to be used in all our cooking and baking. Cracklings was the stuff left after the fat had melted down. With added salt, they tasted like crunchy chips. I had enjoyed them very much before I knew where they had come from.

The next pieces of meat that Bill brought in were chops, steaks, small roasts and ribs. All went into the frying pan or oven and cooked until well done. The cooked meat eventually went into crocks and were completely covered with liquid lard. They stayed in the root cellar and were later moved to the ice house, after Dad restocked it with slabs of ice from the slough.

Every other bit of meat removed from the bones would be canned like the fruits and vegetables. The cut-up meat went into clean jars, seasoned with salt, pepper and garlic, sealed and boiled in the larger canner.

"Write down the time, Heli. We have to make sure that it boils for at least three hours," my mother said with concern in her voice.

"Why?"

Annoyed she said, "If we don't boil it long enough, we could die without ever knowing that the meat had gone bad."

That's a scary thought.

"Why would it kill us, *Mutti*?"

"Don't worry your little head about it."

I knew that meant she didn't know the answer!

That was all the time we had for that day. I knew that tomorrow would be more work.

The following day happened to be Sunday, but we could not waste a day for rest. There was much more meat to be processed. I was shocked to see Bill bring in a bucket of pig's feet.

I didn't remember helping my mother with these before. I must have been away at school the last time.

"Wash those jars and peel the garlic, Heli," she directed me in Hungarian. Because no one in our family or close friends spoke German, my mother and I had stopped speaking it unless absolutely necessary. She translated any Hungarian for me, and I helped her with any English. While I cleaned the jars and garlic, *Mutti* cleaned, inspected and cut the feet into smaller portions to fit in the jars. Filled and sealed, these jars, too, boiled for three hours.

If I had thought the raw pig's feet looked disgusting, then the next part of the pig that came into the house was even more shocking. I pulled my eyes away as soon as I realized what it was—the whole head of the pig. I shuddered! The previous morning's scene replayed itself in my mind. I became queasy and had to leave. As I grabbed a jacket and heading out the door, *Mutti* called out, "Where are you going? We are not finished."

"I feel sick and need some fresh air. I'll be back soon."

Surprisingly enough she said, "Okay."

I never knew how she would react to any situation. When I least expected it, she would pounce on me, bringing to mind the day I had followed the mama cat as she took her kittens for a hunting lesson. The mama cat had stationed herself above a gopher hole, opposite the angle of exit. There, she had listened patiently, then pounced on the gopher from behind as it popped its head out. It didn't see the strike until it was too late. I felt like that gopher many times.

One such incidence had taken place on Mother's Day. We did not have a chance to get into town for me to buy her a present. Instead, I gathered wild spring flowers and thought they would be a nice surprise for her. With my flowers clutched tightly in my hand behind my back, I entered the house. Before I could open my mouth or show her my gift, she yelled at me.

"Where have you been? I have been calling you all morning! You know you're supposed to stay close to the house."

"Sorry *Mutti*, I had to go a little farther to gather these flowers for you." I handed her the flowers. She took them and placed them in a glass of water. No "thank you" or "sorry" came from her lips. I had not expected that and felt extremely hurt. *Come to think of it, I never hear her apologize to anyone.*

Instead, it was, "There's a lot of work here we have to get done, and I need your help."

I had thought that if I was kind to her, she would be more kind to me. That didn't work. When I *was* prepared for a fight or had a reasonable argument ready, she gave in without the slightest hesitation —like now. And yesterday morning, she had been surprisingly thoughtful. There was no rhyme or reason to her actions. *Will I ever understand her?*

As soon as I stepped out the door, Coalie bolted to by my side. I put both my hands behind his ears and gave them a rub, then hugged his neck and breathed in the fresh cold air trapped in his fur. I felt better immediately. After a big kiss on his nose, we headed out for a walk. I told Coalie about last morning's episode. As usual, he turned his head toward me and perked up his ears. *"Yes, yes, I hear you,"* he said. He was such a good listener!

As we walked, I could smell the onions, garlic and grease on me. So did Coalie, for every chance he had, he would lick my hands. I realized that the butchering would not only provide a feast for us, but also for both dogs. I would have to go back to that smelly, steamy kitchen, but now I had a good reason.

"Soon, Coalie, you will have lots of yummy bones and skin to chew on." I patted his head and went back inside.

I washed my hands, put my kerchief and apron back on and began peeling and cutting more onions and garlic. Concentrating on my task, I tried not to look at the big pot that held the head. Eventually, my curiosity got the better of me, and I sneaked a peek. Thankfully, I could only see the snout pointing up past the rim. That was enough, I looked away.

Think of Coalie! Think of all the treats he will get from this thing in the pot!

Around lunch time, Dad and Bill came in with another pail of small bits of meat. They washed up and had a cup of coffee while *Mutti* fried up some of that meat with onions and potatoes. Everyone guzzled down the meal with enjoyment. I tried not to think about what I was eating and pretended that yesterday morning never happened. I could only get a bit of the meat down.

Before they left, Dad and Bill took a slice of bread and soaked up the crunchy, salty, pork left-overs in the frying pan. After that, Bill helped Dad set up the meat grinder while *Mutti* washed some long white tubular things.

"What is that?" I asked, slightly turned off by them.

"These are the guts from the pig that we're going to use as casings for our sausage," she replied without the slightest distaste. *Yuck! Disgusting!* My foster mother had been right when she had said, "Sometimes it's best not to know everything."

Despite my squeamishness, I watched in fascination as Dad and *Mutti* ground the meat, added spices and *kasha* (buckwheat) and used the same grinder to push the mixture into the casings. Once tied and steamed, they began to resemble the product I was familiar with. While they were making the sausage, the pig's head was still boiling in the pot. Now, after a small break, my mother was about to take it out. I didn't want to watch what she did next and excused myself. She didn't object. I went into the bedroom.

A while later she called me back into the kitchen. I dreaded seeing that horrid head again, but had to obey. To my pleasant surprise, the head was gone, and only the meat remnants rested in a large bowl on the table.

"I need you to hold this pillow case open for me while I pour this meat into it," she instructed as she placed the bottom of the case into another bowl.

I held the top of the wet pillow case tightly as the bits of meat and broth splashed into the bottom. When all was in, *Mutti* tied the case as tightly as she could. As she did, the extra juices oozed out. We took the leaking pillow case into the root cellar and headed towards a large ceramic crock. At the bottom of this container was an upside down plate with a board on top. My mother placed the dripping case of meat on top of that first board, placed another board over it, then put a heavy stone on top of that. I could see the juices in the case being pressed out and flowing the open space at the bottom of the crock. With a lid on, it would remain there until no more juice came out. Then it would be ready to be cut into thick or thin slices and served cold on a plate or in a sandwich. It was called "head cheese." It was a *head* all right, but I didn't know about the *cheese* part. *I'll never look at head cheese the same way again.*

It had been an exhausting two days, and still we were not done. I began to realize and appreciate my mother's hard work a little more.

Bacon, bacon, bacon! I loved bacon but luckily did not have to take a part in its making. Dad took care of that when I was in school the next day. By the time I came home, it was already hanging and being smoked in an old covered sled that used to carry his children to school in the bygone winters. About two inches thick, the bacon was mostly fat with very little meat on it. I liked it both fried and as is. The best part was the rind or skin which I could chew on for hours or share with Coalie who swallowed it in one gulp.

I thought long and hard about the morning of the killing. I knew that meat came from live animals like the chickens, but I had not seen or felt the pain of the animal being killed until that morning. It took me quite some time to get that terrifying image out of my head. I talked with Mrs. Ermel about my experience, and she told me about what she called the "circle of life," where some animals die so that others may live. As I looked around the farm, I noted that birds caught insects to feed their babies. The coyotes would probably kill and eat the baby bunnies that Dad had shown me. And closer to home, the mama cat killed that gopher to feed her kittens. So Dad, having looked like a murderer at the time, was really just a provider.

Having gone through this, I now had a greater understanding of how life worked—*I don't like it, but that's the way it is!*

Vicious Virus

Winter—1956/1957

The air grew chilly while the sky turned grey and threatened us with snow. Another terrible winter was upon us. December proved bitterly cold, but by Christmas time, the temperatures had warmed up slightly.

As usual, I knew what I would be receiving for my Christmas presents because I had ordered them from both the Eaton's and Sears' catalogues. Even though it wouldn't be a surprise, to some extent, it was still exciting. I waited, imagined and fretted. Will it fit? Will it look good on me or—the worst of all—will anyone else be wearing the same thing? Normally, I would be able to try anything on as soon as it arrived, but for Christmas, it was wrapped and put under the tree while I was still at school. This time, however, I detected an extra box with my name on it. It was the shape and size of a shoe box but slightly bigger.

Boots! It must be boots, but I don't need a new pair. Strange?

After I had opened all my other gifts, tried on my clothes and beamed with happiness, my parents finally allowed me to open the mysterious box. Skates—not new and not white, but a pair of second-hand, brown, tattered boy's skates. *They are beautiful!* They fit and I loved them!

I barely tasted my Christmas dinner for wondering how I could try my skates out today. It would take some serious work to shovel the snow from a slough. *Hurry up you guys. Can't you see I have more important things to do than eat. I can't believe I just said that!*

Finally everyone was done! I helped clean up, put my outdoor gear and boots on, grabbed a pair of Dad's heavy wool socks, my new skates and started for the door.

"Where can I find a shovel?" I asked Dad on my out.

"What do you need a shovel for?"

"I need to shovel some snow off the slough by the barn so I can try out my new skates."

"Okay, I'll help you," he replied with a twinkle in his eye.

Together, we found the shovel right outside the door and headed to the slough I had suggested. We crunched through the snow with Coalie bounding ahead of us. I hoped it won't take too long to clear the snow.

Wait! What's this? Some of it is already clear? I squealed and looked at Dad who grinned. I hugged him hard. "Thank you." What a wonderful thing he had done for me. Now I could skate to my heart's content.

I put on the extra socks then slipped my feet into the skates. Dad helped tie them up snug, and I was off—right off the ice in one fell swoop—skates in the air, butt on the ice! *Isn't it supposed to be the other way around?*

Coalie and Dad rushed to my help. But Dad barely had me back on my feet when Coalie, in his excitement, bumped against the back of my legs and pushed the skates out from underneath me. Down I went again. I had to order Coalie off the ice. Whining and barking, Coalie watched me struggle from the edge.

"Go slow now. Take small steps," Dad suggested.

An inch of snow still covered the surface of the ice and prevented it from being too slippery. But its rough surface threw me to the ice frequently. I laughed, I moaned, then I groaned, but it was worth it. I imagined myself moving freely, smoothly and quickly. It did not happen that day. I remembered Ethel's words about how true skills required time and patience.

I went skating every chance I had—each time getting better.

Sometimes it was too cold, sometimes I had to clear the snow again, but I went anyway, even if it was just for a little while. It allowed me out of the house and certainly helped the winter hours go by faster.

***

One Monday morning in the new year, I sat at the kitchen table enjoying a bowl of hot Red River cereal with cocoa and cream before I would catch the Bombardier. All of a sudden, my stomach lurched. I had to leave the table and make a mad dash to the pee pail in the bedroom. The walls were moving around and around. Everything came up and out. I immediately felt better, rinsed out my mouth with water and went back to the table.

"*Mi a baj?* What's the matter?" *Mutti* asked.

I couldn't answer because I had to run to the pail again. This time she followed and held my forehead with her hands as I emptied more food. *Oh my God! I hate throwing up.*

"Well, you're certainly not going to school today. Take your clothes off and get back into bed," she ordered.

Today, I had put on my new skirt and top that I had received for Christmas. I had also curled my hair. I looked snappy but felt crappy. More than willing to obey her, I still worried about missing school, but I couldn't go anywhere in this state. I rinsed my mouth again, replaced my wonderful new outfit with a long flannel nightgown and crawled back into bed. My mother pulled the big feather quilt over my shoulders.

"I'm so cold, *Mutti,*" I complained, shivering.

"I'll be back in a minute," she said. "You stay covered."

I pulled my knees up to my tummy, wrapped my arms around them and lay shivering until she returned with a hot water bottle. *Oh blessed warmth!*

A big bowl and a towel went on the floor just by my head. She placed her palm on my forehead. I relaxed and closed my eyes. *Somebody stop this train from moving. I'm getting dizzy, I'm becoming sick again!* My heaving tummy woke me. I leaned over the bed for the bowl—retching, retching, but nothing came.

"*Mutti!*" I called weakly.

She immediately returned with a glass of water in her hand, put it on the dresser and sat on the chair below the window. Her hand again found my forehead, then she was gone. This time she returned with a wet facecloth and proceeded to wipe my face.

"I'm going to make some camomile tea for you. That should settle your tummy."

That horrible sick feeling in my stomach did not go away—nor did the spinning of the room. It wasn't long before *Mutti* brought a mug of tea.

"Sit up and have a sip," she said, as she picked up my shoulders and tucked some pillows behind my back.

As soon as I became upright, the heaving began again. I fell back on the pillow, exhausted and damp with sweat. My mother spooned the tea into my mouth. It was very hot and very sweet. It tasted like honey. I closed my eyes. *I am back on the train, rocking side to side. My tummy is hurting, and I have to go number two, but I can't find the bathroom on this train.*

The cramps woke me. I knew I had to get up but didn't have the strength. Somehow, my mother had received *this* message without any words. She helped me get there in time. As I relieved myself, the retching began again. Luckily, my mother had brought the bowl. She now held the bowl, held me, and I could hear her murmur, "*Yoi, Istenem. Mit kéne csinálni?* Oh my God, what should I do?"

Off the pot, on the pot. Face in the bowl, out of the bowl. Freezing cold, boiling hot. Fast asleep, faster awake. This went on all day and all night.

***

The next time I opened my eyes, I saw bright lights and grey and white shadows moving around me.

One of the grey shadows spoke. "Hey there, Helen, you're in the hospital and we're going to give you some medicine to make you feel better. This will only hurt a little bit."

I saw the needle and remembered that I was terrified of them. This time, I didn't care about them, I only wanted this wretched feeling to stop.

Everyone and everything faded away.

I am lying on my tummy in a bed when I sense a presence standing near me. I am not afraid; it feels like my Guardian Angel. I feel a hand touching my shoulder and hear a whisper in my ear, "It's going to be alright." A most peaceful feeling comes over me.

"Helen, it's time to wake up," someone said.

When I opened my eyes, I was in a room all by myself. A young woman in white helped me sit up because I was still very shaky. My arm itched and I scratched it. Lumps? Big red welts were all over my arm and hand. Now my tummy itched. I grabbed a fistful of my gown and rubbed it hard against my skin.

The lady held my hands. "Try not to scratch too hard or too much, Helen. We had to give you penicillin, and it seems you are allergic to it. Those bumps are called hives."

She wore a long, white, stiff dress almost to her ankles, over which an even stiffer apron wrapped around her. I tried to make out her name but could only make out "Miss..., R.N." A silly looking hat with a black stripe across the front sat on her head fastened with bobby pins at the back. I remembered that these women were nurses who worked with doctors.

Someday I wanted to be a nurse, but right now I was going mad from the itch. She had said they were hives. My dad had hives. That was where the bees made honey. *I sure hope no bees try to make their home under my skin.*

"I'll bring something to help with the itch," the nurse said. "Meanwhile, Helen, you must be terribly hungry. Would you like some soup?"

Food? I didn't know if I ever wanted to eat again. *I never thought I would ever say that.*

I shook my head.

She smiled. "Well, the doctor thinks it's time for you to start eating. I'll be back in a little while. You stay seated and remember, don't scratch. You don't want scars on that beautiful skin, do you?"

She called me beautiful! That made me feel better, but I knew my hair must be a mess; I didn't remember curling it last night.

The nurse returned with a hot bowl of soup. "This is Campbell's Cream of Mushroom. I hope you like it." She placed the tray on the bed table and rolled it close to me.

It smelled divine, like the musky mushroom smell of the earth in my "Eden". I took my first slurp, closed my eyes and let it swirl around in my mouth. *Every part of my body tasted that soup!* After the first spoonful, I guzzled down the rest. The nurse positioned a basin on my night stand. Did she expect me to throw up again? I felt fine. The thought had barely crossed my mind, when up came the soup! *Please, please, no more!*

I started to cry.

"You're going to be alright now, Helen," the nurse reassured me. "You're not throwing up because of the flu any more. It's because your tummy hasn't had any food for quite some time.

I remained weak and exhausted. I rested on my pillows while the lovely nurse rubbed a chalky pink lotion onto my skin. With the itch relieved, I fell asleep again.

Two days later, after Dr. Book examined me, he said the words I was longing to hear. "Today, after breakfast, you can get dressed and go home, Helen. We'll call your mother and let her know. What do you think of that?" He was the same handsome doctor that had operated on my tonsils last year. I liked him.

Mutti, Dad, Walter and Alice came to pick me up.

Alice gave me a big hug and said, "Oh you poor little girl!"

I don't know why she said that. I was better, and I was going home. My hair needed to be washed. In a dim memory, someone had washed my body with a cloth, but no one had touched my hair. I must look a fright.

It felt good to be home. My parents were being exceptionally kind and would not let me do any chores. My mother let me sleep in, served me lunch on the couch and never said anything unkind to me. I kept waiting for the sky to fall, but it did not.

I came home on a Thursday but wasn't allowed back to school until the following Monday. I was getting a bit worried about missing too much school work. *How much could they cover in five days?*

On Monday, the Bombardier stopped in front of the house, and I climbed in, still a little weak and weary. Seeing all my friends perked me up, but everyone seemed to be staring at me. Once in class, Mrs. Ermel made it a point to welcome me back. Again, everyone looked at me like I was a stranger. Before I left for the lunch room, Mrs. Ermel said she needed to talk to me. *What is wrong? Oh please, I'm not up to getting heck!*

She pulled an extra chair by her desk, and we sat facing each other. She leaned towards me and in her kind, soft voice said, "You have missed quite a bit of work, Helen. I know you can't stay after school because you have to catch your bus. I thought perhaps I can help you go over some of the lessons you missed and help you get caught up during the lunch hours ahead."

I was grateful that she was willing to help me because I did not want to fall too far behind the class.

"Thank you Mrs. Ermel, I would like that.

She now seemed to be studying me with a worried expression on her face. She had been very kind and understanding about the "DP" issue, so I decided I would ask her what was on my mind.

"Why is everyone looking at me as if they don't know me. What is going on?"

"My dear girl, you don't know, do you?"

Know what?

"You have been a very sick little girl," she started.

I certainly know that!

She continued as gentle as ever."You had gastroenteritis, and it has certainly been hard on you."

I don't know what gas-to-bite-us is, but I do know it had been downright awful.

"Have you had a chance to look in the mirror?

"My mother has been dressing me and doing my hair the best she could." *Wow! I'm actually defending my mother! No, I haven't looked in the mirror.*

"Well, sweetie, you've lost so much weight that we barely recognized you when you entered the classroom. That is why everyone is staring at you."

"But I've only been gone for five days." *How much can a person change in five days?*

"Oh, my poor girl." Mrs. Ermel shook her head.

That's what Alice had said when she saw me at the hospital.

Mrs. Ermel took my hands into hers. "You haven't been gone for just five days. You've been in the hospital for almost *two weeks!* I guess you don't remember much, do you?"

Two weeks? I must really look a mess if no one recognizes me.

Mrs. Ermel pulled me towards her and hugged me. As she did, she whispered in my ear, "Don't you worry Helen. Everything will be alright."

That also sounds familiar.

We made a plan to meet every lunch hour until I was caught up. *God bless Mrs. Ermel!*

Meanwhile, I needed to find a mirror. I found one in the girl's bathroom and studied my reflection. *Unbelievable! Who the heck is this?* Where were my "chipmunk cheeks" as Ethel called them. All I saw were hollow cheek bones and pasty white skin. But it was my eyes that frightened me most—sunken with dark circles beneath, like a scary ghost. No wonder everyone stared at me.

At home, the special treatment continued, but I had overheard something that bothered me. *Mutti* had been talking to someone on the phone in Hungarian. Perhaps she had forgotten that I now understood it quite well and, therefore, made no attempt to hide her conversation.

The person on the other end must have asked her about my stay in the hospital. I heard my mother respond that I was home and doing fine, but there was a time when they didn't think I would make it.

What? Is that why my Guardian Angel had come and reassured me, "It's going to be alright?"

Bum Steer

Spring—1957

I had heard of Old King Cole who was a merry old soul from a Christmas carol. At first I thought his name was Old King Cold and figured that the name perfectly matched the chill of winter. This year, the King was not a merry old soul at all and had a cold, wicked heart. With his steel blue eyes below his furrowed frosty brows, he sat upon his frigid throne and blew his icy breath across his kingdom. As he stroked his icicled beard, he ordered the castle door to be sealed tight against the coming of Spring.

But one day in March, the beautiful Spring pried the door ajar just enough to allow her tantalizing balmy weather through. I wanted to throw away my boots and mitts, but Old King Cold slammed the door shut again, not to be opened until the beginning of May. I needed that extra time anyway to get stronger and catch up on all the school work.

No matter the weather, the stork arrived on time and babies had been dropped off everywhere. I wanted to be back in the barn to congratulate all the new mother cows, hens, cats and one pig on their beautiful babies but was not yet allowed out. From my window, I watched as the baby robins, sparrows and blue jays ruffled their feathers and flapped their wings, demanding their parents to feed them.

My mother fed me *my* favourites also—egg salad sandwiches with Campbell's cream of mushroom soup; I had told her how much I had enjoyed it at the hospital. A casserole of noodles, mashed potatoes and onions, topped with sour cream, was another of my favourites. I could not believe the change in her. *It is wonderful, but how long will this last?*

Sure enough, once spring arrived and I had begun to gain weight and grow stronger, the spoiling stopped and her nagging resumed. It was time to get out of the house to do my chores. I returned to teach the calves to drink from a pail. One particular Hereford calf with the cutest white face, long white eyelashes and big dark eyes stole my heart. He caught on quickly to suckling my fingers and soon was drinking on his own.

Meanwhile, I still daydreamed and night-dreamed about horses. I wanted to ride horses. No, I *needed* to ride horses! Neither parent would ever allow me to ride Jolan or Gitzka. Besides, these huge beasts didn't resemble the fleet-footed beauties in my dreams. In my dreams, they were delicate, graceful, doe-eyed creatures whose tiny hooves barely touched the ground. I only needed to cling to their long manes while they carried me through sun-splashed glens and deep, dark forests.

When will I ever be able to ride a horse? Likely never. But, maybe, maybe I could train this little calf?

The calf certainly did not resemble the sleek creature of my dreams, but I had learned that you make do with what you have. It sounded like an exciting and achievable plan since the calf was still young and small enough to be handled and trained. However, it had to be done without the knowledge of my parents.

For the next few days, I thought long and hard how to turn this calf into a horse. I knew I couldn't just jump on its back and ride away. That would be foolish for both our sakes. First, I needed to assure him that I meant no harm. As soon as the calves were released into the corral, I hung around him every chance I had until he no longer ran away whenever I neared him. Then came the first contact—stroking his back with my hand. At the beginning, he bolted, but that, too, was soon ignored. The final stage involved pulling myself up across his back on my stomach. He trotted around, but I stayed on him as long as I could.

After a while, even my weight did not bother him.

Through all these actions, I think my parents either didn't see me or thought I was only playing with the animal. If they would have known my real intent, I don't know what they would have done, but I wasn't going to chance it. By the time his training was over, this calf had joined the rest of the cattle in the pasture, and that was where I would finalized my plan. As usual, it was my job to bring the cows home for milking, but this time instead of walking, I wanted to ride home. I found the calf at the back of the herd, approached it and pulled myself onto his back. I sat there with my legs curled under his small belly.

Oh my goodness! He's not bucking me off!

With absolutely no concern, he followed the rest of the herd home. I, however, dismounted as we neared the yard. I had done it—become a horsewoman! I don't know why I *needed* to ride, or how I knew how to train that calf, I just did. I was happy as a pig rolling in mud. Each time after that, I would ride him home. Because he always lagged behind the rest of the herd, I was able to keep an eye on the cows ahead. He was such a slow poke that I named him "SoJo" after a story about a lazy boy. "Slow" Jo would have been more fitting.

***

As SoJo grew, he became taller and his back became broader. Even though he had become a steer, he remained gentle and slow, so I continued to ride him each time I went for the cows. One cloudy day, on our way home with me on SoJo's back and Coalie running alongside, it began to rain lightly. I no longer feared getting wet and neither did the cattle, though by now, it had begun to come down hard. The heavy rain made ghosts of the cows ahead, but I knew they had a good sense of direction. Sojo's back became slicker and slicker, and because he had grown considerably, I could no longer wrap my legs around his belly for support. It was like sliding around on a wet moving table.

The sky rumbled, the cows stumbled and I grumbled. A streak of lightning was followed by another roll of thunder. The herd began a slow trot, and SoJo followed. I closed my eyes and imagined myself riding through the "sun splashed glen" and the "deep dark forest" of my dreams. Another bolt of lightning and a crack of thunder, even closer than the last, shook me back to reality. I opened my eyes to find myself atop a steer in the midst of a full blown stampede! I had no saddle, no stirrups and no reins to stop this animal in a full gallop. SoJo didn't even have a mane to grab unto. One bounce…two bounce…no bounce!

A whimper and something warm on my face—Coalie. I found myself flat on my back in the mud, gasping for air with the rain pouring into my eyes, nose and mouth.

Am I dead? Can't be. I can feel, smell and taste the rain.

Slowly I stood up, wobbled for a second trying to remember how I arrived there and what had happened. I checked for any pain that might indicate injury. Nothing seemed to be damaged but my pride. I had considered myself an accomplished rider and a classy horsewoman. Now I felt and looked more like the simple country bumpkin that I really was. I looked around. The herd and SoJo were gone. Even those dumb cows knew not to be in an open field in the middle of a lightning storm. Coalie was still at my side whimpering. We were both drenched, muddy and getting cold. I hugged his neck and whimpered back, "I'm alright, Coalie, but we need to get out of here."

The rain still poured down, the thunder still rolled and my skin tingled. I removed my shoes and ran full tilt. The heck with thistles, the heck with stubble, I had to get out of this storm. Coalie agreed, and together we hoofed it home.

The cows were already in the barn. SoJo stood beside the granary chewing his cud, totally unaware of his part in this misadventure. He merely considered me a fly on his back. It wasn't his fault. I didn't go into the barn as I usually do but went straight to the house. *Mutti* was just on her way to the barn when I reached the screen door. She took one look at me, shook her head and said, "You look like a drowned rat. Don't get any of that mud in the house! Change, then come to the barn."

I began to shake. Was it from being wet or from delayed fright? As the scene now replayed itself in my mind, I realized how lucky I had been. If SoJo had not fallen behind, I could have been trampled. My fall from him could have resulted in a serious injury or even a broken neck. I could have been hit by lightning. But none of these happened—all due to the work of my incredible Guardian Angel.

Thank you for saving my life! Again!

Inside the porch, I removed my dirty wet clothes and threw them on the bench outside the door. When I glanced into the mirror above the washstand, I laughed. I *did* look like a drowned rat. My hair, flat against my scalp, dripped rivulets of brown water down my body. It would have been easier to just step outside into the rain, and let it rinse me off. Or better still, plunge into the rain barrel up to my neck. Instead, I chose a basin filled with hot water from the stove reservoir and a facecloth. It felt soothing and warm! As I cleaned up and warmed up, I thought about how I would explain my condition to my mother if she asked. With no visible signs of injury, I could simply say I fell in the slippery mud.

It wasn't a lie. I did fall in the mud. *Neither SoJo nor Coalie would ever tell on me.*

This accident in no way changed my mind about riding the steer again. I simply had to learn when it was safe to be on his back and when it was not—like during a storm.

Perhaps, I should give myself the same advice regarding my mother. I have to learn when to argue with her and when to back off. *Or, I might find myself flying through the air and landing in the mud.*

Dad had learned, that for the sake of peace, it was easier to back off than to fight. I hadn't learned that yet, but I would now. All this, I learned from a bum steer in a field!

The Best Of Companions

Early Summer—1957

Whenever the weather allowed, I went to Mary Ann's place. We discussed how we wanted to spend the summer. We could play store, school or house with our dolls, but it was the sloughs with all its creatures that were the most exciting places for us. We looked for twigs that walked under water, and we discovered them to be beetles that had twigs and grass stuck on their backs for disguise. Other beetles skated across on top of the water, dimpling the surface without breaking through.

We also discovered tadpoles which I knew would become frogs because I had read it in my *Children's Digest* magazine. I would catch them in my palm so that Mary Ann and I could study them as their legs grew and their tails shortened. In the spring, their parents had filled the night air with their shrill voices. Their loud partying had interfered with my sleep. *There ought to be a law against noisy neighbours!*

Every time we neared the edge of any sloughs, we couldn't resist skipping rocks across its surface. Both of us became better and better at finding the right shaped stone and increasing the number of skips. The sloughs turned out to be a constant source of adventure and joy if I disregarded the one with my unfortunate raft.

We never seemed bored. We made mud pies, gathered interesting coloured rocks, or picked the wild flowers. Sometimes we gave the flowers to our mothers. Other times, we braided dandelions into golden crowns and pretended we were princesses. If all else failed, we could always turn over dried cow patties and watch little silver lizards as they scampered away.

All those activities made us thirsty, so we would ask Doraphine to make us a drink from the sweet orange syrup that she had bought from the Watkins salesmen. Today, we chatted and giggled as we quenched our thirst. I didn't tell Mary Ann my big secret—that I had become a horsewoman. She wouldn't have understood my desire to ride a horse, but mostly, I was concerned about it getting back to my mother.

Mary Ann's mom, Doraphine, soon joined us. She wasn't her joyful, laughing self today. I soon learned why.

"Did you know we are moving into Regina, Helen?" she blurted out.

"What? Why? When?"

"Joe has had trouble with his lungs from the war," she told me."We think it would be better for him to get away from the dust on the farm. He will probably be able to find a good job in the city."

"But I will miss you all terribly!"

"Mary Ann will be starting school this fall. It is best she start in Regina." Doraphine looked relieved now that this news was out.

Mary Ann didn't look like she understood the full impact of this conversation, but I did. I wanted to cry.

"You must come and visit us in the city once we are settled," Doraphine added. "Maybe we'll celebrate your birthdays together again in August. What do you say to that?"

"Yes, and maybe Mary Ann can stay at our farm for a while." I offered, not even thinking that perhaps my mother would not approve.

"We'll see, Helen. Meanwhile I'll speak to your mother about your birthday parties, Okay?"

Yes, yes, but I don't see how I will ever manage without you both?

***

After that, Mary Ann and I tried to spend as much time together as we could, but eventually the day came for her to leave. We all hugged and cried. I still didn't know if Mary Ann understood any of it, but since Doraphine and I cried, she did too.

With my best friend gone, I had to go back to playing with my imaginary ones chosen from heroes on the radio, comics and books. The Lone Ranger became the one I was most familiar with since I listened to his program every day after school before chores. The musical theme reminded me of running horses, and soon I had became hooked on all the characters. Whenever I jumped on SoJo's back, I would shout, "Hi-Yo, Silver! Away!" If SoJo only knew that I considered him to be a beautiful white horse called Silver, he would have been proud!

When I wanted to play Lone Ranger in the yard, an old broom served as my horse. I cut out my own mask and wore an old hat and shirt of Dad's. The finishing touch was a gun fashioned from wood with my pant belt as my holster. "Tonto" was invisible, but Coalie became "Bullet". I knew that Bullet was Roy Rogers' dog and not the Lone Ranger's, but in my world of make believe, anything was possible.

When my chores were done, I had the rest of my day with the best of companions—me. Me and my imagination, that is.

"Kemo Sabe, we hunt down cattle rustlers, yes?" Tonto would ask me.

"Yes, Tonto. Thieves are bad people and they must be punished. Find some tracks that we could follow, my friend." I waved my hat in a circle above my head, jumped over the broom handle and yelled, "Hi-Yo Silver! Away!" We galloped off in hot pursuit. If anyone had come into our yard at just that moment, I'm sure they would have asked, "Who was that masked man?"

When I tired of being the Lone Ranger, or when it became too hot to ride across the parched desert, I took on the role of Lorna, the Jungle Queen, a girl version of Tarzan. My game was played under the cool shade of our shelter belt within earshot of my mother's call. I built a tree stand out of a discarded small door and braced it across two sturdy limbs about six feet from the ground. Secured it with nails and rope, it was just large enough that I could lie down on it with my legs dangling over the side. I also attached a knotted rope from another limb. As I swung from the "vine", I gave a hearty Tarzan yell that made all the evil creatures of this jungle tremble in their hearts.

My imaginary friends were fun and extremely kind to me. They always let me have my say and my way, but I missed Mary Ann and longed for August.

stormy weather

Stormy Weather

Summer—1957

July came with a fiery desire to cook us all. Every day seemed to be hotter than the day before. Everything and everyone drooped. Our feeble attempts at keeping cool proved fruitless. We had heard on the radio that the temperature would be a screaming 92° Fahrenheit. As soon as we got out of bed the following morning, we armed ourselves against the coming heat. We closed all the windows and covered them with heavy blankets or sheets. The inner door to the house that was usually open, was shut tightly. Along with that came a warning from my mother.

"Makc up your mind whcther you'rc in or out. Don't bc waltzing through the door every minute!"

We all left the house at the same time to do chores and came back together, making sure the inner door closed behind us again. For breakfast, I had Kellogg's Cornflakes with milk, while Dad and *Mutti* had bread with raw smoked bacon. Dad and I fought over the rind. No fire was made in the stove for cooking or baking—giving my mother a well-deserved break. We spent the morning indoors where it was already becoming warm. For lunch my parents had the thickly sliced head cheese we had prepared in the fall. I only wanted some bread, butter and my favourite plum jam—sweet, yet tarty.

By this time, it was getting hotter and hotter in the house, so I decided I would try to catch a breeze outside. As I slammed through the screen door I heard my mother scream, "Don't go out now, it's the hottest time of the day!"

I didn't listen. The moment I stepped outside, I knew she had been right, but I wasn't going to admit that. I would just spend some time with Coalie, but where was he anyway? Usually he would be by my side by now.

"Here, Coalie, Coalie." I heard him barking from the corral north of the barn, so I went to look for him. I was only halfway there when he came bounding up to me—soggy and smelling awful. He must have been in the slough and now decided that I, too, should be cool by shaking himself all over me.

"Yikes Coalie, you silly dog. You're making me all wet." *Hey, just a minute here. That feels nice!*

"Great idea, Coalie. Let's go swimming," I said, even though I didn't know how to swim.

We arrived at the edge of the slough. I looked at that inviting water and remembered my "Huck Finn" misadventure. *I will have to be careful. I can't expect my Guardian Angel to come to my rescue every time I make a stupid move.*

I waded in slowly; Coalie dove in full force and began to paddle around me. Now where did he learn to do that? I certainly never taught him. *I wonder if he can teach me.*

The water was warm at the edge but became cooler the deeper I went. My feet sunk into the soft silty bottom, and I could feel mushy plants between my toes. Something skittered and slithered around my legs. I imagined all sorts of hideous monsters ready to drag me into their deep watery lair.

Stop it, Helen, you're almost twelve years old. You've been reading too many fairy tales! Monsters don't exist.

I continued to wade in only as far as my waist and remained there for a while trying not to think what lurked beneath this murky water. *There, see, nothing is happening.*

I lowered myself until the water reached my neck but made sure my feet were planted firmly on the bottom. Eventually the water no longer felt cold, so I retreated, and Coalie followed my lead. For the first time today, I felt refreshed and comfortable.

I decided to get under the shade of the shelter belt. By the time we arrived there, my shorts, top, Coalie and I were completely dry. We plunked ourselves down on the cool grass and panted. On my back, I peeked through the trees at the cloudless white sky. Not a single leaf stirred. Despite the shade, the heat was making me more and more uncomfortable. It was time to get back in the house. As soon as I stepped out of the shade, I felt the sun prickling my skin and broiling my brain. Relief seemed so far away.

I slowly and quietly opened the outer screen door, then the inner door, and I was just turning around to close it gently, when my mother appeared. *Did she have ears at the back of her head?*

"I told you it was too hot out!" she gloated. Then her face screwed up as her voice rose "You smell like a rotten fish! Honestly child, I don't know what you do out there, but you're always coming into the house dirty. Change and throw those stinky clothes outside."

Stinky? I just finished washing in the slough, but now that she mentioned it, I did smell a bit swampy. Then I realized that the slough was not a pool of fresh rain water, but it was also a watering hole for the animals who often did more than just drink from it. Phooey!

I remained in the house until it was time to get the cows. It was still a scorcher, but chores had to be done come hell or high temperatures. At least the well was on our way to the cows, and Coalie and I would be able have a nice cold drink from it before we headed out.

Once there, I opened the lid and looked down its deep dark depth. A rush of cold air escaped. On a rope, hung a pail containing some butter and cream. We often put food down the well to keep it cold and fresh in the summer. I closed the lid quickly; its depth made me dizzy.

I grabbed the smaller pail from the ridge at the end of the spout and pumped hard and fast as I had seen Dad do it. This was going to be more difficult than I had thought. I broke into a sweat after three pumps. As the cold water finally gushed into the pail, I noticed that the outside of the pail was also sweating. *I wonder what causes that?*

I poured some water into the cattle trough by the well for Coalie who lapped it up while I took a deep long drink directly from the pail. That was the best water in the world—icy cold, clear and wet! What more could a person need? Maybe a little water on the outside? There was a bit left in the pail, so I splashed it on myself and the last little bit on Coalie. He took off running.

Fool! Don't run in this heat!

By the time the chores were done, I was sweating like a pig. No, no! Pigs don't sweat—it was horses that did. At least that what Dad had told me. I was looking forward to supper because I knew it would be something cold. This time, *Mutti* opened a can of jellied pig's feet that we had canned last fall. The cold meat and jelly were delicious as they slid down my parched throat. For the rest of the evening, we all reeked of garlic.

Dad also opened a can of sardines, and as usual, coaxed me to have some. "Here, Helen, have one. They're so good!"

One look at those tiny whole fish packed and glistening in oil with their big eyes staring at me was enough to make me shudder. I had smelled enough of them from the lunches on the school bus. Dad laughed, I shuddered again. Alongside the pork and sardines, we had cut-up fresh green onions, radishes and green peppers. Pickles, bread and butter completed this cold meal.

Even after the sun went down, the heat did not. Dad sat by the radio listening for the forecast for tomorrow. It would be the same. Once I was in bed, my mother handed me a wet facecloth to cool me off. That did help a bit, but I still couldn't fall asleep for quite some time.

As we lay drenched in our beds, I could hear Dad in the next bed talking to *Mutti.* "This high heat is going to bring bad weather. You'll see."

***

Sure enough a few days later, dark clouds gathered in the west. As they neared, they turned a pale green. The temperature dropped; the wind rose. I had been looking out the south window of our living room when I caught chickens flying by six feet above the ground. *I didn't know they could fly that high and that fast!*

The wind lashed all sorts junk across the yard—tools, rags, cans, branches and gravel. I sure hoped Coalie had found a safe spot. Then the rain came. It was similar to that day in the field when the cows had stampeded. It hammered down so hard and so heavy that all I could see was a film of grey. A deafening crack and a distant flash of light, followed by thunder, shook the house. My skin prickled. That was close!

I heard my mother's high-pitched terrified voice in the kitchen. "*Yoi, Istenem, segits minket!* My God, help us!"

I joined her there just as a drenched Dad entered the house. Thank goodness, because right after that, I heard a light *thump, thump* starting on the roof. Before long, the individual thumps became indistinguishable, and a low, deafening thrumming took its place. I saw my mother scream but did not hear her. I watched the kitchen window shatter but did not hear it. Big, egg-sized hail pounded the table. Dad had grabbed the coal oil glass lamp on the table near that window and moved it to the cupboard. Meanwhile, my mother had moved to the farthest corner of the kitchen and cowered there with her eyes wide and her hands clasped in prayer.

Water and hail continued to stream through the broken window. Dad looked towards my mother, but she had covered her face with her hands. He came to me and shouted directly into my ear, "Get some pillows and towels."

I dashed into the bedroom, grabbed the pillows from their bed, found some towels and rushed back. Dad had meanwhile moved the table away from the window. He now took one of the pillows from me and stuffed it into the open hole in the window pane. That was all that was needed to keep the rain and hail out. I used the towels to mop up the water and melting ice and looked around for *Mutti* to help me. She had vanished.

I could hear her muttering in the bedroom. A few moments later, she returned to the kitchen carrying three rosaries. We each took our own, and as the wind howled and the hail drummed, we went down on our knees on the kitchen floor and recited the rosary. She had done this before whenever there had been a storm. This time, however, she acted more frightened and frantic. Every time the thunder rolled and the lightning struck, she screamed, then ducked as she knelt on the floor. I hadn't been afraid, but now I, too, became scared.

Dad must have noticed that and shouted through the noise, "It'll be alright. If it turns into a tornado, we can go into the cellar. We'll be safe there." He gave me a slight smile, but immediately after, I saw his jaw set firm.

In the end, we did not have to use the cellar, but that day, I had been more frightened in that house than I had been in the open field in the storm riding SoJo.

When the storm passed, we went out to check the damage. All the buildings remained standing, though shingles had been ripped off. Trees were shredded but not uprooted. We did find some dead chickens but only a few. The pigs survived. We wouldn't how the cows fared until we brought them in for milking. My biggest concern was Coalie. When I had been on my knees in the kitchen, I was mostly praying for him. He had found shelter and was just fine.

The garden fared the worst. The hail had smashed all the leaves off the plants and ice still covered a large portion of the ground.

"Are we going to have to plant them all again?" I asked Dad.

"No, most of them will recover, maybe not the lettuce, but the root vegetables will be fine."

Several days later, after I had recovered from my fright, I began to think about that storm. It was interesting to discover that my mother had actually shown fear. I had never seen her afraid of anything or anyone before. I had to approach her and ask, "Why were you so afraid of the thunderstorm?"

She hesitated before she replied. "You don't understand because you didn't experience it. But that thunder and lightning sound exactly like the bombs falling and exploding!"

I had forgotten that she had lived through the bombing of Linz. I also realized that my mother was just like that force of nature. Once she began her outbursts and rage, there was no stopping her. Can anyone stop a tornado? No, you just find a safe place to hide until it is over. Then come out and inspect the damage, start up and carry on. Can anyone bargain with Mother Nature? Well, no one could make a deal with my mother either. The more you tried, the more angry and stubborn she became. Her storms were becoming more frequent and more terrifying. No one was safe.

Fairy Godmother

Summer—1957

I only saw my brother Bill when Dad needed help, like the day of the butchering. Most of the time, he came and went without my knowledge. But during the seeding and harvesting, he would also stay on the farm. He had been the one to inform me about which crops he and Dad seeded and how they were used. He explained that wheat, barley and oats were our main crops, and that oats fed the horses, while barley was crushed for chop and given to the cows and pigs. Wheat was sold on the market for income. I was interested in that information, but I tuned out when he went into details about the Harvester International W-6 tractor that they used. That was the extent of all I knew about what Dad and Bill did in the fields.

Although my interest in the details of the crop production was less than enthusiastic, I did play a very important role. I was their runner—running out to them in the field hauling water, lunch or whatever was required. During the planting and harvesting times, neither Dad or Bill participated in any other chores in the farmyard. Those all fell to my mother and me.

I began to realize that Bill had some sort of influence on my mother. When he was in the house, he did a lot of talking, joking and teasing. Usually she did not like that kind of foolishness, but she didn't mind Bill's. Was it because he was tall and handsome? She had often told me she liked tall, handsome men. Or did he remind her of Ziggy from Linz whom she adored? Whatever the reason, I was happy to have someone around who could make *Mutti* laugh. She never had any of her storms when Bill was there.

I even I fell for his flattery, his easy manner and his handsome smile, but he was always getting the best of me with his pranks. One spring morning, I stood at the kitchen window, as usual, watching for the school bus coming from the east. He snuck up behind me and bent his six foot frame until we were cheek to cheek.

"Whatcha lookin' at?" he asked, rubbing his stubbly chin against my face.

I screeched and pulled away.

"The bus, when I see it top the hill at Kallichuk's house, I know I have just enough time to run to the road to catch it." My senses were alert for any possible prank.

He grinned. "Did you know that there used to be a family by the name of Fefchuk who lived in Walter and Alice's house?"

I looked directly into his big blue eyes. *Is he lying? I can't tell, but he isn't going to fool me this time!*

"I don't believe you. That name sounds silly, too much like you made it up."

"No, honestly, it's true!"

"No way!" I replied, laughing at him as I rushed out the door to catch my bus. *I'm going to remember that name so you won't be able to fool me again with it, Bill. I'm getting too smart for you.*

A few weeks later, my mother and I had gone into Cupar. I was coming out of the restaurant and saw *Mutti* chatting with a woman on the sidewalk. She waved me over and when I reached her, she said, "Heli, say hello to Mrs. Fefchuk. She used to live where—"

I didn't let her finish. I started laughing and pointing at her. "Oh *Mutti*, you know there are no such people as the Fefchucks. Bill has fooled you too."

My mother looked horrified. "What are you talking about? Of

course there is, and you better apologize to Mrs. Fefchuk."

Oh my God! There really is a Mrs. Fefchuk! I apologized over and over again, blushing and stammering, trying to explain that Bill had played a trick on me.

Mrs. Fefchuk just shook her head, laughed and said, "*Az bolond Magyar*, that crazy Hungarian!"

That darn Bill had gotten the best of me again without even knowing it. Or had he?

***

On some of the weekends that Bill spent at our farm, he also brought his girlfriend, Pauline. She was a rather short, chubby woman with a very round face—actually round all over. My mother got along well with her. It helped that she spoke Hungarian and that she happened to belong to Bill.

Pauline had been eager to please my mother. It wasn't *what* she did that pleased her, it was the fact that she *wanted* to please her. Yet, one day after they left, I heard my mother's mind speak out loud. "What is a good looking man like that doing with such an ugly looking woman?"

Oye! I thought she liked her, but I was discovering something new about my mother. She did not like women. Never had I heard her say anything nice about *any* woman, no matter if that person was kind or smart. She only respected people who were either good looking or rich, and then it was best if they were men. Around them, she acted extremely well-behaved and gracious.

Because Pauline got along so well with my mother, I could not trust her. She began to come out to the farm more and more often with Bill, and each time she would bring something nice for *Mutti* and me. I had always been a sucker for bribes, so I wasn't surprised when soon I began to warm up to her.

Now, she was out again and sitting with my mother finishing their coffee at the kitchen table. We had finished lunch, and I was wiping the last cup and hanging it on one of the hooks under the top cupboard.

Mutti and Pauline seemed to be in an earnest conversation—all in Hungarian. I knew it was rude to listen in, but after hearing my name being mentioned more than once, my ears perked up. Their discussion had to do something with my upcoming Confirmation.

I couldn't stand it any longer. "Why are you talking about me? Did I do something wrong?"

Pauline said something to my mother then spoke to me in English. "Put away that dishtowel and come sit here with us. We have something important to talk about."

I sat down between them, my mother to the left and Pauline on the right. I studied my mother's face to get some sort of indication of what was to come, but she appeared calm as she leaned back in her chair. No evidence of any storm clouds. So far, so good.

I felt Pauline touch my hand, so I turned to her. She was smiling broadly when she said, "You know that you will be Confirmed soon at the church."

"Yes, I still don't know what Confirmation is, but yes I will be," I replied. *Why is she so excited about it?*

"Well, everyone who is Confirmed needs someone to stand up for them. They are called godparents. Your mother has just asked me to be your godmother. How would you like that?" Her eyes went wide with excitement as she squeezed my hand.

"What does 'stand up for' mean?" I asked.

"It means that, God forbid, something should happen to your parents, Bill and I will take care of you." Her smile grew wider and wider. She had lovely teeth. "Would you like that?"

Why didn't my mother ask me about who *I* would like to care for me? My choice would have been either Ethel or Big Helen. But Ethel, according to my mother, was not a worthy Christian because she had married outside the Catholic Church! Big Helen, on the other hand, was even more evil with a husband like Frank. For reasons I still did not understand, he was apparently the devil himself. I guess that left Pauline.

My whirling mind was interrupted by my mother's voice. "Answer her, Heli."

The only godmothers I had ever heard of were the ones in my fairy tale books. They had always been kind and generous in the stories. I assumed Pauline would be too, so I said, "Yes."

Pauline jumped from her chair and hugged me. "You will have to come to Regina and stay with me for a while. We can go shopping for your dress. Then there's the veil and shoes. Oh, I can hardly wait. Aren't you excited?" Before I knew what was happening, she had planted a big wet kiss on my lips. *Yech!*

I smiled, hugged her back and said, "Yes."

Mutti had burned all my other bridges!

***

Before long, I found myself in Bill and Pauline's tiny one-bedroom apartment in Regina. It felt even tinier because all the walls, shelves and tables were crammed with nicknacks. *I'm sure glad I don't have to do the dusting here.*

As soon as Pauline had time, we rode the bus to the Eaton's store to find an outfit for my Confirmation. This store was definitely larger than Harry's in Cupar. I had never seen so much merchandise in one building—floor, after floor, after floor. As we entered the elevator, a uniformed, white-gloved young man asked us what particular items we were seeking, then he pressed the correct floor button where this article could be found. A few moments later, the door flew open, and he called out, "Fifth floor! Children's apparel and shoes. Watch you step, please."

Shopping with Pauline turned out to be great fun. She would find a dress, bring my attention to it, then ask if I liked it. I was grateful that my mother had not come with us. She would not have given me any choices. We finally found one made of sheer flowing material, plain but still elegant. However, its short sleeves went against the rule of the church—no bare arms. Fabric had to be added from the bottom of the short sleeves to my wrists. It worked and looked great. Then came a gorgeous veil. I gasped at my reflection in the mirror. I looked like a bride and said so.

"You *are* a bride, Helen. A bride of Christ," Pauline replied.

That's weird. According to *Mutti,* I was only allowed to marry a Hungarian and a Catholic. These grown-ups, they say one thing and do another. Grown-ups indeed, more like g-r-o-a-n ups!

On the same floor but a different department, we found a pair of crisp white shoes and socks. Now I was outfitted from head to toe.

"One more thing, Helen, we need to find a white purse. It will be my gift to you for letting me be your godmother." She decided on a lovely, small, box-shaped purse with a delicate gold handle. It was so different; I loved it. I thanked her with a big hug and kiss on her cheek, but I turned quickly before she could plant another wet kiss me on my lips again.

"It's almost time for lunch. There is a cafeteria on the top floor. Would you like to eat here?" Pauline asked.

Yes, yes, yes! It was always exciting to eat out. We were waiting to catch the elevator to the cafeteria when the most impossible thing happened. My nose picked up a familiar scent that I didn't recognize right away. But as it became stronger, my heart started racing. It was the same soapy scent that I associated with *Mutter*, my foster mother in Austria!

Is she here? She can't be!

I almost unscrewed my head as I craned my neck trying to find the source of the scent. There! Right behind us—a woman in a long dark dress with her hair tied in triangular scarf. Walking beside her was a tall, thin bearded man in black. I heard the unmistakable sound of a few German words but couldn't quite make out their meaning. I couldn't breathe! Tears began to well in my eyes as I watched them walk past. I had to fight the urge to run and fling myself upon them.

I tugged on Pauline's sleeve with urgency and demanded, "Who are those people? They look and smell like my foster parents in Austria."

"They're Hutterites, Helen, but that's all I know. Are you alright? You look like you're going to faint."

My heart pounded, I began to shake. I heard a wailing—it was coming from me! I couldn't stop it, this heavy feeling in my chest. I had to let it out.

Pauline pulled me away from the elevators, handed me her hanky and patted my shoulders. "I don't understand, Helen. Are you afraid of them? They won't harm you."

I tried to talk but couldn't. I just kept sobbing, gulping for air.

"Let's go to the washroom," she suggested as she led me away. Once in the bathroom, she continued. "Okay Sweetie, try to calm down. We'll talk about this later. Wash your face with some cold water. It will make you feel better."

As I was drying my hands and face, Pauline chatted on about what lovely foods Eaton's offered in the cafeteria. I calmed down but was totally bewildered. I didn't know what had happened, but I did not want to visit that feeling again, so I concentrated on Pauline's menu suggestions.

As we entered the cafeteria, the aroma of the food soon masked the earlier scent in my brain. A hot dog with onions and relish, plus fried chips with ketchup soon soothed my tummy and my aching heart. A glass of 7-up replenished the liquids lost. The raisin pie with ice cream, which I shared with Pauline, also helped. By the time we reached the apartment with all our packages, I was myself again.

The following morning, I returned from the bathroom down the hallway outside the apartment. Pauline poured milk into a bowl of Cheerios, a lovely change from the cornflakes I always had at home, and I gobbled it down.

Pauline took the empty bowl to the sink, turned and asked, "Would you like anything else for breakfast, Helen. Maybe you'd like a square of Puffed Wheat Cake?"

I loved that chewy brown cake made with puffed wheat cereal, syrup and cocoa. I accepted. As I pulled each individual puffed wheat kernel from its sticky neighbour and popped it in my mouth, Pauline sat beside me at the table with a cup of coffee.

"Maybe we can talk a little about what had happened yesterday,

Helen. We don't have to unless you want to."

I was really beginning to like her. She always asked for my opinion and respected my choices—unlike my mother. She was also extremely generous with hugs and gifts. *Maybe she will make a good fairy godmother, I mean godmother.*

I nodded. I, too, wanted to find out what had happened and why.

"Yesterday, you said something about those Hutterites who had looked and smelled like your foster parents. Can you tell me a little about that?"

I explained, as best I could, how I had originally thought that my foster parents were my real parents and how *Mutti* had taken me away from them. I told her how I had been alright with that because she had always let me see them in the summer. But then, when we were ready to leave Austria, I had no chance to say a proper goodbye to them. I had felt really bad about that, but what had made matters worse, was that I could not even write them to explain. They must have thought that I had not loved them enough to do either of those things.

"I feel so guilty, and I miss them so much still. I hate *Mutti* for losing their address." The same rush of emotions returned.

"I guess that smell let out all these feelings still inside you." Pauline reached across the table and squeezed my sticky hands. There were tears in her eyes.

That did it! All the rage towards my mother erupted. I blurted out all the bad things that my mother had ever done to me, everything that she hadn't done, and everything I wished she would do. When finished, I was exhausted but felt lighter. Pauline listened and never interrupted. When I stopped talking, she hugged me and said, "I know how you feel, Helen."

"How can you know? Did you have a mother like mine?" I asked.

"No, my mother was nothing like yours," she replied "But mine did not have the time for me. There were too many of us.

"Well, my mother only has me, and I know that she has the time," I spat out. "She just doesn't like me or love me, that's all.

Pauline shook her head, took my hand in hers, and, with the other, turned my chin to her face. "I'm sure your mother loves you, Helen. Think about it. She protects you, feeds you, clothes you. She had enough courage to bring you to Canada so that you could have a better life. Maybe, in her mind, and her time, that is all that was required of good mothers, and she may think that she's doing a great job."

"But she's not!" I complained. "I wish she would praise me when I'm doing a good job or encourage me when I don't. I wish she would hug me and tell me she loves me like everyone else does. I wish she wouldn't yell at me for days on end for things I didn't even do."

Pauline looked at me sadly. "Sometimes, for whatever reasons, people can't love us the way we want them to." She gave me another big hug, let go and turned away. I heard her murmur, "Sometimes, Bill doesn't love me the way I want him to."

Confirmation

July—1957

Before I could be Confirmed, I needed more than just a dress, veil and shoes. I needed catechism at the Holy Trinity Hungarian Church. Again, I would have to stay at Big Helen and Frank's farm where I had stayed for my First Holy Communion.

But will Helen and Frank take me in again after my mother has been so awful to them?

They did, and I was surprised and relieved to find myself back in their home. A great amount of time had elapsed since my mother had attacked Frank, but I felt that I needed to apologize for her bad behaviour. I still did not understand the reason for her rage towards him that day. All he did was hug me goodbye.

My opportunity came one afternoon when Big Helen and I were sitting alone on the couch, each crocheting a doily. She enjoyed doing that as much as I, and she had begun to teach me to read patterns, so that I could make pieces for end tables, coffee tables and even larger pieces like tablecloths or bedspreads.

I didn't know how to bring up the subject, so I just blurted out, "How come you still let me stay here after *Mutti* was so mean to you guys. And, what did Frank do to make her so mad?"

Her crochet hook stopped. She looked puzzled. "Oh that? Don't you worry about it, Helen. We've already forgotten about it." With a giggle, she added, "Your mother thinks *everyone* is out to get her." She went back to her crocheting.

I noticed she hadn't answered my second question, but I let it go and carried on with my real reason for asking. "I'm so sorry she had been so unkind to you. You both have been so nice to me, thank you." *I'm relieved I could finally apologize.*

She placed her crocheting on her lap and put her hand on my knee. "Don't you apologize for her, sweetie. It's not your fault. And it's not our fault either; we did nothing wrong. She does that to everyone."

I sighed. "I don't know why she is like that."

Big Helen paused. "You know, Helen, it seems that she doesn't want to share you. She gets jealous when anyone else loves you, or you love someone other than her. I think your mother is a very sick puppy."

I never thought about it that way. She could be right. Maybe that's why *Mutti* wouldn't allow me to go to Ethel's wedding. She was envious of our love for one another.

Then I remembered something that my godmother had said to me. "Pauline says that we can't always expect to be loved the way that we want. What do you think?"

She thought for a while. "Well, I think she's right, you know, but a person still has to take some responsibility for the way that people treat them. For example, Frank and I don't hate her, and our family appreciates all she does for Dad. If she would only be a nicer person, everyone in this family would bend over backwards for her. But, instead, she seems angry all the time and causes nothing but grief."

Yes, that she does.

My opinion of Big Helen just went up tenfold. *She is so forgiving. Wish I can be more like her.*

I don't hate my mother either, but I am the only one that had to put up with her "storms" on a daily basis. On several occasions, I did love her much less than other times. When that happened, I believed I had broken the fifth commandment—love thy father and mother. Often, when my mother had been unkind, I would ask my Guardian Angel,

"Are you sure I have to love her now?" I never received an answer, so I assumed it was still "yes."

I wonder if I am ever going to be able to obey that commandment!

***

The day before the catechism lessons started, we went to visit Frank's parents who lived about a mile or two north of their place. I met his two younger brothers, Ernie and Tony. Ernie, I figured, was a year or two older than I. Tony was not yet twelve. I had not played with any boys since Willi, but thank goodness, both accepted me readily. I guessed being a tomboy helped. As we scampered around, I noticed that Tony had worn a long-sleeved shirt on this particular warm day. I paid no attention, but when his sleeve accidentally rode up, I saw the reason why. It revealed a very badly scarred arm that wouldn't straighten out all the way. Of course, I had to ask him what had happened.

He looked slightly embarrassed and answered shyly, "Ernie and I were pouring gasoline from one container to another when suddenly my sleeve burst into flames, and we couldn't put it out. I was in the hospital for a very long time." He stopped, shivered, then continued in a different controlled, proud voice, "They said I had third degree burns to my arm and back."

I remembered how much it had hurt when I burned my finger on the stove from making toast. I shuddered when I tried to imagine that pain all over my body. That was first time I had seen a true hero.

The real reason for this visit, I found out, was to introduce me to Ernie who would be picking me up and walking me to the church for our catechism every day. I was surprised and looked at Ernie who grinned and winked at me.

The nerve! I don't need a protector! As Lorna, the jungle queen, I can make lions cringe in fear!

The next morning, I was barely ready when Ernie showed up. Still a bit miffed that they felt I needed a babysitter, I gave him a cool greeting. *He better not think that he can boss me around!*

The morning had already become warm, and the sky threatened rain. Big Helen handed Ernie an umbrella and reminded him not to lose it because she didn't have another. Off we trudged on our three-mile journey down a dirt road. As we walked, the silence between us became heavier—as did the air. Dark clouds dipped lower and the sky grumbled. A fine mist began to fall, so we hurried our steps. We had a long way to go with no houses or shelter anywhere near this road. Soon heavy drops of rain raised little dust clouds as they hit the dirt road. Ernie opened the umbrella. We crouched beneath it and broke into a light run.

I stopped Ernie. "Wait, I have to remove my shoes. This mud will ruin them. I'll never hear the end of it from my mother."

I placed my hand on his shoulder for balance and looked up in his face to see if he objected. He had a grin from ear to ear. It was the first time I noticed his incredibly blue eyes and thick curly hair.

I tucked my socks into the shoes and tied the shoe laces to my Roy Rogers lunch box.

"You have a good idea," Ernie said, and he leaned down to remove his shoes and roll up his pant legs. This time, he leaned on my shoulder. I liked that.

I took my lead from him and pulled the back of my calf-length skirt toward the front and tucked it into my waist, the way I had done when I had climbed the cherry tree in Austria. It brought the hem above my knees, well above the mud.

Ernie burst out laughing. "That looks funny, but you are smart. We better make a run for it, or we'll drown like gophers!"

By this time, the rain pounded on our umbrella, and the road had turned into mud soup.

"Give me your lunch pail and shoes," he said. "You hang on to the umbrella with one hand and give me your other. I don't want you to slip and fall in this mud."

Hand in hand, with Ernie steadying me, we ran as fast as we could, stopping every once in a while to catch our breath, laugh and carry on again. It became difficult for both of us to remain under the umbrella without bumping into each other. As a result, Ernie became quite soaked.

Of course the rain stopped as soon as we neared the church. The moment we entered its yard, Ernie let go of my hand, returned my items and moved slightly away from me. I handed him the umbrella, but he said, "No, you take care of it. I'll probably lose it. I'll meet you at the bottom of the steps after Catechism. Okay?" He didn't wait for my answer but was gone to join some boys at the back of the church.

Is he embarrassed to be seen with me? I must look a fright with my muddy legs sticking out under my tucked up skirt. My lovely curls are stuck to my face. I'm sure I look like Cinderella after she had just swept the hearth.

On the other hand, the rain had only made Ernie look more handsome. His thick curls, heavy with rain, had fallen over his forehead. The moisture on his face emphasized his angular cheeks and jaw. His wet shirt had been plastered against his broad shoulders and slim waist. With his pant legs rolled up to his knees, he resembled a dashing buccaneer in my comics.

Not fair!

But, I had better things to do than think about Ernie. I had to remove the mud off my feet and put my shoes and socks back on. With no water or towels available, I cleaned my muddy feet by rubbing them in the wet grass. Once most of the mud had been removed, I sat on the steps of the church, dried my feet with my socks and put my shoes back on.

God, I hope I'm not the only girl here! Oops, I just used the Lord's name in vain!

Despite my sin, God granted me my wish. After hearing some giggling around the corner, I followed the sound to find a group of girls. I recognized only two of them. One was Irene Antol whom I knew a little. She and I, along with her brothers, Ernie and Roy, had played baseball together while our parents visited. The other, Helen Sentes, whom I liked very much, was my classmate at school.

I sidled up and hugged her. "Hi, am I ever glad to see you here. When do you think we'll be able to go into the church?"

"I'm glad to see you, too. I don't know any other girl here," she replied as she hugged me back. "I think the Sisters will let us in once everyone gets here."

I guessed everyone had arrived because we heard the unmistakable clang of a school bell coming from the front of the church. Everyone gathered on the steps and began pushing and shoving to get in. Two women stopped our progress. They looked like mirror images of each other with long-sleeved grey dresses that almost reached their ankles. The only thing that broke the dreary grey was a crisp white collar. When my friend Helen had mentioned "sisters", I had expected real nuns with their black and white habits and veils.

One of them clapped her hands to get out attention. "Hello boys and girls. We are the Sisters of Service who will be preparing you for your Confirmation. My name is Sister Agatha and on my right is Sister Beatrice," she said loudly and clearly. "Girls, line up on my right and cover your heads. Boys to my left and be quiet."

I put on a small kerchief and lined up with the rest of the girls.

Clap, clap! "Ladies first," barked one of the Sisters.

Once inside, we girls piled into the pews on one side of the aisle, the boys on the other. I made sure I sat close to my friend Helen. The lessons began almost immediately with a prayer from Sister Beatrice who became our instructor, while Sister Agatha tended to the boys. I couldn't help but peek over to where the boys were. I noticed there were only six of them, while there were eight of us girls. I found my Ernie immediately and recognized Irene's brother, also called Ernie. Then there was my classmate Jerry Sentes, and Gary Kayter who rode on the same school bus with me. The other three I did not know.

"Helen, eyes to the front!"

Which Helen did she mean?

The drill remained the same for the rest of lessons. We had to sit and listen to the drone of the Sisters while the interior of the church became what Ernie called "hotter than hell". The required dress code of the church for women meant that I had to wear a long skirt or dress, long-sleeved top, full slip, socks, shoes and a kerchief. I tried to pay attention and be interested, but the only thing I was interested in was Ernie. I wondered why he was so friendly and kind on our way here but then completely ignored me when we reached the church.

Everyone suffered from the heat, and some had not brought anything to drink. The thirst drove some boys to check out the slough near what everyone called Sparrow Shit Hall, a building just down from the church where the families of the congregation gathered in the fall for Fowl Supper. It didn't get used much the rest of the year, hence the name. The boys came back, their thirst quenched with slough water. That night, Gary Kayter must have been told by his relatives that anyone drinking from the slough might have swallowed some eggs. These in turn might hatch in their guts and become adults. Thus the following day, Gary warned all who had ingested that slough water that they may find adult frogs and lizards in their poo. That put an end to *that* water source, but another soon took its place—holy water! The boys found it behind the sacristy and guzzled it down. They said it tasted extremely flat. Flat or not, I was sure God was going to smite them down, but He didn't.

The only ones that did the smiting were the Sisters of Service. I noticed that Sister Agatha, who taught the boys, was more stern and harsh than our Sister Beatrice. She wielded a yardstick that came down on any unsuspecting boy if she caught him talking, laughing or fidgeting. *Whap! Whap!* Never too hard, but hard enough to get their attention. She reminded me of my third grade teacher in Austria. I noticed, however, that her whaps ceased the moment Father Barton appeared and began anew immediately after he left.

We girls were perfect angels of course, or perhaps, we were more fearful after witnessing the boys' situation. I was desperately trying to understand the "Holy Trinity". How can God be three people—the Father, the Son and the Holy Ghost? I didn't even have a relationship with God the Son. My idea about Him was that of a stern, forbidding image not to be messed with. I preferred the kind, gentle image of a guardian angel who safeguarded two children across a bridge. Hence, I never spoke to God directly only through my Guardian Angel. It had worked well so far.

Now, these Sisters were telling me that the Holy Ghost, along with the Father and the Son will come upon me and make me strong to practice and defend my faith. I would become a soldier of Christ and "promise to dutifully fight the war between good and evil, light and darkness and between the human race and the powers of hell". I didn't understand what they wanted me to fight, but I sure hoped my Guardian Angel would be at my side should that time come.

We were also required to pick our confirmation name. This had to be a Christian name, one from the bible, but not like Judas or Jezebel, more like saints or heroes of the bible. I chose St. Theresia, the only saint I had any information on. This name was to be added to my baptism name. I was happy with that because it meant that I would now have a middle name like anyone else here in Canada.

During those ten days or so, Ernie and I had at least two hours each day where we walked, talked and laughed together. We discussed many things, and I found we had a great deal in common, especially our love of animals. I had chattered about Coalie; he talked about his horse. That gave me the opportunity to talk about how I had trained my calf, SoJo. It felt good to finally be able to tell my secret to someone. His eyes opened wide, then he bent over and howled. He didn't believe me! It was difficult for me to prove something no one else knew about.

Why do boys always think they're the only ones capable of knowing or doing anything, while girls know nothing and do nothing?

Despite the difference in our opinions, I began to look forward to seeing him every morning. It was a chance for me to actually talk to a boy, which was something I knew my mother would forbid. I liked his calm manner, his quick smile, easy laughter and the way his blue eyes twinkled when he looked at me. I felt happy and beautiful when I was around him. But I still didn't understand why he always became so cool once we reached the church. I was too timid to ask him directly but would have to talk to Big Helen about that.

So, I was both happy and sad when the last day of catechism arrived —happy that the grueling lessons were over, but sad, knowing that my time with Ernie would also end. On that day, as Ernie dropped me off for the last time at Big Helen's house, I knew we would probably not see each other for a very long time. There would be no chance to say goodbye to him tomorrow with all the people around, so I made my move. I stood on my tiptoes and gave him a quick hug and kissed him on his cheek. He pulled back, looking at me, not moving. Then he smiled his wonderful smile. My heart beat faster and I blushed. A second later, he bent over and planted a kiss on *my* cheek! He ruffled the top of my hair, turned quickly and ran off like a jack rabbit.

Big Helen saw all of this and giggled. "Make sure you don't tell your mother about any of this, including Ernie walking you to the church. We don't want another war on our hands, do we?"

I thought it a wise decision also.

That evening I approached Big Helen with my question about Ernie. She concluded that he was just too shy to let the other boys know. "They would have teased and laughed at you both. I think he was trying to spare you from that. He is a very kind lad, just like his brother, my Frank."

I agreed and accepted that explanation.

***

The following day, Thursday, Helen and Frank drove me home so I could get ready for the big day tomorrow. It was very hard to say goodbye to them. I wondered if they knew what a lovely respite they had provided.

Back at home the next day, my mother made sure I was washed and dressed by the time Bill and Pauline showed up to drive us to church. I must admit, I thought I was beautiful, but then that would mean that I was vain, and no sins were allowed on this holy day. *Okay, Okay, I'm ugly, God! Are you happy now?*

Pauline, on the other hand, looked beautiful. But before I could say anything, she drew near, gave me a hug, a wet kiss and murmured in my ear, "You look absolutely lovely, Helen. God bless you."

Hey, I was going to tell you the same thing!

We arrived at church in plenty of time, and Pauline grabbed my hand and headed over to where Frank and Helen were chatting with Ernie, Tony and their parents. *Mutti* hung back and wouldn't let Dad come with us. She must have still been upset with Frank.

I casually said my greetings to the rest of his family, but couldn't keep my eyes off Ernie. *Boy, if I thought he had been handsome before, he looks amazing all cleaned up and in his suit!*

I blushed, and my heart gave a flutter. We greeted each other coolly, or at least I tried. Soon everyone was heading to the church entrance. As Ernie passed me, he leaned over and whispered in my ear, "You look beautiful!" Before it had sunk in, he was gone. *He thinks I look beautiful! Let me not be vain! Let me not be vain!*

I found it difficult to concentrate on anything else for quite some time.

There was no regular mass, only a ceremony, and being Friday, not all the congregation had come. Mostly only the family of the Confirmed were present. I had asked Big Helen before why it wasn't held on a Sunday. She had explained that the Sisters of Service had to teach at the next parish on Monday. It would not give them enough time to prepare if they left on Sunday.

A bishop had been brought in for this special occasion. *We must be pretty important! There I go again with the pride...I'm hopeless.* There were several prayers before the actual ceremony, but soon it was time to receive the Sacrament. I, along with others to be Confirmed, approached the altar. We all stood in line with our sponsors, waiting for the bishop, in his strange hat and red vestments, to give us our Sacrament. He finally stood in front of Pauline and me. She put her hand on my shoulder and gave him my new Confirmation name.

The bishop made the sign of the cross on my forehead with oil and announced, "Helen Theresia Kish be sealed with the gift of the Holy Ghost."

"Amen," was my practised reply.

"Pacem vobiscum. Peace be with you."

"Et cum spiritu tuo. And with your spirit.*"*

I was worried about getting that reply right, but we had practised this one often enough. A few more prayers, and then it was over! I now had the strength necessary to fight the devil.

After, our newly confirmed class and the bishop grouped to have our photos taken just outside the church. I looked around to see if I could catch a glimpse of Ernie, but he had left as soon as the pictures were taken. Instead, I found Helen and Frank and thanked them again.

"Remember not to say anything about Ernie at all. And most of all, for heaven's sake, just shake Frank's hand, don't hug him. I'll hug you extra for him, okay?" She laughed, but I sensed the caution in her voice.

I still did not understand any of this, but I made sure I never breathed a word to *Mutti*.

***

There was another incident at Big Helen's that I did not breathe a word about. She and I often worked in the garden, and this morning it had become quite hot. There was not a breeze to be found for the garden was surrounded by bushes. To my surprise, Big Helen removed her blouse and tied it around her waist. She was not wearing a bra! This did not alarm me for I had seen my mother naked many times at the *Lager*.

"Why don't you take yours off if you're hot?" she said. "The dog will warn us if there's anyone coming into our yard. We'll have plenty of time to slip our tops on before they see us."

Even though I had been topless before, I had never been topless outside. I hesitated. My mother would not approve. *But I am really hot.*

If Big Helen can do it, so can I. Off came my blouse and bra! A breeze, which I had not felt before, blew across my chest. At first, I felt vulnerable and unguarded. Then, something stirred within me—it was absolutely exhilarating! I felt free and natural. *I like it! I love it!*

Big Helen smiled and carried on with her hoeing, but I couldn't stop dancing in the sun. I finally settled down and watched my stepsister. She looked so beautiful. And even though my breasts were mere bumps compared to hers, I felt beautiful too.

Out of the blue my mouth said, "Where do babies come from?"

Big Helen stopped hoeing and stood up. "What brought that on?"

"I don't know. It just came into my head. I asked my mother, and she told me that the stork brings them, just like the animals in the barn. I've never seen a stork here in Canada, so I don't believe her."

She laughed and let out a long, "Yoi!" She shook her head and became serious. "Have you had your periods yet?"

"Yes." I knew what they were. I didn't like them, but I had started my periods earlier that year. I was too embarrassed to talk about it. Besides what did that have to do with my question?

"Well, that means your body is ready to make a baby. It will grow in your belly. It means you have become a woman."

So babies grow in a woman's belly. I sure hope my body doesn't start growing one now without my permission like my breasts did.

But my mother had told me that a woman was unable to have babies until she was married, so I didn't have to worry. I didn't plan on getting married for a long time. When I would marry, I would like it to be with Ernie.

Oh well, at least Big Helen has confirmed that I am a woman now. Maybe that's why I feel so beautiful.

***

Back home, whenever I had time or before I fell asleep, I would think of my time at Big Helen's. I remembered the wonderful talks she and I had, and remembered our mutual experience in the garden. I would also recall every detail of my walks with Ernie. These were perfectly happy memories to use in my Eden whenever I wanted or needed them.

One evening, *Mutti* and I were in the kitchen preparing a cool summer supper—canned chicken, fresh green onions, green pepper, cucumbers and homemade bread. I was washing and cutting the vegetables to make a platter when she asked me, "What did that boy, Ernie, say or want from you outside the church?"

Oh, my God, she knows everything. Who could have told her?

I needed some time to collect my wits, so I pretended I didn't know which Ernie she was talking about.

"That Ernie Kovach, Frank's brother. You know who I mean."

"Oh, that one. He was congratulating me on being Confirmed." I tried hard not to reveal my lie.

Her voice rose. "You stay away from him. He is no good, just like Frank."

But you told me that if a man was a Hungarian and a Catholic, he would be good enough to marry!

Instead, I answered back. "You don't even know him well enough to say that!" *This is not the first time I talked back to my mother. What is happening?*

"I know men, and they're all up to no good! So, you stay away from them."

I didn't know what she meant by that, so I just said,"Yes, *Mutti,*" and let my breath out.

Oye! I am so relieved you don't know what really happened, and my joyful secrets are still intact!

> *The Sisters of Service was a community of Roman Catholic religious women who brought the Catholic faith to outlying districts in Canada. Founded in 1922, the Sisters abandoned the traditional religious habits and large convents. They provided a Catholic presence among the immigrants from the ports to their*

homesteads. They were teachers, nurses and social workers. Thousands of children were instructed in their faith through the summers by these women who had "Come to Serve".

Bambi

August—1957

Soon after my Confirmation, Doraphine had phoned my mother and, as promised, invited me to stay with them for a while in Regina. Remembering how badly my mother had reacted the first time she had suggested it, she did not inform her about us celebrating our birthdays together. Smart woman! As a result, *Mutti* allowed me to go. Not having been in touch since early summer, we were pretty excited about seeing each other and eager to have some fun together.

I slept on the couch in their living room. One morning, some very loud and annoying crunching sounds woke me up. I followed them to the kitchen,where I found Mary Ann merrily munching on her cereal. I was so angry that she had interrupted my sleep, I yelled at her. “You’re not supposed to eat with your mouth open. That’s bad manners. You woke me up with all your noise!”

As soon as I hcard mysclf, I kncw *it* was wrong and *I* was wrong! I was her guest and I had just insulted my host. On top of that, I was twelve and had just bullied a six-year-old girl. It seems I still hadn’t learned the lesson that just because I *could* do something, didn’t mean I *should.* And worst of all, I sounded just like my mother! Tears streamed down Mary Ann’s cheeks. I felt sick! I knew how hurt she must be because my mother had done the same to me many times.

How can I make this better?

I apologized, but were mere words enough? Penance was due, and that did not mean ten Hail Marys. It meant that I owed her a lot of gentleness, kindness and generosity. If all else failed, grovelling and bribing should not be beyond my dignity. For the next week I had plenty of opportunities to do just that.

Here in the city, unlike the farm, our roaming was reduced to the house, yard and front steps. Outside of that, we had to be with an adult. In order to make up for my sin, I allowed Mary Ann to choose what she wanted to do and let her win at most of the games.

Our combined birthday party included some neighbouring children close to Mary Ann's age. Cake, ice cream and balloons were passed around. The best present came a few days later when Doraphine took Mary Ann and me to a movie called *Bambi.*

At the theatre, my excitement grew when I realized it would be a cartoon like Snow White. As the room darkened, the screen filled with a lush green forest split with shafts of sunshine. I gasped and forgot my popcorn as I recognized my forest of Austria. I became swept along a path with birds swooping and singing above, and leaves moving aside to reveal a mother deer and her baby. All the animals in the forest had come to see the baby deer. *Wow! No people in this movie—great!*

Mary Ann and I laughed and laughed as Bambi played with his forest friends—a rabbit named Thumper, and a skunk named, of all things, Flower. Being from the farm, both Mary Ann and I knew from experience that no skunk smelled like a flower! Along with a girl fawn named Faline, these friends played and taught Bambi about the forest, other animals and what things were named. It reminded me of the time Ethel had taught me the English words for articles around the house and farm.

Mary Ann, Doraphine and I roared as Bambi tried to walk on an icy pond and ended up flat on his tummy, twirling like a top, while Thumper skated around him with the greatest of ease. I probably had looked just like him the first time I had tried to skate on our slough.

I sobbed at the death of Bambi's mother and his mournful calls of "Mother, Mother!" I cried for Bambi and me. I also had lost my foster mother, *Mutter*. Turning to Mary Ann for support, I realized she seemed just as distressed. I looked at Doraphine and found her giggling, but I was sure I saw tears in her eyes too. Relief flooded over me when this sad scene finally ended, and we were introduced to the "Great Prince of the Forest," Bambi's father.

What about *my* father? I hadn't thought about him since I moved here. I wanted to know more about him. *I will have to brush my mother's hair soon, so I can pry this information from her!*

I held my breath during the terrifying scene of the forest fire as the flames raged around Bambi and his father, and I was swept along with the other panicked animals. My heart rate returned to normal only after Bambi and all his friends survived and lived happily ever after.

By the time we left the theatre, I felt like a wrung-out dishrag! Never have I had such a range of emotions sweep through me in such a short period of time. I looked at Mary Ann and saw her red nose and eyes, and I began to laugh.

"We must look a mess!" I said to her.

"Well *you* do," she replied, smiling.

Teasingly, I imitated Thumper. I put my hands on my hips, stuck out one foot, thumped it down in rhythm as I repeated Thumper's words, "If you can't say something nice, don't say nothing at all!"

I could have used that advice before I had hurt her with my ugly words that morning.

I will try never to forget Thumper's words.

New Outlook

Fall—1957

Preparing for the next school year had always been thrilling for me. New clothes, shoes, books, new teachers and maybe even new friends. My clothes had been chosen and ordered during the summer holidays from either the Eaton's or Sears catalogue. This gave us enough time to exchange if necessary. The text books required for that year were provided by the school and handed down from the previous year. We were instructed not to damage them in any way.

"Teacher say you no lookeen so goot," my mother informed me a few days before school started.

I didn't think I looked that bad, but a girl always wants to look more beautiful. It soon became clear she had not been referring to my physical looks but rather to my poor eyesight. I *did* have what they called a "wandering eye". I assumed it was also trying to escape from my mother. Even when that eye took off, I did not feel it had affected my vision.

Are they going to give me a new eye?

We took a bus from Cupar to Regina where Pauline helped us get to an eye examination. It went well—although sometimes, I couldn't tell if one image was clearer than the other. Fortunately, my wandering eye did not have to be replaced, and only glasses were required. It had been fun to pick out my frames, so many to choose from. Thank goodness

Pauline convinced my mother to allow me to get the latest "cat eye" frame. I was sure these would have me "lookeen so goot."

A week or so later, we returned for the fitting. I loved them! There was only one problem. I couldn't see a thing with them on! I was in a fish bowl with walls of glass closing in on me. The rest of the day was a nightmare; the glasses made me dizzy and sick to my stomach. I wanted to rip them off, but of course, wasn't allowed. But the moment I was alone, off they came! Once school started, the teachers made sure I wore them. I didn't think the new glasses made me see any better or look any smarter, but my friends thought they were "cool", so I kept them on. Soon they became a part of me, and I no longer fought against them.

I had hoped to make new friends this year and considered myself lucky when I found a girl named Delma Langford. She invited me to her home in town for lunch a few times. She had the kindest mother and family and, for the first time, I understood what envy was. I very much wanted to return her kindness and have her sleep over at the farm, but *Mutti* would not allow that. Nor would she allow me to stay over at Delma's place. She claimed she had never heard of such nonsense.

Both Delma and I were happy to discover that Mrs. Ermel would again be our teacher. This time she introduced me to another favourite subject, Biology. She taught us the parts of a flower—pistil, stamen, calyx, sepal—and what each part played in the creation of a seed and its growth into a new plant. Every time I learned how things worked or what purpose they served, the more magical the world became.

Whether it was the result of the glasses, the Biology classes or becoming a woman, I began to notice more of my surroundings. Before, I had paid attention only to the thoughts banging around in my "little head" and the feelings affecting my heart. Now, for some reason, I sensed everything differently. This fall, for example, I noticed that the days had become shorter and the nights longer. Every morning as I waited for the school bus on the east side of the house, I would stand still and look for changes around me. The sun now cast a more pinkish hue on the sides of the buildings, unlike summer, when it had appeared a more burnished gold. I wondered why? Even the air had changed—more brisk, with the musky scent of mushrooms.

Fall had truly become one of my favourite seasons. One morning, I caught the grass wearing a furry white coat of frost. Most of the trees had already put on Joseph's coat of many colours. Gone were the robins, the swallows and the crows. The only birds remaining were the rowdy sparrows, the chattering chickadees and the swooping blue jays. I couldn't understand why their tiny feet did not freeze solid. Despite the protection of wool mitts an socks, my hands and feet were always getting cold.

The ravens replaced the crows. At a distance, I couldn't see if that big black bird was a crow or a raven, but I could certainly distinguish their calls. There was no mistaking the deep hollow-barrelled voices of the ravens.

The beckoning honks of the geese would always made me look up and watch their V-formations until they eventually melted into the sky.

I wish I could soar with them.

Losses

September—1957

On a cool Saturday morning that fall, I was busy doing my weekly job of cleaning the house when I heard the screen door slam and Dad calling my name.

"Come quick, Iluska, I found something for you."

I wasn't too happy to be interrupted. I needed to get this boring dusting done, and I still had to mop and wash the floor. Reluctantly, I went to the porch. Dad stood there with his jacket slightly open. Something was moving inside it. He zipped it down farther to uncover a wild duck!

"This is a young mallard that can't seem to fly," he said. "I don't know what is wrong with her. Can you take care of it until it gets better, then we'll let it go so she can fly south."

Would I? Yes, yes, yes!

But I realized, that everything I had ever done or would ever do, was controlled by a person called *Mutti*. "What will *Mutti* say?"

"Don't worry. I'll talk to your mother. Meanwhile, the safest place for her is in the house. You'll have to be extra careful not to let it escape when you open the door to go in and out." He handed me the frightened bird. "For now, I'll get you a mixture of grain, and she can pick what she likes the best. She'll need some water, too."

I pulled the flapping, squawking creature towards me and secured its wings under my arm. Cooing softly to this beautiful brown mottled duck, I carried it to the bedroom and released her under my bed. She would feel safe somewhere dark and covered, but she would also require a nest and some newspaper for her business. I found the right box size, cut one side down, filled it with straw and came back to the house. She was still hunkered under the bed, and as I approached, she hissed. Dad quietly came up behind me with a mixture of grain in a shallow bowl and a special container for water similar to the one we used for our chickens. If we had given her a bowl of water, she would have used it for swimming.

"It's time to leave it be, Iluska. If she survives the night, she will be alright. If we bother her too much, she could die from fright."

I have never heard of that, but if Dad said so, then it must be true. He might not know everything like my teachers, but he knows about animals and the land.

I went back to cleaning the house with my heart singing. My day of drudgery had become a day of glorious adventure. When *Mutti* came back in, I assumed Dad had spoken to her so I thanked her for letting me keep this animal in the house. Even our dogs and cats were never allowed in.

She looked upset. "I don't understand that man. He didn't take very good care of his animals before we came here. I was the one who washed and disinfected the cows' teats so they wouldn't get infected. I was the one who made sure the dogs were fed and housed properly in the winter. Yet here he is, bringing in a wild wounded bird into the house. Where is it right now?"

"It's under my bed, but Dad said we shouldn't disturb her," I answered, hoping that she wouldn't change her mind.

She washed her hands, put on her apron and began preparing lunch. "Well, alright, but I hope you realize that if it messes anywhere in this house, you will have to clean up after it."

I won't mind that at all as long as she makes it through the night.

She made it through the night and many nights thereafter. Slowly, surely, she gained her strength. There didn't seem to be a broken limb or wing. She began to trust us enough to follow us around the house. We all laughed at her cute waddle. She wagged her tail feathers, flapped her wings and stretched her long neck, all the while issuing a constant stream of nattering squawks. Even though there were three languages spoken around this house, none of us understood Duck. Dad got a great kick out of her and laughed every time he saw her. I even caught *Mutti* smile as she coaxed her to eat some left over vegetables. The duck was thriving. She was a total delight to everyone who saw her.

I should give her a name, but what? The Hungarian word for duck was *kacsa*—sounded like "caught cha." *Kachi. We'll call her Kachi!*

We were all very careful that Kachi would be kept safe inside. She did not use the newspaper as intended, but rather, she shredded it with delight and scattered it about the bedroom. So, not only did I have to clean her watery poop, but also her toys. She slept under my bed in the box provided but was usually the first one up, loudly demanding that everyone else get up too.

One morning I needed to go outside to do my chores. As usual, Kachi was right behind me, so I made sure I pushed her back from the open door with my foot. Suddenly, there was a grey blur which was followed by a most horrendous squawking. Before I could react, one of our cats from outside had rushed through the open door, grabbed Kachi by her neck and dragged her across the yard. The poor duck, even although she was bigger than the cat, and squawked and flapped her wings wildly, could not free herself. I ran after them screaming and flapping *my* arms. To no avail. Before I knew it, they had both disappeared under the granary. Kneeling down, I tried to reach in but could see nothing in that darkness. No more sounds came from Kachi.

I knew what that meant, and I thought my heart would break. I had known enough not to let the duck out, but I hadn't expected a cat to come rushing in. I should have checked. She had been under my protection, and my one moment of carelessness had cost Kachi her life. Sobbing, with despair and guilt, I went to find my parents and tell them the horrible news.

Mutti's response was "I knew this was a bad idea." But her voice sounded sad.

Dad's comment was much kinder. "It's not your fault, Iluska. That could have happened to any one of us. It's not the cat's fault either. It's the way of life."

Neither one of their answers consoled me.

I concluded that "the way of life" seemed darned unfair.

***

Life turned out to be even more unfair and downright cruel one day late September. As usual after school, I went to get the cows for milking. On my way, I was thinking about SoJo and how big he was becoming—so big that I had difficulty staying on his broad back. Soon he would become too large and too dangerous for me to ride. Our relationship and secret would come to an end. I found the herd quickly because they were closer to home, but something was wrong. There didn't seem to be as large a herd as before, just our regular milking cows. Where were all the young heifers and steers?

Oh my God, where is SoJo?

I looked around to see if they had somehow managed to slip into another field and hadn't found their way back. I saw none. These cows needed to get home for milking, so I had no time now to look for the missing ones. Maybe cattle rustlers had stolen them just like in the Wild West stories of the Lone Ranger or Roy Rogers. This was the first day for a long time that I actually had to *walk* home.

As soon as the cows entered their stalls, I told Dad about the missing others. He did not appear surprised. "They are not missing, Iluska. They were sold this afternoon."

"Sold? Sold to whom?"

"To the slaughter house," he explained. Then he looked at me curiously. "Why? What's the matter? We always sell our animals in the fall. Pigs, chickens, *and* our cows. You knew that, didn't you?

Of course I knew. Trooper, the runt pig that I had nursed back to health, had also been sent to market the same year he was born. In previous years, I had no reason to be concerned about where the extra cattle went. Now, however, I was deeply concerned.

I ran out of the barn, not wanting Dad to see my tears. I headed to the chicken coop to do my chores, all the while choking on my tears. Coalie sensed my feelings and nuzzled his cold wet nose into my hand. I dropped down, buried my head in his neck and hung on tightly. *At least I still have you!*

In the fall, only a few cows gave milk, and those that did, only gave enough for our personal use, so I knew that their milking would not take long. *Mutti* would soon be calling me to help with supper. That would not be enough time for me to gather my self-control. Above all, I did not want my mother to see me cry because then, I would have to explain my tears, and she would disapprove. I tried to stretch my time in the chicken coop by washing out the water container, adding more food, cleaning out the nest boxes and changing their straw. Finally, there was nothing for me to do, so I gathered the eggs, took a deep breath and heading towards the house.

Before I even made it through the door, my mother asked, "What took you so long?"

I didn't answer, but instead, I turned away from her. I didn't want my face to trip me up. Either I was not very good at hiding my feelings, or mothers have a third eye, because before long, I heard the dreaded words, "*Mi a baj?* What's the matter?"

"I lost my pet calf, today and I'm sad." I didn't say how much of a pet he had been.

"How many times have I told you not to make pets of these animals. They are for work and food only. By getting too close to them, you cause yourself a lot of grief!"

Is that why you won't let people get close to you? Thank goodness my mind did not talk out loud like hers did!

She was right of course. We did use our animals for many things. We ate our chickens, gathered their eggs, and used both to pay the grocery bills, doctor bills and even a haircut. Most of the litter of pigs went to market for money. Last fall, one of them had provided us with food for the year. Our cows gave us milk, cream, and butter, and now I had to come to terms with the fact that SoJo was just another animal that brought in some money.

I had seen many natural deaths on the farm. Old Puppy, Dad's dog, had died of old age. I had been sad but not heartbroken. None of these animals had touched my heart, but Kachi and Sojo had been different. *Mutti's right. Love has a price. I need time to wrap my mind around this.*

My heart ached through supper, through homework and the rest of the evening. I went to bed early trying to escape my emotions. To take my mind off SoJo, I concentrated on the sounds in the attic and the walls. Was that sound a mouse, a rat, or a bat? I hoped it was not a squirrel. Dad had said they were the most destructive. I then turned my attention to the cheery chirping of the crickets outside my window, but even they did nothing to lift my mood.

Maybe I'll feel better tomorrow.

The next day my Saturday chores of cleaning house had to be done, and my grieving would have to wait. I was determined that as soon as I had finished them, I would go to the hayloft to deal with my feelings. The hayloft had become my new Eden. The original one in the pasture could only be used on warm, sunny days. Now, in the cold wet fall, the hayloft above the barn served as a more convenient and practical hideaway and was within ear shot of my mother calling. It was also warm and dry enough that I could remain there for as long as I needed.

As I cleaned, I thought of how that hayloft had always allowed me to gather my thoughts, work through my heart, and come out feeling better than when I went in. The moment I would scamper up the vertical ladder and pull myself through the opening, the sweet fragrance of the dried grass would hit my nostrils. With that scent would come memories of the time Greta and I helped my foster parents gather their hay. These memories, in turn, were always accompanied with feelings of love and security.

Now with my work done, I headed straight for this Eden. No human or animal was in sight, only Coalie, who whimpered as I climbed the ladder. He was the only thing missing in my perfect hideaway, but he was too big and heavy for me to hoist him up there.

As I brushed away the numerous cobwebs that constantly popped up everywhere on the farm, my mind automatically turned to spiders. There were many kinds, and I liked none of them, except the ones they called "Daddy Long Legs." Their small round bodies swayed to and fro when they moved on their long thin legs, making them look as if they were doing a slow waltz. The other spiders appeared dark, ugly, and darted much too quickly for my liking. Unfortunately for me, my mother believed they brought good luck and would not brush them off if they landed on her. It made me shiver in horror. I never tested her belief.

Once through the opening of the loft, I had to be very careful so as not to slip and fall back down since there was no trap door. I peeked between the wide gaps in the weathered wood wall and scanned the farmyard for anyone heading toward the barn. No movement was detected. Turning to face the other way, I purposely launched myself unto a high, soft heap of hay, disregarding all risks of those dreaded dry thistles possibly embedding themselves in my body. I found a comfortable spot and lay back. Shafts of sunshine pierced through the gaps in the old wood wall. Fairy dust danced in their beams. When the sun touched the hay on the floor, it spun it into gold like Rumpelstiltskin had done in my fairy tales. I thought about how hard Dad and the horses had worked to cut and gather all the tall grasses from anywhere they could—around the yard, the ditches and the sloughs. He would have loved to see it turn to gold. Today though, not even this magical place brought me peace.

Sojo! I will miss you. Poor Sojo! I feel so guilty. Is this the reward you get for being my loyal, fleet-footed companion?

He had been special to me, so it never occurred to me that they would treat him like any of the other cattle. If they had known of my secret and my special love for him, would it have changed the outcome? Most likely not! I was finally able to let my tears flow freely. I remained there until no more fell.

I had come to only one conclusion. *In the future, I will have to be more careful to what and to whom I give my heart, or develop some hard callouses around it.*

Fire Fire

November—1957

Throughout the year, one of my many chores had been to fill the wood box beside the stove. Almost every day, especially in the winter, I carried in armloads of split logs from a wood pile just a few steps north of the house. There were two huge piles—one, already chopped and available for immediate use, and the other, stove-length round logs that still needed to be split into appropriately sized pieces for the stove.

On this particular day near the beginning of November, I had just finished a hot bowl of *Mehl Suppe*, a hearty thick soup made from browned flour and added caraway seeds. *Mutti* was still enjoying hers. She was always the last to sit down to eat and the last to finish. Being that Dad had been served first, he was finished eating and now strolled over to the stove to light his after-meal cigarette. A small decorated tin box on the wall near the stove held a box of *Eddy's Red Bird* matches. He pulled out a wooden match and struck it on the stove's cast iron surface. As he lit his cigarette, he glanced out the small north window nearby and commented, "That woodpile is getting low. I guess I better do some chopping soon."

I heard my mother grunt in agreement.

"Yep, I think today's a good day for chopping wood," he said as if he hadn't heard her.

He often used that expression when he was considering doing a job. Every task would only be completed if it was a "good day". At first, I thought that his decision depended on the weather. Soon though, I began to suspect that it had more to do with his mood or desire and less to do with the weather.

I looked at him and gave him the most pitiful look that I could muster up. He caught my look and winked. Turning to my mother he spoke in Hungarian. "I have to go and sharpen the axe, but I will need Iluska to help me with the wood chopping. Can you spare her this afternoon?"

I heaved sigh of relief; he had received my message.

"I guess so. She's not much help around here!" *Mutti* replied.

And you wonder why I don't like helping you. But then, if you did consider me helpful, you wouldn't let me go with Dad. Sometimes, not being appreciated has its benefits.

I almost smiled with glee but turned so that my mother wouldn't see. By the time I finished clearing the table and washing the few dishes, I could hear Dad already working by the woodpile. I glanced at my mother.

"Go, he'll be waiting for you."

Any time Dad asked for my help, I was more than happy to oblige, no matter what the task—even cleaning the manure out of the barn. My job today, however, would only require me to supply him with the round, uncut logs from one pile and heave the freshly chopped ones on the other. My most important duty, however, would be to stay clear of the swinging axe and flying wood. You could never tell from which direction a piece of wood or axe part might come. Between the work, we could have a nice chat and visit without interruption. Whenever my father and I began a conversation with my mother around, inevitably it would be taken over by her.

I watched as Dad used a very wide log as a base and placed one of the rounded logs upright on its flat end surface. That was my cue to back off. Once I was clear, he raised the axe over his head and with a loud whack, drove it through the middle of the log. Two more whacks and we had firewood which I gathered and threw on the right pile. I was amazed how he hit the mark every time. The thicker logs, of course, took more whacks.

I was wondering why he hadn't invited me to go with him to cut the trees for these logs. So I asked him, "Are these logs from our field?" I knew that he had cut the fence posts from our land. "I could have helped you. You know that I'd go anywhere just to get out of the house away from my mother."

He placed another log but did not raise the axe. He looked at me, shook his head and laughed. I knew he was amused with my comment about *Mutti.* We were both of the same mind about avoiding her sharp tongue at every opportunity.

He pulled out his big red handkerchief from the back pocket of his overalls, wiped his eyes, and blew his nose. He wagged his finger at me. "Don't let your mother hear you say that. We'll both be in trouble." He tucked the handkerchief back in his pocket and answered the other part of my question, "No, I don't get the logs from our land because we don't have any decent hard-wood trees here. The Touchwood Hills Reserve, just north of here, sells pre-cut poplar poles. I go up there every winter to pick them up with the horses and sled."

A sleigh ride in the winter! Sounds like fun!

"May I go with you this winter?"

He shook his head. "Sorry, Ilushka, but this time even I have to say no. It's too far, too cold and too dangerous. Besides, I always have to leave very early in the morning so that I could be home before dark."

It was the first time he had said "no" to me. But then, it seemed to be given in a different tone from my mother's. Dad's "no" had an explanation, a good reason, and a tender concern attached to it. Instead of being angry about not being able to go, I felt safe and secure in his decision. I had never felt that way with any of my mother's.

"So why do you have go there in the winter? Can't you pick them up just before you need them? And how come you didn't let me help you cut the poles?" I wanted to stress how eager I was to assist him.

He looked at me, sat down on one of the logs, pulled out a rolled cigarette, lit it, inhaled deeply and let out the smoke through his nose. He began in Hungarian. Whenever he had to explain something that was a bit more complex, he reverted to his native tongue. I understood it better than his English by now. "You sure do ask lots of questions, don't you?"

Don't be silly, Dad. I know you love to explain things to me and I love listening.

He didn't wait for me to verbalize this thought. "Let me explain about what needs to be done to get good firewood. My father taught me what I needed to know. Hardwood is better than softwood because it will burn longer. That's why I buy poplar. I pick it up in the winter because I'm not so busy then. Also, the wood needs to season or dry for at least several months before it can be used. This decreases the build-up of oil in our stove pipes that can cause chimney fires. So I get the poles in the winter and let them dry. In the spring, a neighbour makes his rounds with his circular saw and cuts them into stove-length logs that we are splitting now." He took a couple more drags from his cigarette. "Can you see now why I didn't ask for your help?"

"Yep," I replied. I got more than I bargained for! I hadn't really been interested in a lecture about wood cutting. All I had wanted was the assurance that he hadn't purposely avoided my company. And, I was content that he hadn't. In the process, I also learned that things were never as simple as they first appeared. Who knew that a chunk of wood for burning required all that knowledge?

***

Except for some hot summer days, that wood burned in the stove on a daily basis. Cooking, baking, laundry, ironing, bathing, preserving or just heating the house all required the burning of the wood. I did not know that this miraculous process had its down side.

I stepped outside the screen door one day and was heading towards the chicken coop to gather some eggs. As usual, Coalie greeted me with a lick to my hand. I stroked his head and rubbed his ears. He loved that and showed it by uttering a doggy moan of pleasure. As I straightened up, I saw white flecks drifting around me.

Darn, don't tell me it's snowing already!

It was only the beginning of November and it didn't seem that cold outside. I checked the sky. It wasn't snow. It was ashes from the dark smoke and sparks that spewed from our chimney! I ran back into the house waving my arms, pointing to the ceiling, all the while screaming, "Egermancy, Egermancy!" *Mutti* and Dad,sitting at the kitchen table, did not move, just looked at me, puzzled.

Egermancy? Maybe that didn't come out right.

I yelled, "*Feuer, Feuer!*" and hoped that would get a response.

My mother's eyes widened as she recognized the German word for fire. Her voice rose as she translated it to Dad. Both jumped up, now. Dad stepped into his boots and headed to the door while *Mutti* grabbed the pails that always sat in the porch. They ran outside without putting on coats. I followed. Two, fifty-gallon metal drums filled with well water sat on a stone boat just outside the porch. From one of these, my mother now drew a pail full and handed it to me.

"Put it on the bench," she ordered, "then come back for another."

Dad arrived with a ladder and leaned it against the side of the house directly in line with the chimney. He grabbed one of the pails and hoisted himself up the ladder. Once on the roof, he used the horizontal strips of wood that had been bolted to the shingles to keep himself from slipping backwards. I had never seen him move so fast. He emptied the pail down the chimney and came down to the edge of the roof for the next full pail. *Mutti,* already up the bottom ladder, exchanged a full pail for the empty one. The process of filling, transferring and pouring down the chimney continued until Dad was satisfied that the fire was out.

All three of us huddled outside the porch door and heaved a collective sigh of relief. Dad looked quite pale and shaken. He didn't say anything and just came over and patted me on my shoulder. I think he wanted to say thank you, but *Mutti's* words cut in.

"How many times have I told you to clean those #!&?#! stove pipes?

You always keep putting things off!" In Hungarian, swear words were much more colourful. Ethel had claimed that my mother's were the worst she had ever heard. I felt sorry for Dad, but at least this time, she wasn't yelling at me.

"I hate taking those damn pipes apart," he declared. "They never seem to fit together properly after!"

"Well, now you have no choice! Now, it's going to be even more of a mess to clean them," she said with a heavy sigh.

We gathered the pails, our wits, and headed indoors. None of us wanted to face the mess that would surely be there.

Ethel had previously described to me how one day in winter, a long time ago, high winds had pulled the flames from the stove and up the pipes until they glowed red. Dirty stove pipes had almost cost them their home. She had gone into great detail, cursing and swearing throughout the whole story. "You should have seen the goddamn mess we had to clean up!"

At the time, I had laughed at her misfortune, but now it didn't seem so funny. We stood in the entrance between the porch and the kitchen in silent horror. I wanted to swear too, but *Mutti* was doing a much better job already. In one breath she cursed God. In the next, she begged Him for help. "*Jó Istenem, segits meg engem!* My dear God, help me!"

We were definitely going to need all the help we could get. The kitchen had been turned into a black dripping cave. Inky dark water leaked from every joint in the stove pipes that crossed the ceiling, writing its journey across everything beneath it. Long, shadowy fingers oozed from the chimney insert, down the wall and onto the floor. This sooty liquid now crept slowly across the kitchen toward us.

Where do we begin?

Dad looked defeated, but *Mutti* sprang to action and barked out orders. "Heli, get some newspapers, some buckets, soap and rags. Jóska, get over here. Before we can clear up this mess, you and I need to remove and clean these pipes."

By the time *Mutti* and I changed our clothes, covered our hair, and spread the newspapers on the floor, the fire in the stove had been put out and the pipes had cooled. As each pipe was separated from the other, clouds of soot and residual black water rained down on Dad. I heard him grind his teeth and swear under his breath.

"Stop your cursing. This is all your fault. If you would have done these pipes when I told you to, this wouldn't have happened!" Nothing ignited my mother's wrath as much as when she knew she was right.

Every one of the pipes had to be separated from the other, carried outside, scoured and brought back to be reassembled in the kitchen. As predicted by Dad, the refitting had become just as traumatic as their removal. There was very little wiggle room or sufficient light behind the stove where the first two pipes had to be inserted. When that was finally accomplished, the pipes went up to the ceiling, then across to the chimney opening. And, because none of the pipes were marked in any way to indicate their order, much trial and error, accompanied by much cursing followed, until each pipe found its proper fit. Once joined, they had to be supported by wires from the ceiling. As soon as the last pipe elbow went into the chimney opening, Dad took off, a cloud of soot wafting behind him.

Mutti and I stood looking at each other. We knew it would be only us who had to clean up this devil hole. She pronounced it as the "debil hole". She relit the stove, heated large pots of water, then we just had to get on with it. That black oily residue just wouldn't come off. Each wipe smeared and spread the stain. Bucket after bucket, hour after hour, we battled this demon. Even after gallons of elbow grease, we were only able to make the kitchen look half decent. By then, *we* didn't look so decent. Black from head to toe, we could have passed as chimney sweeps. My mother and I had talked about them while we were cleaning. She told me that they were an ever-present service available in Austria, but they didn't seem to have them here in Canada.

During all this time, she had actually been talking *with* me and not *at* me! As we removed our sooty clothes and washed up, we talked about how lucky we were that this had happened in the morning, otherwise we would have been working in the dark through the night.

"Hee keels me!" she said in English as we finally flopped down on the clean kitchen chairs.

"What do you mean by that?" I asked her in Hungarian.

She confided in me that sometimes, like today, she felt that she worked too hard. Surprised that she shared her feelings, I wanted more. "Are you sorry we came to Canada?"

"Oh, no, never. I just didn't expect to work this hard. Everyone in Austria told me it would be easier here."

I didn't know what to say. I had not seen her at work in Linz, therefore could not compare, although I had to admit that she did work really hard here.

Before I had time to reply, she continued. "I do miss the beautiful things I used to be able to buy in Europe. They just don't seem to make quality clothes, shoes, jewelry or perfumes here. I can never find something I like. When I do, it costs a fortune."

I didn't know anything about quality, but I knew that the few things she had brought from Linz were beautiful. Her jewelry, made of gold, was intricate and delicate. She had one blue dress that I thought looked very fashionable and expensive. I loved her perfume and her fur coat. She had also owned good leather gloves, purse and shoes. I often wondered how she had been able to afford such things on a cleaning lady's salary. Perhaps she had free room and board at the Stöbers. Or maybe she had suitors that wooed her with gifts.

I imagine all kinds of love stories these days.

Again, I didn't know what to say. This was the longest time I had spent alone with her for months. Was it the fact that we had shared these miserable hours of cleaning that she shared a little of herself? Or was it because she was tired and her guard had been down?

I learned something new about her today and it made me hopeful again. Perhaps, if I made an effort to spend more time with her, we could at least learn to respect one another, then maybe, maybe even love each other. *I must consider this, but will she dowse water on this small flame of hope again as she had so many times before?*

I had also learned something new about Dad today. He wasn't the hero or the perfect Dad I had fashioned in my mind. His habit of putting things off had cost my mother and me hours of hard labour without so much as a thank you or "could I help". Worse yet, we could have lost our home. It seemed that he couldn't handle emergencies very well, nor work when he wasn't in the mood for it. He literally ran away from it. He also showed this trait by not standing up to my mother any more, and would head out the door the minute an argument started.

I guess he's just as human as the rest of us.

the clothesline

Dirty Laundry

Winter—1957/58

In summer, *Mutti* would do laundry every Monday. But in the winter, this task became grueling and painful, and she put it off as long as possible.

Whenever we required a large quantity of hot water in the winter, we would not use the well water in the fifty-gallon drum that had now been moved into the kitchen. That had to be saved for drinking and cooking. Instead, early in the morning of a bath or laundry day, we filled a large canner with clean snow. More snow was added until that large container was full of water. On laundry day, this hot water was carefully transferred from the stove to the washer tub in the porch. *Mutti* then shaved some homemade soap into the water.

The first part of this nasty business involved starting the motor of the washing machine. Its ghastly smell and ear-splitting roar reminded me of Ziggy's motorcycle. Because of this, and despite the cold, *Mutti* had to open the door of the porch to keep us from being overcome by the gas fumes. But she could do nothing about the grating, headache-enducing rumble of the motor for the rest of the day. It was so loud that all the neighbours a quarter of a mile away knew we were doing laundry.

My mother attempted to show me how to separate the clothes, but I could not figure out her plan. Not only did the wash have to be separated by colour but also by grunginess. Hence, Dad's dirty overalls always went in the wash last. Our delicates, like bras and panties, never went into the machine. They would never survive such brutality and had to be done by hand—my hand!

Each load went into the washer and agitated until *Mutti* decided it was clean. *Splish-splosh, splish-splosh.* Then all of the clothing was passed through the wringer—two rubber rollers attached to the side of the washer. My mother would bring the articles close enough until the rollers caught it, then they would be pulled through on their own, pressing out the excess soapy water

That looks like fun. "May I do that, *Mutti*?"

She looked at me in horror. "No, you'll catch your fingers in that contraption!"

Surely, I wouldn't be quite that clumsy, would I?

Once through the rollers, the clothes dropped into a tub of clean warm water beside the washer. There, I rinsed the clothes, but was not allowed to pass them back through the ringers again. I did catch them on the other side and put them into a basket to be hung to dry. While all that was going on, more hot water and another load of laundry was added to the washer tub. When the white sheets came through to be rinsed, *Mutti* added blue liquid called 'Mrs. Stewart's Liquid Bluing'.

"What is this for?"

"You always ask too many questions."

I'm sure I had only asked one.

I kept looking at her until she finally answered. "Alright, alright. That stuff makes the whites look whiter. It keeps them from looking grey or yellow. Happy now?"

I am never happy when you are like this.

She ordered me to hang some of the smaller clothes on lines strung across the corners of the kitchen and living room. The larger articles like sheets, Dad's long johns and overalls had to be hung on the clothes line outside. In summer, this had been a relatively easy task. In winter, it became absolute torture. I helped her carry the basket of wet materials to the clothes line. As I handed her the clothes pins, *Mutti* fumbled with the half frozen sheets and clothes. I could see her face contort with pain as she tried to blow on her fingers to keep them warm. She could only do a few at a time before having to to go inside to warm her hands.

By the time each load was washed, rinsed and hung, the sun had begun to set. The clothes on the line had to be brought in. Again, I saw my mother wrestle with the iced-up pins, the clothes that froze to the line and the ever increasing darkness. This was where I came to the rescue. These large, rigid items could not be folded. So I grabbed one end and she the other, and together, we had to hold them upright like sheets of plywood and manoeuvre them through the narrow doorways, around sharp corners without bending them or dropping them. This might cause the material to break, resulting in a tear.

Once inside, they were draped across any available furniture until they softened and dried. Dad's long johns usually started on the couch upright and stiff. As they thawed, they slowly drooped into the seat, eventually looking like two headless gentlemen discussing the affairs of the world. With very few seats left for us in the living room, we all ended up in the kitchen where more laundry swung over our heads. Their clean fresh scent filled the house as though Spring had invited herself in for a cup of tea.

***

Getting into town was a hardship in the winter months. We still didn't own a vehicle and were dependent on other people's goodwill. Because they were family, had a car and had to pass by our place in their way into town, Walter and Alice were the ones we continued to depend on mostly.

Dad and *Mutti* rode in with them to do their own shopping, but sometimes when there were only a few items, my mother gave Alice her list. When this happened, my mother would always complain about what

Alice had brought home for her. It either wasn't the right kind, the wrong size or colour, too ripe, or it was a piece of junk. After a while, Alice caught on and only purchased items like salt, sugar, flour or a brand specified by my mother. If the brand was unavailable, Alice would not substitute. The result was that my mother frequently ended up with nothing, which also made her bristle.

In March, I had a very bad cold, and my mother insisted that I stay home from school that day. I hated that! But, the queen had spoken, and she ruled the land.

But what in God's name could I do all day? Bake a chocolate cake —yes? I pulled out the bowl, the baking pan and checked the ingredients. With no recipe to follow, I asked my mother which ingredient I should add and when. She wouldn't tell me. Instead, she grabbed the measuring cups and spoons and added the ingredients herself, then told me to mix it.

How am I ever going to learn from my mistakes if you won't let me make them?

I was already mad at her for making me stay home, now this made me crazy. As usual, I kept my mouth shut and instead, I beat the batter bitterly.

"You're stirring it the wrong way," she said. "You have to stir it clockwise, not counter clockwise."

Some nasty comments had formed in my mind and were just about to fall from my lips when we heard Coalie bark. Most of the time that meant a vehicle had pulled into our driveway. I ran to the north window and recognized Walter's car.

I always enjoyed Alice's company. She was such a funny person. Whenever she saw me, she would greet me with the name my mother called me, except she would exaggerate it. She would shout out "Hell-lee!" and stress the last syllable with a really high pitch. Then she would laugh and laugh. I thought she was funny, but I didn't think *Mutti* appreciated it. I was anxious to see them and expected them to come through the door any minute now. Only Dad came in carrying mail.

"Where is Alice and Walter?" I asked.

"They were in town and had picked up our mail," he replied. "They said they had lots of work to do and didn't have time to come in and visit."

Oh, drats!

Dad took off his bulky jacket, hat, mitts and boots in the porch. He dropped the mail onto the table and sat down. My mother poured him a cup of coffee, as I poured the batter into the round bake pan. I knew she wouldn't allow me near the oven, so I let her put the cake in.

As Dad slurped his coffee from his saucer, my mother and I joined him. I loved coffee, especially with a lot of cream and sugar. I filled two cups from the pot that was always on the stove. I noticed we were almost out of doughnuts for coffee. On a farm, you should never be out of any baking. Visitors never phoned to ask if they could or would come. They just arrived. No one left without being offered some kind of food, be it just baking or even a full meal if it was near dinner or supper time. No one ever refused the invitaion. Good thing I had made the chocolate cake.

As *Mutti* drank her coffee, she glanced through the mail for anything interesting. Without warning, she jumped up and yelled, "*Yoi, Istenem*! Oh my God! They've opened our mail! Look, the flap is open. That's why they didn't come in to say hello. That *kurva!*" She spit that last word out like it was poison. Alice wasn't even near, yet my mother carried on as if she were.

That woman can pick a fight in an empty room!

I quickly took the offending envelope and studied it. It was indeed half open, but the unsealed part of the flap had new glue. That meant that it had never been properly sealed to begin with. With it being partially sealed, no one could have seen any of the contents. I tried to bring that to her attention, but she would have none of it. I turned to Dad for support, but his face was obscured by cigarette smoke. I tried to reason with *Mutti* again, but no success.

"Dad, help me here," I begged.

Dad, already in the porch, was putting on his jacket and heading out the door.

Chicken! I wanted to scream at him.

This was exactly why I never liked staying home. Sooner or later, she would realize that Alice was not here and would then turn her anger on me. What to do? I could only think of two options—hide outside like Dad, or distract her.

I decided to distract her by offering to brush her hair. She always calmed down when I did that for her.

"*Mutti,* let's finish our coffee in the living room and I'll brush your hair, okay?" I said very softly and slowly, practicing a calm voice.

"She has no business in our business! Why do people do this to me? I'm always kind and generous, yet look what I get in return," she muttered, this time adding a small sad sniffle.

Kind and generous? You've got to be kidding! Generous—yes. But kind—not a chance!

I couldn't stand this any longer, and before I knew it, my mouth said, "How can you say you're kind when you just finished calling Alice a bad name? I heard you." I was shocked that I would again be questioning her actions, but I wanted to see what she would say if caught in the act.

"Well, that's just a saying. It doesn't mean anything," she replied. By the innocent expression on her face, I think she truly believed that.

Can you not hear what comes out of your mouth?

That's what I wanted to say, but concluded that she either did not see her guilt, or if indeed she did, would never confess it. So I merely said, "Here, let me carry your coffee."

I took her cup and steered her into the other room. When I went back into the kitchen for the doughnuts and my coffee, I slipped all the mail into our Fibber McGee and Molly's drawer. Out of sight, out of mind, I hoped.

One never brushes one's hair in a kitchen, nor does one do it without something around the shoulders—another one of my mother's laws written in stone. So, now in the living room with a towel over her dress, I finally had her settled down on a chair a little away from the dining table. I removed her hair pins and loosened her braided bun. Her hair had become whiter and thinner now. I no longer used a comb for this procedure but rather a brush which had been purchased from one of the Fuller Brush salesmen. *Mutti* loved the rough massage of the bristles and soon slouched in her chair in anticipation. I began to brush using slow, gentle strokes. She heaved a sigh, folded her hands across her stomach and began breathing evenly. I thought she had calmed down until I heard her repeat some of her earlier words under her breath, including the word, *kurva.* I brushed a little harder and faster thinking to distract her. It worked. She moaned with delight.

I knew the Hungarian word that my mother used was a bad thing to call anyone. My mind returned to the movie *Bambi* and Thumper's words about kindness. *"If you can't say something nice, don't say nothing at all."* She sure could have used that expert advice. With my thoughts now back on that movie, I remembered there was some promise I had made to myself. What was it? I rolled through the scenes in my mind and came to the place where Bambi met his father. Father! That's it. I need to ask my mother a little more about my real father.

My mother, in her dream world, did not move an inch. I wasn't sure if it was a good idea to disturb a sleeping ogre, but I knew from past experience that this was the most relaxed state I would ever find her in, and those moments were far and few in between.

"*Mutti,* what was my real father like?"

Her eyes opened partially, but nothing else moved. "What?"

"What was my real father like?" I asked again, a little more anxious now.

She didn't appear disturbed by my question and simply mumbled, "Well, he was a very nice man. He was very attentive to me and very generous."

"How long were you married for?"

"Married?" She shifted in her chair but answered in a matter-of-fact tone, "We were never married. He was a German soldier stationed in Hungary where I lived at the time."

My hand paused in its brushing. "Not married?" I asked. "I thought a woman was *incapable* of having babies without being married!" Had I misunderstood her when she had explained this to me the first time?

She squirmed a little. "Yes, yes, but there was no shame. I was a widow, and it was war time. You grabbed what happiness you could. Who knew what tomorrow would bring."

So, she had been married before I came along? Something else I don't know. Is that why our last names were different—mine Kiraly and hers Méhész.

She had answered, but that hadn't been my question. I was confused.

Before I could rephrase my question, she continued. "I really liked him. He was a big gentle man. He explained that he had a wife back in Germany, but I didn't care. I had been a widow for so long and was lonely for some attention."

"Did he know that I was in your tummy?" At least I'd learned that much about babies, but didn't know any more than that.

"Yes, he did, but he had been ordered back to Germany to protect the Fatherland."

I was so stunned by her answer that I stopped brushing altogether. "Oh my God! You told me he died! He could still be alive! How could you keep such a secret from me?"

"Everyone has secrets."

Yes, I have many secrets now, too.

She carried on. "You were too young to understand these things. I didn't want you to worry about what you couldn't change." Then she reminded me to keep brushing.

I did, but my mind was in a whirl.

There she goes again, making excuses for not telling me the truth. How many other things has she kept from me or lied to me about. For instance, did she really lose my foster parents' address?

There were so many questions bouncing around my head, but they weren't forming any words. Thank goodness because she continued without prompting. "I prayed to God to give me a girl, and He always heard my prayers because He knows I am a good Christian."

I chuckled out loud, but thought, *God granted you a girl, not because you're a good Christian, but because even He didn't want to bear the brunt of your tantrums!* My heart was being truly unkind!

"Boys require men to raise them," she said. "Girls only need their mothers. Having a daughter meant I would have a good companion and wouldn't have to be lonely any more."

That was the kindest thing she ever said about me! Trust her to say something nice after I just finished hurling a nasty thought. Was I being a good companion and a dutiful daughter?

With all these lovely compliments coming, I decided it might also be a good time to ask about her childhood, my grandparents, aunts and uncles. So I did. But I was wrong. I could sense the change in her mood.

In a cool, even tone she said, "Don't you know it's rude to ask personal questions? If there is something you needed to know, I would have told you."

My questions stopped and so did the brushing. I made one long braid that I folded into a bun at her nape and anchored them with the U-shaped hairpins. While I cleaned the brush and carried the cups into the kitchen, *Mutti* got up to shake the towel outside. She was on her way back through the kitchen when I heard her say, "I have a photo of your father. Would you like to see it?"

She caught me completely off guard. I thought any new revelations were done for the day. "*Ja, bitte, bitte!* Yes, please, please." I didn't know why I reverted to German.

We had a photo album of all our pictures from Austria, but I had never seen a picture of my father in there. Why would she hide that from me? Did she consider it bad taste for Dad to see it. Or was she just being private?

"You stay here, I will bring it to you." She went into the bedroom and in a few moments returned with a well-worn photo. It showed a man in a German soldier's uniform standing outside a house. He looked like nothing I had imagined him to be. I wouldn't have called him handsome, but he was tall, as she liked them. Rather plain in his spectacles, he appeared to be smiling. I couldn't take my eyes off him! A very strong longing to know him better overcame me. What did he like or dislike? Did he like children? Most of all, would he have liked me or loved me?

"You can put it into the photo album now if you like," she added.

I would like that very much. Then I can look at him any time I want.

"How come you wouldn't put his photo in the album before now?" I asked, baffled as usual with her decisions.

"Anyone would have recognized that German uniform in the photo. It would have been dangerous for me and you if anyone knew I was going out with what some people would have called the enemy. Besides, one doesn't hang one's dirty laundry on the line for everyone to see."

I didn't know what laundry had to do with all this, but I understood that revealed secrets could be both enlightening and enraging.

Ironing Out the Wrinkles

March—1958

Regardless of how carefully we spread the clothes, most of them, because they were made of cotton, became wrinkled and required ironing. Only the most important clothes received this preferential treatment. Dad's white shirts, dress pants, our cotton blouses, skirts or dresses fell into that category. Everything else had to make do.

Mutti used "flat irons" which looked like flat-bottomed boats with detachable handles. These, however, would never float in a million years for they were made of cast iron. Three were heated on the stove to the right temperature—too hot and they would scorch the material, too cool, and they wouldn't do the job. As these heated, my mother sprinkled the clothes with water and covered the kitchen table with two or three folded blankets over which she placed a white sheet.

I offered to do the ironing, but was flatly denied. As I watched her, I knew I would never have been able to do it anyway. She fitted one of the irons on the stove with the handle, jostled it to insure it was snug, and hoisted it over to the table to place it in its special cradle. If that handle ever gave way, she would have no toes left. To insure that the bottom of the iron had no dirt on it from the stove surface and was the right temperature, she ran a trial run on the top white sheet. If no scorching or staining appeared, she began with the real clothes. If a particular piece was heavily wrinkled, steam was required. This was achieved by placing a clean white wet cloth over the required material, then using the iron atop that. As one iron cooled, she replaced it with another hot one on the stove, alternating until all the ironing was done.

Again, what appeared as a simple task, proved to be not only tedious, but downright arduous and hazardous. I remembered, how in that first hot summer, I had witnessed Ethel sweating and swearing as she slaved by the hot stove in order to iron the clothes. The air inside the kitchen had become bluer than the sky outside.

With all the hard work involved in having clean, ironed clothes, I concluded that it was frugal both money-wise and work-wise not to have too many of them. Now I understood why my mother would get so upset when I dirtied my clothes.

***

I had wrinkles of my own to iron out. My mother and I had been arguing more frequently and more intensely. One evening after supper, it began again. I wasn't sure what started it, but I had became more and more angry. Dad began gnashing his teeth, and I knew I couldn't carry on this quarrel. Slipping on my outdoor clothing, I slammed out the door.

Where to go? The sun had not yet set, but the snow had already put on its evening attire—a shimmering light blue gown. I could go to the hayloft, but it was too dark and a lantern up there would be too dangerous. I looked around for a possible substitute for the hayloft and noticed the straw stack by the barn. *Perfect!* As Coalie and I plodded through the snow, I spied the full moon rising from behind the stack.

That man in the moon is grinning at me. The nerve of him! I'm going to sneak around the stack and punch his nose.

By the time Coalie and I arrived there, he had risen too high for me to reach him. After clambering up the slippery stack, I pulled Coalie up too. I threw myself unto my back with Coalie beside me. I watched the sky darken from steel blue, to indigo, to inky black.

Up here was where I had first searched and found some of the constellations that the *Children's Digest* had talked about. Now, I hunted for the Hunter, searching for the three bright stars in a neat row that made up his belt. I knew his name was Orion and that he could be found in thc south eastern sky. There he was—three stars of his belt, the two stars that made out his shoulders, two stars below that represented his knees and row of smaller ones, arched like his bow. Next, all I had to do was find the Big Dipper in the northern sky, follow the line of the stars that formed the edge of the pot to find the North Star which is at the end of the handle of the Little Dipper. The clear night made it easy for me to find both. The two dippers faced each other, making the Little Dipper look as if it was spilling something into the bigger one.

I'll need to read up on their stories.

I had read that the North Star had been used to guide travellers in the past. I wondered that if ever I became lost, would it help me find *my* way? That thought brought me back to the real reason why I was here. I was lost and confused. Why *was* I so angry at my mother these days? Was I becoming like her—angry all the time? What started it, and how can I make it stop? I lay there on my back with one hand on Coalie's back, stroking him gently but thinking hard. In the past, I had believed her ways were those of all parents and grown-ups. But once we came to Canada, I began to see that people acted and thought differently. Here, they smiled and laughed more easily and often. Open to new ideas, they did not put too much importance on ceremony. Mostly though, in my experience with them, they were less scornful and judgmental. That was what I wanted to become.

In Austria, I had not seen the volatile side of my mother. I did, however, remember her constant nattering, but she had never ranted and raved as she did here. I guessed that, due to my prompt obedience, she never had any reason to become agitated. However, once we arrived here, the first person who didn't do as she asked had been Ethel. I had seen the consequences of that—much cursing and screaming from my mother, and much cursing and crying from my sister. That had escalated into the scene where my mother had become a raging woman with a stick, chasing Steve and Ethel across the farm yard because she thought they should not marry.

But Ethel was not the only one who felt her wrath. Big Helen and

Frank also saw and felt her rage. I had never seen such fury nor heard such foul language as the day my mother had almost physically attacked Frank after he had given me a hug. That day, shocked by her behaviour, and unaware of her reason, I had trembled.

Because we dealt with Alice and Walter more frequently than the others, they, too, became her targets more often. Yet, they continued to drive us wherever we needed. Didn't she know she was biting the hand that helped her?

Doraphine had also been severely reprimanded for sending over baking that was moldy. I knew for a fact that it had come out of her oven just before I headed for home with it.

No one was safe—it seemed the harder they tried to please her, the nastier she was towards them—especially my family and friends. Strangers were not excluded. If she did not attack them directly, she would certainly batter them to a pulp in their absence.

I sighed and ruffled Coalie's ears. He moaned and laid his head on my tummy and rolled his eyes at me.

God, I love this animal! Why can't I love my mother in the same way?

I knew she wasn't evil because I *had* seen her good side. Whenever I had been ill, she had devoted herself totally to my care and comfort, both at the *Lager* and here. There had also been those precious times when she had almost acted normal, showed concern and even shared her feelings, like the time we planted the garden, preserved food, or more recently, when we had cleaned the chimney fire mess. Why couldn't we have more of those? She had shown me kindness and concern, but not often enough for me to forget the bad times.

Is it me? Am I the problem, or her?

I thought about all the discussions I had had with my family about her. All agreed that she was not normal. Big Helen had even gone as far as calling her a 'sick puppy' and felt sorry for her.

What did she mean by that?

I knew Ethel's feeling towards her were not good, but she had no obligation to her. For me, she was my mother—although at times I still wondered about that! I, too, had begun to sense that something was terribly wrong with her thinking, and that drove me crazy. I couldn't reason, explain or even reach her.

Why is she like that? What can I do? If adults can't deal with her, how can I?

I patted my best friend's head and tried to come up with a solution. Big Helen had suggested that my mother just wanted me to herself. Plus, my mother, herself, had just recently commented how she'd prayed for a daughter for a companion. Perhaps if I gave her what she wanted, and with some time and patience, maybe she would be happier. Then maybe, maybe, she might love me in return.

It was not a new thought, and I knew it might not work. Pauline had mentioned that, "some people can't love you the way you want them to." If that was going to be the case, I would have to be content to claim it from my family. I felt confident they would give me as much as I required.

I heaved a sigh of relief that I had a chance to search my heart and mind and come to a decision. Coalie stirred, but did not move. Still on my back, I gazed at the dark sky filled with stars that popped out like diamonds, just like in the song *Twinkle, Twinkle Little Star—like a diamond in the sky.* These seemed so close, I was sure if I sat up, I could pluck and put them in my pocket. Another choice had just presented itself. *Grab these diamonds, take Coalie, and run!*

Displaced Person

Summer—1958

School had been out for almost a week. I loved creating new adventures around the farm, but I missed my friends. I also knew that each year, as I became older, I would have to take on more chores. If they were outside, I didn't mind. If they were inside, I detested them, no matter what they were.

One day at breakfast, I was busily munching away at my Kellogg's Cornflakes while *Mutti* and Dad were chatting in Hungarian and drinking coffee. Usually, I didn't pay much attention to their chatter, but today, I overheard the words "buying the house in town", and my ears perked up. When they noticed I had begun to listen, they stopped. I knew then, that something important was indeed up. I had to ask them directly, "Why are you buying a house in town?"

My parents exchanged glances, then my mother shrugged. "We didn't want to tell you just yet and let you enjoy your summer. But now, you might as well know. We are buying a house in town because we have to sell the farm. Dad is getting too old to work it anymore."

I sat there dumbfounded, my food unchewed in my mouth! My parents returned to their discussion, and this time I was all ears. They talked about how much to pay for it and what changes they needed to make to it.

Dad turned to me and asked, "We are going to ask Walter to take us to town after breakfast to look at the house and maybe make final arrangements for its sale. Would you like to come with us and see it?"

I couldn't respond, my mind had turned as soggy as the cornflakes in my bowl. Unable to come up with an excuse not to go, I mumbled, "Yea, sure." Everything I did after that was automatic—cleaned up the kitchen, washed the dishes, changed my clothes and made myself presentable.

When we finally reached the "house in town", it turned out to be more on the edge of town and looked like a granary. Walter left us to visit his mother in the house next door. The three of us went inside and saw floors, ceilings and walls—nothing else. The space, divided into two rooms, would have fit into our bedroom on the farm! I heard my mother mutter something to God. Dad must have heard her too, for he immediately tried to console her by telling her that these two rooms will serve as the kitchen and living room, while two more rooms will be added for the bedrooms.

"All the work will begin immediately and will be done by the time we move in near the end of August," he reassured her. "The best thing about all this, Lisi, is that there will be running water and electricity! We will also have a cement basement with a cistern for water. There'll be lots of room for storage and room for an electric washing machine."

I saw her face relax a bit.

Just then Walter poked his head in the door and said, "Hey, Helen, look at that big back yard. You'll have lots of grass to cut." Then he chuckled.

Don't be silly. How can I cut the grass without horses?

Dad came to my rescue. "Don't worry, Iluska, the whole back yard will be made into one big garden." More good news for my mother.

What about me? There's nothing here that makes me happy. There's no trees to climb, no hayloft or straw stack. And there's no shelter for Coalie.

Walter drove us to Main Street, three blocks away. *Mutti* and I went to the Café while Dad and Walter went to the bank. We both ordered a cup of coffee and shared a cinnamon bun.

"Are you happy about this move?" I asked her, remembering that I had made a promise to be kinder to her. I was talking with food in my mouth.

She took a slurp of her hot coffee, put the cup down and answered with a sigh, "I will miss the farm, but here in town, there will be less work. I'm not getting any younger either."

I knew she had been born in 1902. That made her almost fifty six years-old. She wiped her mouth with a napkin. "We might even have more time to visit people and do other things."

My being kind to her is working. She's revealing her feelings again. What else can I say to keep this conversation going?

"Can Dad build a dog house for Coalie in town?"

She looked startled. "What?"

"Coalie will need a dog house when we move into town. Can Dad build him one?"

"Oh that? Yes, yes, of course" she replied rather absentmindedly, then looked away.

A new shelter for Coalie makes me happy.

Back on the farm at the kitchen table, it dawned on me how almost all important discussions and decisions, including the most recent one, had taken place on this oil cloth covered surface. Most had not made any difference to me, while others had significantly affected my life, yet no one had consulted me.

I don't like being a child. I will have to speak up more often or stop complaining that I have no choice.

I needed to go outside and think things through with my buddy by my side. We ended up behind the woodpile. I sat down on a log and pulled Coalie close to me.

"Come here, my dear friend, I have to tell you something. Can you believe they're making us move to town. Can you imagine us in town?" He cocked his head and lifted his ears, then let out a little whine. I knew how he felt.

No more farm? No sloughs to explore or swim in, no pastures to run in, no trees to climb, and no hay lofts or straw piles. No more cute baby animals wild or tame, to marvel at, cuddle or feed. What will happen to Jolan? No more bribing carrots in exchange for the feel of his velvety nose. In the winter, there will be no sledding, no skating, no warming up in the sweet scented barn.

Will I be able to find another Eden?

Now I truly understood the meaning of "precious". All these things were now painfully precious for they would be taken away. I was being forced out of my true home and made to live in a strange new place, again. Wasn't that the definition of being "displaced"? That's what Mrs. Ermel had explained.

Now I am becoming really sad. Stop it Helen! Don't panic. It can't all be bad.

I tried to think of something good about moving into town. The best one was that I would be attending the same school and be able to maintain my friendships. Maybe there, my mother would let me stay overnight at Delma's. Perhaps I could also participate in some extracurricular school activities, like sports. With only a house and a garden to take care of, my chores would be substantially diminished—although it would be the outdoor ones mostly, the ones I liked the best. Also *Mutti* would have more time to spare for me. Perhaps, we could finally find time get to know each other better.

That would be nice. Best of all though, I'll still have Coalie.

I had noticed the open field across from our house in town. "You and I can romp to our hearts content out there. Maybe we could find another Eden in that tall grass." I hugged Coalie hard. He licked my face. Perhaps my Guardian Angel would again come in my dream and tell me, "It's going to be alright."

***

"Coalie! Coalie! Where are you? Come, boy! Coalie!"

I called and hunted everywhere. I was beside myself. He would never leave me, so where was he? Surely he would show up tomorrow. There was only a week left until we move. What if he came back and we were not here?

Tomorrow came, no Coalie. Another day went by—no Coalie. Frantic, I wanted to ask *Mutti* but did not trust her to tell me the truth, so I asked Dad. "Have you seen Coalie? He's been gone for several days now and I'm worried about him." I could barely get the words out, my throat was aching so.

"*Yoi,* Iluska, I think he ran away and may have gotten killed by a car. That is why he hasn't returned." He quickly turned his head.

I could tell he had tears in his eyes. Was he sad for Coalie or me? That was when I sensed that I would never see Coalie again!

The sight of Dad's tears made my own gush like a dam had burst. "How could this have happened?" I cried. "He has never taken off like this before. What if he is lying hurt somewhere, unable to come home?"

That bundle of fur had captured and enraptured my heart like no one or nothing had ever before. I could not believe the pain as my heart broke! I ran out of the house at full speed, and kept running and screaming until I found myself in the glen under the trees where Coalie and I had created our first Eden. I threw myself on the ground. I heard an agonizing howl and realized it had come from me. My shoulders shook. My stomach heaved. Out came the bile, the pain and the anger, until I collapsed.

I stayed there for a long time, but eventually I got up and headed back to the yard. Everything reminded me of him! The sobs began again.

I could die. Everything I truly love is gone! I don't want to move. Not without Coalie.

Dad came toward me as I entered the yard. "I'm so sorry Iluska. I know how you feel. I love my horses the way you love your dog." He put his arms around me and hugged me, then handed me his big red handkerchief. "Maybe Coalie wouldn't have been very happy stuck in the small yard. Dogs can't run free in town, so he would've been tied up."

That made me feel a little bit better, but every day, every night and in between, I could feel shards of glass slowly shredding my heart. I still sobbed in front of my parents, and wailed when I was alone. True to her form, my mother did not respond the way I had expected her to. I was sure she would say something like "I told you so," but instead, she, too, cried a little. Every time they saw me, they would look at each other and shake their heads sadly. Meanwhile, Coalie took over my mind, making me useless for anything else. Neither of my parents demanded anything of me.

In Town

August—1958

I functioned in a dream state for the next week. My brain could think of nothing but Coalie. My heart longed and ached for all the things he did for me and with me. I did whatever was asked of me without arguing or questioning anything. Pack this. Carry that. Put these things there. "Yes, *Mutti*." "Yes, Dad." "Okay." Exhausted, I would collapse on to my bed each evening, not really caring if tomorrow came or not.

The move was inevitable, the busy-ness distracting, and one afternoon I found myself standing in front of our house in town. The house had been fixed exactly the way Dad had promised. Four tiny rooms, each just large enough for essential furniture with not an inch to spare. I didn't care. I finally had a room of my own. The running water turned out to just be rain water, pumped up from the cistern in the basement. Drinking water had to be brought in from Alice's farm and stored in a ten gallon crock. I had hoped we would at least have an indoor toilet, but no such luck. An outhouse was erected at the end of our lot, far from the house.

By this time I had come to terms that Coalie was most likely dead, and that perhaps it was for the best. At least he would be in heaven with my Guardian Angel looking after him, and not suffering in a ditch somewhere. He would be in the true Eden created by God with all the other animals. Every night along with my prayers, I would talk to him as though he were near, telling him how much I loved him and missed him. He would come in my dreams and we played together again. It was very comforting.

Living in town definitely had its benefits. Less chores for all of us. I still cleaned the house and shoes every Saturday, but it took half the time and energy. We no longer had to depend on someone to drive us into town, church or even school. All were within walking distance. *Mutti* liked that part the best. The only problem now was that we had to pay for our meat, eggs, milk and almost everything else. The huge garden in the back provided us with the enough vegetables, but it had to be dug up by hand.

The biggest benefit had to be electricity. No longer did we need wood and all the work that went with its supply. The stove was on only for cooking and baking, not ironing or heating the house. Electricity afforded us a forced-air furnace with oil as fuel. Never again did we have to wake up to a cold house. Unfortunately the cold drafts coming in through the single-paned frosted windows remained the same. *Mutti* and I enjoyed the new quiet electric washing machine in the warm basement.

She beamed. “Dis ees berry ni-ess!” Then she reverted to Hungarian. “But, we still have to carry the clothes up the stairs and hang them on the line, whether it’s summer or winter.”

I did the carrying, the hanging and also the ironing with the electric iron. I enjoyed my new task, remembering the horrid way *Mutti* and Ethel had to iron in the farm kitchen. Dancing to the tunes on the radio while ironing also helped.

With less work, my parents had more time to spend with friends. There were several Hungarian families near our house, and a visit with them required nothing more than a stroll across the back lane. Each time, though, I heard my father complain. “What? Why do we have to see them again? I don’t want to go. You go.”

“Don’t be silly, I’m not going by myself. It’s good for us to get out of this house.” She fussed to get him to change his shirt. “Please,

Jóska, we couldn't do this before. The Dolhas have invited us over. It's impolite to refuse."

I spent my extra time with friends or involved in after-school activities—volleyball, baseball, soccer and track and field. I also had more free hours for my favourite activity—reading! All this would not have been possible if we had remained on the farm. The cloud of despair had begun to lift.

Dad secured a job collecting the garbage in Cupar. He drove a small tractor with a trailer, picked up the garbage, and deposited it at the nuisance grounds just outside of town. He really liked his new work because being on the tractor reminded him of being on the farm. Another plus included the opportunity to find some hidden treasures that others had discarded, but that we could use. Anything at all—tools, kitchen items, and occasionally even beautiful clothing that actually fit me. But sometimes, I became concerned that the ladies who had discarded them would recognize them on me. What would they think? They weren't "garbage" clothes to me. Some were classy clothes I could never afford to buy, and I loved them!

No one ever stepped forward to claim their property.

Time, life and friends began to crowd in and ease my heart. Sharing my sorrow about Coalie with others also helped. During a quiet moment of reflection, I reviewed my life, from Austria to Cupar, and came to a realization.

I am not the first, and I won't be the last person to lose someone, some place or some thing they loved. And for every dark moment I had to experience, my Guardian Angel gave me a bright and happy one to balance it. I'm now a lot more ready for the future. I wonder where my new journey will lead?

Epilogue

Everyone adjusted and everything went well once we moved into town. Dad and *Mutti* appeared much happier and relaxed. I had begun to enjoy all the things that the town offered, especially having my friends at my fingertips.

Then tragedy struck! Dad became a diabetic, and suffered a stroke a few years later. Our financial situation—tenuous to begin with—now became dire.

Mutti and I had to find work to sustain us. My mother found a position at the Cupar Hotel as a maid, cleaning the rooms and bringing home the linens for laundering. She did the washing; I did the ironing.

I also brought in regular money by doing weekly house cleaning for Mona Moscovich—the lady who had cut my braids. At the same time, she hired me to babysit for her and recommended me to her friends. Cleaning the dusty shelves at Harry's Store was another source of income. Every penny counted!

As our financial situation deteriorated, so did my mother's mental health. I must admit my decision to speak up more often, along with my teenage angst, did nothing to help her or me. None of her physicians had picked up on her illness. It was not until she had moved into the nursing home many years later that she was finally diagnosed with paranoid, histrionic, narcissistic and obsessive personality disorders, including delusional disorder. Once I understood her illness, I realized that she really had no control over her thoughts or actions.

As an adult and mother, I know that she did love me in her own way, otherwise she wouldn't have protected and provided for me. She just couldn't love me the way I wanted and needed as a child. As a result of her illness, sadly and regretfully, my mother and I never shared a mutually respectful or satisfying relationship. Perhaps in heaven we may finally touch each other's hearts.

I am however, forever and immensely grateful for my mother's great courage to uproot herself from everything familiar for the chance of a better life for both of us. Her hard work and sacrifice allowed me to grow up and live in a country that has given me everything I have and everything I am today.

That same sense of gratitude applies to my Canadian family, friends and teachers. Without their positive feedback and support, I do not believe I could have managed nor survived the intractable, destructive, albeit unintentional influence of my mother's undiagnosed illness. Their love and guidance kept me on a steady, normal loving path. They taught me that I was *not* responsible for what happened to me as a child, but I *am* responsible what happens to me as an adult.

My experiences on the farm also shaped my life. The most precious gift given to me was a deep reverence and recognition of the force of nature—its truth, beauty and healing powers. I still require and seek it out to this day. The simplicity and frugality of life on the farm taught me that my happiness has nothing to do with what I own, but has everything to do with the relationships I have with people around me. My years on the homestead developed in me a sense of self-discipline, self-respect and team work—lessons I did not learn from books.

Despite my mother's misgivings about their marriage, my beloved Ethel and her husband Steve Sulea have loved and respected each other deeply to this day. They had no children, but when her oldest sister Margaret passed, they adopted her newborn boy, Jack. He grew into a tall, strong, good man who loved to cook. Ethel has since become an artist in her own right, selling beautiful paintings of mostly prairie scenes and prairie life.

Helen and Frank Kovach moved on to the homestead site, and a little later, adopted two beautiful and intelligent girls, Patsy and Marge. Big

Helen finally had the chance to become the mother she so desperately wanted to be. Both girls brought her extreme joy and pride.

Alice and Walter Kallichuk were blessed with one more lovely baby girl. All three, Lenny, Susie and Allyson, grew up to be responsible, kind adults.

Doraphine and Joe Kish gave Mary Ann three more siblings to play with—two brothers, Patrick and Steven, and a sister named Betty. After playing house with her so often and knowing her so well, I have no doubt that Mary Ann became a loving mother herself.

My lovely godmother, Pauline eventually married Bill and had Alex, a son she could now shower with her wet kisses.

I did not have the opportunity to meet or come to know my other two brothers, Frank and Zoltan Kish in Ontario. However, I had briefly met my brother John Kish and his family from British Columbia just shortly after we had moved to town.

There was one other person who played a crucial role in my life. Without realizing it, Mona Moscovich had become my mentor. As my employer, we spent a great deal of time together, and soon she began to be sympathetic to my difficult situation with my mother. It was her intervention that allowed me the opportunity to move to Winnipeg where I resided and worked for Dr. Book and his family while I finished my grade twelve.

Once in Winnipeg, I was steered by Dr. Book towards graduating in the field of Medical Laboratory Technology. During my twenty years or so in the lab, some as a Chief Technologist, I obtained my Bachelor of Science degree through night classes at the university. Later, I opted to teach the medical secretary course at one of the leading colleges in Winnipeg. Eventually, I returned to the medical lab, part-time only, so that my husband, Lawrence, and I could do some traveling.

Somewhere between all that, I managed to create a most beautiful, free-thinking daughter, Helena Currie, and am now the lucky and proud grandmother of three lovely girls, Charley, Lara and Emma. Born and living in England, they did not have the opportunity to get to know from where and whence I came.

It is for them, that I have written my journey.

BIOGRAPHY

Born in Linz, Austria, she emigrated to Canada in early 1954, grew up on a small farm in Saskatchewan, and spent her teens in the nearby town of Cupar. Adopted by her new family, she was known as Helen Kish.

An opportunity arose for her to move to Winnipeg, Manitoba where she graduated from a Medical Laboratory Technology course. From there, Helen worked in various medical labs and eventually managed the lab at Mall Medical Clinic for 20 years. During this time, she married and became Helen Wells. After the Clinic closed, she was recruited by Success Business College to instruct the Medical Secretary course.

During this time, she had a daughter and achieved her B.Sc. Degree from University of Winnipeg.

Many years later, she met and married her present husband, Lawrence Hastman. She eventually returned to work in a lab in Beausejour, but only partime, so that she and her husband could travel.

No longer a displaced person, Helen lives with her husband on a small acreage outside Selkirk, Manitoba. She enjoys her retirement and is persuing her other passion of Nature photography. She hopes to do more traveling and, of course, more writing.